My Naked Safari

From Maine to Africa

Adventures of an Amateur Sportsman

Peter Edward Popieniuck

North
Country
Press

My Naked Safari

ISBN 978-1-943424-03-0

Library of Congress Control Number 2015941545

Cover photography by Sylvia Stagg-Giuliano

North Country Press
Unity, Maine

For Uncle Peter.

Killed in action in World War II. April 1945.
Dad always said you were the hunter and fisherman in the
family. We would have had quite a time together.

Acknowledgments

Many of my outdoor adventures have been solo affairs. Others have been with friends, family, and, in some cases, complete strangers. Regardless, I have been supported by many people before, during, and after these experiences. I owe all of these people my gratitude.

At the top of the recognition list is my loving wife, Molly. Not only has she encouraged me to embark on my various expeditions, but she has also graciously allowed me to place various taxidermy mounts in strategic locations in our home. Not many non-hunting spouses would be so accommodating. Anyone who puts up with all my eccentricities has earned special recognition. I'm immensely grateful to Molly.

Thank you also goes to Mom (Marjorie) and Dad (Alexander), my siblings (Andy, Iris, and Liz), as well as my children (Jason, Alex, Matthew, and Lara) for their collective encouragement, patience, instruction, and inspiration. I've learned much from each of them. And still do. I hope it's been a two-way street.

The owners of Fins and Furs Adventures, Carroll and Lila Ware of Skowhegan, Maine, deserve credit for connecting me with outfitters of the highest quality and integrity. I regard Carroll and Lila as trusted friends and recommend their services without hesitation to anyone looking for the best in a memorable hunting, fishing, or outdoor experience. I've never once been disappointed. Carroll is also a pretty fair cribbage player and doesn't mind too much being separated from his cache of quarters. He might contest that last point.

Jim and Lori Geib, owners of New Frontier Taxidermy in Solon, Maine, are owed a debt of gratitude. Their painstaking attention to detail in preserving my animal trophies has been exceptional. Not only do I value their skills, but also their creative suggestions. Every time I look at one of my examples of their handiwork, I can't help but recall the events surrounding it. I smile a lot.

Guides can make or break an outdoor adventure. I've been fortunate to have had many outstanding guides. Several deserve special recognition. Each has demonstrated that he sincerely cares about satisfying his clients. Guiding is more than just their job. Roland (Rol) Burry of Gander, Newfoundland, was my guide on my first two caribou hunts. He set the standard by which all my future guides have been judged. None have surpassed him. Remi Laprise comes close. Remi was my 2013 caribou guide at Leaf River Lodge. His shore lunches of fried potatoes, fresh-caught salmon filets, and tender caribou heart were unforgettable highlights of that trip. Dan Davis of Corinna, Maine, shepherded me to and from many deer hunting stands during several November visits to Northern Outdoors at The Forks in Maine. Dan made those stays enjoyable and memorable for both Molly and me. Conroy Hallgren of Safari, S.A. and his associate, Brian Kelly, saw to it that Molly and I had an unbelievable safari experience in South Africa. They put together an unforgettable and perfect balance of safari excitement, sightseeing, and hospitality. I am forever grateful to them.

I've also had the pleasure of connecting with some exceptional outfitters. If it wasn't for them, I wouldn't have half of these tales to tell. Among these great outfitters are Leaf River Lodge and its owner Alain Tardif. Whether you're on a quest for caribou or a fantastic fishing experience, Leaf River leads the list. They treat their clients like respected guests, not just as numbers. Double Buck Lodge and its owner Conrad Rollins offer superior black bear hunting adventures. Conrad has a magic bear elixir attractant with a secret recipe. Simply said, it works. With exclusive access to an area that's loaded with big bears, success rates are unusually high. Finally, if you like northern Maine deer hunting with a blend of big woods remote wilderness and lodge comfort, it's hard to beat Northern Outdoors at The Forks,

Maine. Quality guides are available, or you can do your own guiding and scouting.

Whether named above or not, a well-deserved thank you is extended to all the individuals and enterprises that have helped me pursue my outdoor passions of hunting and fishing and in becoming a better sportsman. Each of you is remembered and appreciated.

Foreword

The title of my book was derived, in part, from the 1966 Hollywood film entitled *The Naked Prey*. The movie stars Cornel Wilde as its unnamed hero. Mr. Wilde is leading a party on safari in colonial-era South Africa when they cross paths with a local tribe that expects gifts in return for infringement on their territory. While Mr. Wilde's character suggests the group abide by the harmless extortion, the rest of the safari party rudely rebuffs the natives and sends them away.

The tribesmen later return en masse and capture the entire group. All except Mr. Wilde are brutally killed. Mr. Wilde is stripped naked, given a short head start towards freedom, and then chased over several days by a number of the more aggressive warriors. Their intent is to catch and kill him. The story revolves around the chase and Mr. Wilde's use of his wits, good fortune, and his eventual safe arrival at a colonial outpost. As he reaches safety with only seconds to spare, Mr. Wilde's character turns and exchanges a salute of respect with the last of his pursuers.

While my own sometimes harrowing outdoor experiences, including my time spent on a South African safari, pale in comparison to those dangers faced by Mr. Wilde's character, they do share the common thread of frequently not knowing what's coming from around the next corner or up from behind. Learning the hard way, and also by trial and error, have been typical of my life as a self-taught sportsman. More often than not, Lady Luck has generously smiled upon me. At other times, she has just put her hands over her eyes, turned the other way, and shaken her head in disbelief before bursting out in laughter.

Today, as I look back over the obstacle-strewn as well as humorous path I've traveled in New England and elsewhere to become a better sportsman, I raise my own hand in salute to the people and experiences that got me this far. Keep up the good work. My naked safari is ongoing.

Introduction

"Thank you, Professor Roche."

Professor Roche was my college English literature instructor. I remember him for two reasons. First, he always managed to carefully point out the juiciest and most salacious parts of the novels we read. This was much appreciated at an all-male private university. More importantly, he urged all of his students to start and keep a journal of their life's activities and thoughts. That was close to 50 years ago. It took me 40 of those years to start my journal. I'm somewhat of a slow learner.

My Naked Safari is that journal of my life's experiences as an amateur hunter, fisherman, and outdoorsman. The emphasis is on the word "amateur". Robert Ruark, Peter Capstick, Theodore Roosevelt, and other more contemporary professional adventurers need not worry. I believe that I'm more like the average Joe or Jane sportsperson and just want to see what I can experience and accomplish with limited means, support, and skills.

My Naked Safari also describes many of the people I've met and known during my adventures. I've tried to recount those experiences accurately and honestly, warts and all. When appropriate, I've attempted to use humor to tell the stories. At other times, more serious and factual writing was called for. Above all, I've tried to make the stories interesting, even to those who may not be avid outdoors people. The reader will have to determine if I've succeeded.

I had almost no formal training in preparation for any of these adventures. I did attend a one-day fly fishing class at an L.L. Bean store in Maine. I also had a total of about six hours of instruction in fly-tying techniques. That's it. The rest has all been informal, seat-of-the-pants, learn-as-you-go, trial and error. And as you'll read, there have been plenty of errors, but overall, more successes. I've learned from both. I'm grateful for both. Looking back, I wouldn't have had it any other way, though at times, when in the moment, I might have.

The single most significant aspect to these adventures, what they all have in common, has been in sharing them with other sportsmen. Boating a huge fish, downing a trophy-class animal, or witnessing a magnificent vista such as the northern lights is wonderful enough if you're by yourself. But if you're accompanied by close friends or family, these events can take on bigger-than-life, epic proportions. The experience is enriched and the memories are heightened and amplified.

Professor Roche was in his mid-sixties when he suggested I start keeping a journal. It's highly unlikely that I can thank him personally or that he'll have the opportunity to read *My Naked Safari*. However, if he and I did meet today, I think he'd say "better late than never."

Thank you for reading my book. I hope you enjoy the experience and find it stimulating and entertaining.

Our relationship with Peter Popieniuck began about a decade ago, when Pete asked to join our group of caribou hunters in Quebec. Since that first hunt, Peter has joined us on many, many adventures and has become a dear friend and hunting companion. It never fails that when Pete joins us, Murphy, of Murphy's Law fame, seems to consistently appear.

Pete first mentioned his desire to write a book about his exploits and adventures several years ago. When he told us that the book is done and that we are included in it, we were indeed honored and proud. Peter's book is a funny, candid, sometimes touching account of his adventures (and misadventures). For Lila and I as Maine Guides who have enjoyed the company of many hunting dogs, of various levels of ability, the chapter describing Diesel really put its hand on us both.

We have shared endless moments of successful and not so successful hunts with Peter Popieniuck. Cribbage games, trophies taken and missed, and above all else, the camaraderie that our relationship has provided have made for great memories. We are very proud to have played a small role in Pete's outdoor adventures and look forward to many more.

Pete, remember; you do not need a shooting stick!

Carroll & Lila Ware
Master Maine Guides
Fins and Furs Adventures
Skowhegan, Maine

I first met Pete and Molly in the early 2000s at Northern Outdoors where I was a registered Maine hunting guide. For more than a decade Pete and Molly would show up for the third week of hunting season. At Northern Outdoors we hunt from tree stands which are already up and in place when the hunter arrives. Flagged trails lead the hunter to his stand. My stands are all marked on GPS and many times throughout the day I would circle around my hunters trying to push a deer onto them, only to get to their stand site and see NO hunter. This was not the case with Peter, not ONCE did I ever find Pete OUT of his stand. I have never had or heard of another hunter, sitting in a tree stand like Peter Popieniuck.

Pete always wanted to spend as much time as possible in his stand, causing him to walk to and from his stand in the dark. Pete never shot a deer at Northern Outdoors, but not for lack of putting his time in. Pete did see deer, but not always something he wanted to shoot. One night as he came out of the woods, he shared, "I saw the biggest buck of my life but it only had one antler." Why is it that sporting camps judge bucks by the size of their antlers? The top 10 bucks listed in the "Maine Sportsman" magazine are listed by weight…. Pete you should have shot it.

The hunts run from Monday to Saturday morning, if that's what it takes. I could always plan on hunting on Saturday morning if Pete hadn't scored yet. One Saturday morning almost paid off. Pete was in his stand when a nice buck stepped out, but it was to Pete's left. I think he would have shot this deer, but in these tree stands your range of motion is limited, and Pete was skunked again.

When I heard Pete was writing a book, my first thought was it must be a book titled, "My Life in a Tree Stand." After reading some of his manuscript and knowing Pete like I do, I would have to say this, he did it his way. Sometimes it paid off in a physical reward and other times great memories were created to ponder, to treasure, and to be passed on. I haven't seen Pete and Molly for a few years now, but it was always a pleasure seeing them and spending the week hunting with Pete. I still hear from Pete once or twice a year with Pete keeping me up to date on his activities.

This book is an excellent read, it made me laugh and it made me cry. I felt just like I was present on the fishing, camping, and hunting expeditions and having a great and entertaining time. My hunting and fishing experiences are significantly limited, but I thoroughly enjoyed reading this. Diesel I'm rooting for you and there will be tears in Maine when you go to meet our maker.

Dan Davis
Master Maine Guide

Table of Contents

Part One : Buck Naked

Like Mr. Wilde's character in *The Naked Prey*, I began my journey as an outdoors sportsman literally without even the proper clothes on my back or the skills to succeed. "Buck naked" might also be used to describe my many years—more than I care to admit—of frustration at deer hunting. Anyone that thinks a hunter just nonchalantly strolls into the woods and calmly bags a trophy deer without half trying is in for a rude awakening. The same holds true in fishing.

But perseverance paid off. I slowly learned new skills and became more adept at attaining my goals. Modest success encouraged me. Failures made me that much more determined.

The chapters in part one describe my early efforts. I believe about 2,600 years ago the ancient Chinese philosopher, Lao-Tzu, said that a journey of a thousand miles begins with a single step. Here are my first baby steps. I think Lao and I could have hunted together. After all, didn't the Chinese invent gunpowder?

Fishing Memories

To most people, the words jitterbug, goldfish, and daredevil bring to mind a popular dance from the 1930s and 40s, a tasty Pepperidge Farm snack cracker, and an iconic comic book hero (or a Ben Affleck movie flop). But not to me. They are the names of legendary fishing lures from my childhood.

First memories

My first memory of fishing involves standing on the bank of a pond with a fishing rod made from a six-foot-long sapling, a short length of white string, a hook tied to the end of the string, and a writhing worm on that hook. (Tom Sawyer had nothing over me!) And I even managed to catch a couple sun fish, but was unhappy because Dad, fishing beside me with his beloved Shakespeare President reel and rod, caught considerably more fish than I did. Even at that early age, I determined that fishing was a competitive sport.

Despite that first experience, I must have enjoyed it more than I thought at the time because my next early fishing memory is of waiting patiently on the staircase of our home at 4:00 a.m. By waiting on the steps, Dad couldn't get past to go fishing without me knowing it and then he'd have to take me with him. And he did take me.

Dad was big into brook trout fishing in the local streams near our Massachusetts home. Most of these spots were secret and known only to him. I use the word "streams" rather loosely. These were mostly little trickles of water that moved fast and deep, but were narrow enough so you could straddle them with your legs. Dad would gingerly sneak up to their banks, dangle a worm over the edge, and often be rewarded with a wriggling native brookie on the end of his line.

I had my jobs on these excursions. The first was to carry the worms. Dad had one of those green metal worm boxes that clipped to your belt and I faithfully trailed him through the swamps and over the tussocks of grass carrying that box of worms. Whenever Dad needed fresh bait for his hook I opened the box's metal lid and delivered the new worm. Job number two was carrying any fish that were caught. These were threaded neatly through the gills and mouth on a stick that Dad would whittle from a sapling with his yellow-handled KA-BAR pocket knife. He'd leave a stump of a branch on the end to keep the fish from sliding off.

When we weren't fishing for brook trout, Dad would take me fishing for suckers. We didn't eat these bottom-feeding fish because, as Dad said, they had a tendency to get wormy, especially later in the season. Bait consisted of a few slices of white bread. We'd break off a small piece and roll it between our fingers to form a dough ball. Then, with the dough balls threaded onto our hooks, we'd drop our lines over the embankment and watch the suckers hoover them up from the bottom. Sometimes the suckers weighed several pounds and were huge catches for a young fisherman like myself.

Middle years experiences

After those earliest fishing memories, I graduated to more advanced techniques and equipment. Among other things, this involved owning my first official rod and reel. The reel was a Planet brand closed-spool spinning model. (I'm pretty certain this was even before the days of the first Zebco reels.) With that Planet reel securely fastened to a hand-me-down five-foot steel rod, it seemed like I could cast a lure or a weighted hook for miles. I also acquired my own small metal tackle box which Dad helped stock with hooks, bobbers, weights, and a few of his bass lures. With this equipment in hand, I embarked on my first fishing expeditions.

One such destination was a local pond that had a small cabin on a point of land that jutted out from shore. In front of the cabin was a small cluster of maple trees that had fallen sideways into the water. The horizontal tree trunks enabled my brother and me, and any friends with us, to get farther from shore and have a convenient bench seat to rest on. We caught a lot of hornpout (catfish to some) from those tree trunks. We even gave names to some of them. The bigger the fish, the more awesome-sounding the name. Once we fileted one of the hornpout and tried to grill it on the metal cover of a coffee can in the cabin's fireplace. It tasted awful. Maybe that was because the coffee can had been used to carry our worms.

Another early fishing hot spot was below a dam on the Assabet River in a neighboring town. Aside from a few perch and sunfish, the main attraction was the suckers that lurked in the river. In addition to a few youngsters like myself that fished there, the location also drew some inner-city fishermen to its shoreline. Even at my young age, I realized that these people were not fishing just for fun like I was. They were fishing for their dinners.

Once, I caught a large sucker that weighed about five pounds. I never intended to eat it, but did plan to bring it home to show to Mom and Dad for bragging rights. Shortly after landing the sucker, one of the city fishermen asked me if I'd sell him the fish for a dime. I immediately agreed. Then my "customer" handed me a nickel and told me that if I came back the next day he'd give me another nickel. As far as I was concerned, I was a nickel to the good. I didn't go back the next day. To this day, that transaction represents my one and only "commercial" fishing experience. Obviously my bargaining skills needed work.

The Assabet River in Maynard and Stow, Massachusetts offered other fishing adventures. It was possible to fish in the pool directly below Ben Smith Dam when the river was especially low in the summertime. On one occasion I'd been casting unsuccessfully for about 30 minutes at the silhouette of a large fish in the pool. I'd managed to drag a worm past the fish's nose several times to no avail. Eventually, I had to leave the pool for fresh bait. When I returned, an adult fisherman had stolen my spot. He made one cast with a red and white Daredevil spinning lure and instantly hooked *my* fish. It was a nice fat rainbow trout. I can still see its iridescent colors shimmering in the sunlight as that carpetbagger fisherman put it in his creel. Since it was the middle of summer at the time, I hoped that trout tasted muddy.

The river also held sunfish, calico bass (crappie to some), yellow perch, pickerel, and largemouth bass. Every now and then we'd catch an eel. I never liked eels. They'd always swallow the hook and I'd have to cut the line and lose my hook after landing one.

Mom and Dad claimed that eels were a delicacy. I brought one home once and Mom cooked it. I don't recall eating it. I do recall handling the slimy beast and the chore of cleaning the "snake". At least I got my hook back on that one. I'll stick to trout, thank you very much.

Henry Thoreau's Walden Pond on the border of Concord and Lincoln, Massachusetts was another favorite fishing haunt. I went there many times with Dad and, later, by myself or with my brother. This was back in the days when the fishing season opened annually on the third Saturday of April. Walden was always freshly stocked with trout just before opening day and drew large crowds of anglers. If you didn't get there before 4:00 a.m. all the prime fishing spots were already taken. By dawn, the entire pond was literally lined with eager fishermen spaced about ten feet apart. Tangled lines were the order of the day. Every once in a while there was some excitement when a fish was landed. Most likely, it had just gotten hopelessly entangled in the web of hundreds of lines.

Being on the water itself at Walden Pond was little better. Imagine trolling through a maze of hundreds of boats and lines all crammed onto a small body of water. It seemed like rush hour in Boston only wetter, but with all the same curses and single-digit hand gestures.

Though I didn't partake in those days, liquor consumption was quite rampant on Walden Pond during those opening-day events. One example of its consequences stands out vividly. John Lewhank, one of Dad's friends, was often seen fishing at Walden, standing on his favorite sandbar, chest-deep in his waders. John had the unfortunate nickname of Moose Face. This was due to both the massive size as well as the redness of his nose. Imagine the old vaudeville comic, Jimmy Durante, but double the size of his schnoz. John's deep booming voice matched the size of his nose.

This particular opening day, Moose Face was casting from his usual sandbar and standing in four feet of water about 50 feet from shore. He was continually hollering to friends on shore while he fished. It was rather obvious from his slurred speech that his footing wasn't the only thing quite unsteady that day. In an attempt to make an extra-long cast, John totally lost his balance, toppled over, and went completely under the surface of the water. He rose from the 40-degree depths seconds later, hat still in place, rod in hand, and still bellowing. He resumed fishing as if nothing at all had happened. It probably wasn't the first time, or the last, that Moose Face took such a dunking. I was in awe of any man so tenacious in his dedication to fishing.

Atlantic adventures

Dad also had a passion for saltwater fishing. He owned and managed a bar in our home town. (In those days it was called a "social club." It wasn't a sports bar and didn't serve meals other than pickled eggs, pork hocks, lambs tongues, and steamed hot dogs that the "regulars" downed along with their whiskey shots and beers.) During the summer months Dad organized fishing trips for himself and about a dozen or so of his customers. They'd charter a boat in Rockport, Massachusetts, once a month and head several miles offshore to fish for cod, haddock, and pollock. Every once in a while there would be a last-minute cancellation, and I or my brother would fill the empty spot. The trips were great adventures, though I did sometimes wonder why one or more of the fishermen would stay below deck all day and occasionally come topside only to lean over the rail and heave "chum" on the water's surface. Perhaps it had something to do with staying up all night drinking before the trip began.

Eventually Dad bought his own boat. It was a red and white 18-foot fiberglass Lone Star runabout with a six-foot beam that allowed plenty of room for fishing as well as the ability to handle Atlantic swells. The boat was named the *Lizabee* in honor of my youngest sister and her family nickname. The *Lizabee* was initially equipped with a 40 horsepower Evinrude outboard motor that was later upgraded to 100 horsepower. Over the years we made literally hundreds of family fishing trips out of Gloucester, Beverly, and Marshfield, Massachusetts. And did we catch fish!

Dad had his system down pat. We had a 30-gallon galvanized trash can sitting amidships and it, in turn, sat inside a large galvanized wash tub. Several gallon-size milk jugs filled with ice provided refrigeration. With all six family members fishing, it was not uncommon to fill the entire apparatus with fresh fish in a few hours. Once the fishing was complete, Dad pulled out his fish-cleaning kit. This consisted of a Rapala fileting knife that he kept razor-sharp with frequent use of a handheld sharpening stone. The cutting board was one of Mom's old pastry boards. The entire catch would be cleaned on the spot and all the filets put in five-gallon plastic pails. With a still-frozen jug of ice placed on top, the catch was chilled and made it safely home at the end of the day for individual filet wrapping and freezing.

Needless to say, we ate a lot of fish in those days. What we didn't immediately eat, we froze. Once the freezer was full, we gave fresh fish away to the neighbors. It got to the point that they knew when to expect our return home and would be waiting for us with plastic bags in hand and leave with cod and haddock filets fresher than any that could be bought in the supermarket. In later years, Dad brought several of the neighbors and his friends with him on these fishing trips.

In all the years we fished offshore, there were only two downside events. One was being stranded several miles from shore on two consecutive weekends because of fuel that had been accidently contaminated with water. On both occasions we were towed to shore, once by a group of divers and their boat and the second time by a lobster boat. After the second occurrence, Dad realized that it had to be the gas station's underground tanks that caused the problem. I don't believe he purchased gas from that station ever again, but he did add a small "kicker" motor to the *Lizabee*'s transom. We were never again stranded.

The second event was a bit less dangerous. Neither I nor my Dad, sisters, or brother ever got seasick. The same cannot be said for Mom or the aunt who once ventured out with us. I always thought it was an exaggeration that a person's complexion turned green when they suffered from seasickness. It's not. It really turns green.

That boat meant a lot to all of us, but especially to Dad. So much so, that it sat under a carport at Dad's house for many years even after he stopped going on his Atlantic fishing trips. Eventually, he fittingly sold it for a small sum to a couple guys who were looking for a good seaworthy craft to use for their own offshore trips. I hope it served them as well as it served us.

Still fishing, still learning

Fishing is and always will be in my blood and in my head. I've managed to learn some of the most important truths of the sport in my several decades of practice. Among these are that any knot not checked will always come loose at the most unfortunate time. Fishing line left in direct sunlight for extended periods of time reverts to a tensile strength of three ounces. Hip boots or waders will always be one inch shorter than the water depth of the next step you take. If the fish aren't biting, grab a sandwich. The ensuing tug on your line will be almost instantaneous.

I enjoy traveling to fishing trade shows. I marvel at the changes in technology that have happened over the last 60 or so years. I can remember when fiberglass rods were "the thing" to have. Now it's boron or carbon fiber rods. My old Planet spinning reel, which I still have sitting on a shelf, has been replaced with fishing reels that look more like they were designed by NASA. I recall when monofilament line was new. I'm pretty sure that some of today's fishing lines are the laboratory products of competing mad scientists. Lead sinkers have been updated by fishing weights made from elements rarer than some precious metals. Dad's original Raytheon flasher depth sounder has been replaced with electronics that notify you not just of the presence of unseen fish, but also their depth, size, numbers, and the water temperature. And where Dad used his eyes and a compass to triangulate landmarks on a printed nautical chart to remember approximate fishing hot-spot locations, today's GPS systems not only show their exact coordinates, but will automatically take you there.

Lest I sound like I'd prefer caveman-style fishing, I do admit to taking advantage of some of the newer technologies. I use hybrid fishing line for its combination of strength and durability. My boat has an LED electronic fish finder, though mine is a 25-year-old model. A few years ago I traded in my old two-cycle outboard motor for a new super-quiet and gas-efficient four-stroke model. And someday I'll have to spend some time figuring out how to use the handheld GPS I bought. I think I know what a waypoint is so that's a start. Until then, Dad's original Airguide compass will stay securely mounted to my boat's dashboard.

Not everything has changed. I'm fairly certain that most fishing lures and other innovations in tackle are designed to catch more fishermen than fish. It's still always a thrill to land "the big one," regardless of species. I never grow tired of watching the wide-eyed excitement on a child's face when he or she has a fish on the end of their line. I believe the vivid colors displayed by a freshly landed brook trout, rainbow trout, arctic char, or salmon, either Atlantic or landlocked, are some of the most wonderful of nature's gifts.

I still fish as often as possible and have had many more memorable experiences since those early days. I've taught myself how to tie my own streamer flies and have been pleasantly surprised that they do, in fact, catch fish. I'm working on becoming a better fly fisherman. I've taught my children how to fish and intend on doing the same for my grandchildren. I've long since reached the stage in my fishing experience where actually catching fish is no longer that important. What does matter is the experience itself, whether it's with a fellow fisherman or by myself. I now keep only what I will eat and happily release everything else. And I'm still a big fan of Jitterbugs, Goldfish, and Daredevils. Worms too. Thank you, Dad.

Camp Life

The car crammed full of people slammed on its brakes and came to a skidding stop in the middle of the road amid a cloud of dust directly in front of my camp in Andover, Maine. Out jumped the driver with a big, questionably sober, grin on his face and a hearty "Hi! How ya doin'?" followed by something like, "When's the party start?"

Even in his somewhat inebriated state, he could probably tell by the puzzled look on my face that I had no idea what he was talking about. When I told him I was the new owner of the camp, his expression quickly saddened and he got back in the car with his friends and slowly drove off. Apparently, my newly purchased camp in the Maine woods came fully equipped with a local reputation.

Finding my Maine Garden of Eden

I'd done a lot of hiking, fishing, and camping in Maine and New Hampshire with family and friends and even though I was only in my early 20s, I'd already decided I wanted to own remote property in the north woods. My preference was for about 20 acres of woodland where I could eventually build a cabin. However, during several real estate hunting trips the only land I found that I could afford already had all of its significant timber cut and looked like anything but pristine wilderness.

Dad stepped in. He knew two friends who were selling their camp in Maine. It was on approximately five acres of land versus my desired twenty and was camp-style instead of cabin-style, but it was fully equipped down to the dishes in the cabinets and silverware in the drawers. If I bought it, I could begin using it immediately. The current owners were selling it because one of the three had recently passed away and the other two were not interested in keeping it.

I eventually learned that a significant reason for the sale was that one owner was the widow of the deceased partner and it seemed that the camp was the local party house when the men were all there. The widow wanted no part of the place. Several of the guys had local girlfriends who apparently liked to party as well. That explained the car that stopped in the road and the frowns as they departed. Their hideaway in the woods was no more.

Dad and I took an inspection drive to view the place and I still remember our reactions as we went in. As soon as we crossed the threshold of the front door we turned and just smiled at each other. This was the place I'd been looking for.

There was a building-long combination dining room/kitchen/living room. The kitchen had a propane stove with oven and a propane-fueled refrigerator, as well as a kitchen sink. Connected to this room were two large bedrooms, each with homemade double bed bunk beds. And best of all, a high-ceiling, pine-paneled room with a massive fireplace had been added on the opposite side from the bedrooms. There was even a small bathroom off the fireplace room, though running water had not yet been made available. Gas lights, a large utility shed, a wood shed, an outhouse, and several overstuffed chairs and sofas rounded out the camp's buildings and furnishings. A green felt-covered card table turned the fireplace room into the game room. And the price was very reasonable. I was sold instantly.

There was no municipal electricity available, but I viewed that as a plus. There was, however, a very old electric generator which the owners occasionally used and a gas floor furnace for heat. While the place wasn't quite as remote as what I had originally been seeking, the lack of power made up for a bit of that in my eyes. The unpaved road that dead-ended at Lower Richardson Lake and the presence of a state-maintained boat ramp there also contributed to the wilderness atmosphere and my anticipated fishing adventures.

Raising a camp family

Within a year of buying the camp, I was married and at the same time adopted my wife's four-year-old son. We quickly added three more children of our own, two boys and a girl, and the camp became our vacation spot. Swimming in the lake, fishing in the brooks, exploring logging roads, and looking for wildlife like deer, bear, and moose became our routine.

One of the kids' favorite activities was walking on fallen logs through the swampy area next to the camp. As they'd go out the door I'd always tell them not to get dirty, knowing full well that they'd all come back soaked and wearing mud up to their knees. The nearby local swimming hole, dubbed The Devil's Den, offered the best clean-up opportunity in mild weather. Thousands of years of running water had carved a whirlpool bath into the granite rocks and we took frequent advantage of it.

Over time, I added a chimney and a wood-burning stove for heat, since I had a virtually unlimited supply of firewood. I also hand dug a well outside the kitchen window and installed a hand pump beside the sink. The ready accessibility of this form of running water made washing and cleaning easier and filling five-gallon pails to empty into the toilet tank simplified the use of the bathroom, at least in the warm weather. The outhouse was kept in good repair for cold weather use since the camp was unheated when no one was present. In later years, I even added a wood-fired steam bath, though I've yet to experience rolling in the fresh snow after getting all steamed up. Maybe someday.

As the local logging operations expanded, so did my explorations. Topographic maps that showed inaccessible streams and ponds gradually gave up their secrets as the logging roads were extended. One prime example of this was Mettalack Pond.

According to the topographic map, Mettalack Pond was about a mile long and up to about half a mile wide. It was a sure bet for fat native brook trout if only we could get a canoe into it. Within a few years, the logging roads provided that access. Accompanied by my sons, my brother, and his stepson, we hauled two canoes, our fishing gear, and a picnic lunch through the woods to the pond. We were in for quite a surprise.

While we crisscrossed the entire length and breadth of the pond several times, we found not a single spot where the water was more than about four feet deep. It undoubtedly froze nearly to the bottom in the winter. Even hardy Maine brook trout need a bit of year-round running water in order to prosper. We spent the day on the pond and had fun exploring anyway. Late in the day my brother and I hauled out the canoes while the boys threw handfuls of mud at each other and, later on, removed the leeches they'd picked up. Everyone, except the leeches, was happy.

While Mettalack Pond never lived up to our trout fishing expectations, its shallow depths, abundant lily pads, and other aquatic plants made it an ideal place to watch feeding moose. The children and I spent many a summer afternoon sitting on the shore watching moose feed on those plants. Ducks and geese often cruised the pond's surface and kingfishers and hummingbirds constantly darted among the shoreline spruces. We've even hauled in a canoe once or twice more just to cruise its surface. The place was, and still is, so idyllic to me that I've often told my now-adult children that if I ever vanish without a clue as to my whereabouts, they'll probably find me in a small, hand-hewn cabin by the shore of Mettalack Pond.

During those early camp years I also introduced my children to trolling for salmon on Lower Richardson Lake. We spent many hours and days catching little or nothing. Years later, one of my sons told me they all believed there were no salmon in the lake at all. I prefer to believe it was merely time spent perfecting my technique. Since those days, we've actually done quite well at catching the elusive landlocked salmon on Richardson. Looking for the resident bald eagle and the occasional osprey have been other pastimes.

We went through a variety of boats on Richardson. The first was Dad's 12-foot aluminum boat. It worked well and the little 9.5 horsepower outboard was adequate if there were only a couple people aboard. But the prevailing wind direction on Richardson was north to south and thus enabled the waves to build in height for the lake's entire several-mile length. For safety sake, a larger boat was required.

Next in sequence was a secondhand, homemade, wooden outboard boat I purchased from a friend. It was deeper and broader, but it's nearly flat bottom made for quite a rough trip if there was anything more than a ripple on the lake.

Boat number three was actually quite good. My then-father-in-law gave me the 16-foot Old Town boat he owned but no longer used. It came complete with an ancient 18-horsepower Johnson outboard and a trailer. The only issue with the boat was that the transom was completely rotten. It was made seaworthy by shortening the boat by six inches at the stern and the application of a little carpentry work and some fiberglass cloth and resin. The Old Town served me well for about 10 years. Eventually, after more rot threatened to turn it into a submarine, I sold the Old Town and got $300 for the whole package, which was just a bit more than what it cost me to replace the broken driveshaft in the Johnson after its final outing and tow back to the boat ramp.

Since then, a relatively maintenance-free, 16-foot Sea Nymph boat with a 50-horsepower four-stroke Mercury outboard fills the need for a lake-capable water craft. It allows me to concentrate all my efforts on fishing rather than having to devote at least half my time to keeping the boat afloat. I view this last boat as a well-earned luxury. I paid my dues with its predecessors.

The camp as corporate retreat

After owning the Andover camp for a few years, my boss suggested that we might try a fishing trip there. Not being one to pass up an opportunity to fish, and maybe impress the boss at the same time, I agreed in a flash. That first year it was just me, my boss, and one other guy from the office. We had the three of us in Dad's 12-footer and between the bad weather and choppy water, we were on the lake for only about four hours and caught nothing. But the precedent had been set.

The following year we had six fishermen; the next, nine. One year I think we had four boats and about 15 people. The crew ranged from experienced fishermen to a couple guys that not only had never fished, but didn't even own any equipment. There was always plenty of extra tackle in camp. While the fishing success was up and down, we always had a good time. Where else except at a New England fishing camp would you be able to experience a group of guys sitting around a five-inch, battery-powered, black-and-white TV watching the Boston Celtics win an NBA championship in early June? We cheered just as much as if we'd been high up in the nose-bleed seats of Boston Garden.

Whenever we weren't fishing we were playing cards, eating, sleeping, consuming the occasional (!!) beverage, or telling each other tall tales and bragging about the fish we wished we'd caught. Once we even panned for gold in a stream. While we didn't find any gold, we had the fun of looking for it. Another time, one guest brought along his art supplies. I can still see him at his easel, sitting behind the camp on the stump of a log, mosquitoes and black flies swirling around his head, painting a picture of a storm-tossed clipper ship. I can only guess how his mind's eye envisioned that ship while he was in the middle of a spruce forest.

Another time, one of the neophyte fishermen wanted to proudly show the rest of us the new streamer flies he'd just purchased. Unfortunately, he chose to do this while we were zipping along the water at about 20 miles per hour. When he opened his tackle box the flies literally took flight. They might have worked better had they been attached to a trolling line at the time.

The next generation moves in

The camp and its surroundings have been upgraded over the years. Not too long after I purchased it, the road was paved all the way to the lake. Gone were the days of hauling the boat to the launching ramp and finding its contents covered with dust. Changes were also made to the camp itself. More efficient wood-burning stoves replaced the earlier models. Second-hand furniture and carpets replaced the original fourth-hand furnishings. New asphalt shingles on the roof stopped the leaks from rainstorms and melting snow, though I was surprised at the asphalt roof when I'd actually told the contractor to install a metal roof.

Then a really big change took place. About ten years ago Central Maine Power ran electric lines up the road. I had mixed emotions about this. It would likely mean I'd have year-round neighbors which did, in fact, happen. While electricity would certainly make many things more convenient, hooking up to it would also diminish the camp's rustic character that drew me to it in the first place.

In the end, convenience won out over character. Out went the gas lights and propane refrigerator to be replaced by their electric equivalents. The battery-powered TV gave way to a secondhand plug-in color set which, on a good day, can pull in two channels if the rabbit ears antenna is pointed just the right way.

The conversion to electricity was made all the simpler by the fact that the original owners had completely wired the camp to take advantage of their generator. All I had to do was bring street power to the fuse box and it was done. But the gas range and hand pump beside the sink are still there for two reasons. First, I can still cook and have water even if the power fails. And second, I don't want to give up every last vestige of camp atmosphere.

The biggest change at the camp is in the midst of happening now and it has nothing to do with the physical structure or its environment. It has to do with who's using the place. When my children were young, we'd visit the camp on weekends or on week-long vacations. Then, as my kids reached their teens and early 20s, like most young people, they developed other interests and weren't quite as interested in traveling to rural Maine as they once had been.

But when they got into their 30s, a wonderful thing happened. They started to miss the place. I'd get asked about going on springtime fishing trips again. A weekend visit to the camp in the middle of winter became an annual ritual. The hike to the summit of Lookout Rock and whether or not the "Old Man" (me) could still get there became a friendly challenge, though I'd sometimes hear it was their crafty means to an early inheritance. And eventually they started to bring their own friends and families to the camp for their own good times.

I like to think I've done something right by instilling an appreciation for nature and things less modern in my children. When I see them passing that along to their own friends and my grandchildren, I know I've done right.

Maybe someday when my mind is a little less sound than it is now and I'm confused and happen to drive by the camp in Andover, Maine, I'll stop and holler out the window and ask, "Hi! How ya doin'? When's the party start?" And, when that day comes, even if my short-term memory is somewhat addled, but my sense of direction is still intact, I hope I'll be greeted with, "You're just in time, Dad. Come on in. We've been waiting for you."

I've had a lot of fun being a terrible bird hunter. By that I mean my bird hunting skills (I hate to even think of them as expertise) took many years to develop, over several species. I also had a lot of frustration as well as excitement during that time.

Woodchucks and crows and ducks...oh my

My efforts at bird hunting started while I was still a young teenager as a sideline to woodchuck hunting. The same fields that held the woodchucks, also known as groundhogs, were often visited by flocks of crows. Both the woodchucks and the crows were considered solely as pests in those days. I'd occasionally take a shot with my .22 rifle at a crow on the ground and every now and then would hit one. I learned early on that crows always have a lone sentinel posted in a tree ready to sound the alarm if anything unusual appears. And with crows' sharp eyesight, it was almost impossible to outwit them. In response, I developed the technique of sitting under a leafy tree with my P.S. Olt crow call and wait for whatever showed first, a woodchuck popping its head out of its den or a crow responding to my call and landing in the field near my homemade crow decoys. I fashioned these out of reshaped wire coat hangers and black cloth. I bagged a lot more woodchucks than crows.

Later, I took to wing shooting at crows with my 12 gauge shotgun. By hiding under a canopy of oaks or maples and blowing into the call and trying to sound like a crow in distress, I'd occasionally hit the right series of notes and the black birds would dive-bomb me through the branches. The action was fast and furious and nearly all of the time I'd miss. But it was a lot of fun. Less so for the crows. To this day I carry that P.S. Olt call when I bird hunt and tell my wife that if I get the chance, I'm going to take a crow and, true to my hunting ethics, cook him up and eat him. Happily, as far as my wife's concerned, it hasn't happened yet.

From crows, I graduated to ducks. I knew absolutely nothing about duck hunting and didn't have a dog to assist me even if I ever did manage to knock one of them out of the air. But I didn't let that stop me.

I bought a half dozen hard plastic mallard decoys at the local Mal's department store, strung some heavy-duty monofilament fishing line on them, and tied some cast iron plumbing fittings to them for weights. My expert decoy pattern consisted of throwing the decoys out randomly in a loose bunch from the canoe and then pulling the canoe into the nearby cattail reeds and camouflaging it by draping an old army poncho over the gunnels. In addition to the decoys, I got another call from P.S. Olt. This time it was a duck call.

It took a long time before I took my first duck. I had to learn how to lead the birds. And I had to learn how to speak duck. A Duck Commander I was not. Eventually I was rewarded and soon the ducks began to fall with somewhat greater frequency. But not without new frustrations.

A beacon in the night

My primary duck hunting haunt was the local river which had been dammed up in the 1800s to provide power for the textile mills. Behind the dam, what once had been a swift running watercourse became a slow and spread-out waterway filled with flooded meadows and huge beds of cattail reeds. High concentrations of nitrogen from decades of fertilizer runoff and ineffective sewage treatment from the towns upriver encouraged the growth of the water plants. This, in turn, provided cover and food for waterfowl. While the river had long since ceased to be a clear, swift-running New England waterway, it at least partially redeemed itself as a great duck-hunting destination and was only a mile or so away from home.

Unfortunately for me, I was not the only local sport that knew of the river's duck-hunting potential. More than once after I'd been careful to get to the river well before dawn, scatter my decoys, and pull into the reeds to patiently wait for the legal shooting time of 30 minutes before sunrise, I'd be surprised by the earlier-than-legal shotgun blasts from other hunters who had paddled their canoes and boats to nearby concealed locations. This was particularly frustrating because due to my weekday work schedule and prohibition of Sunday hunting in Massachusetts, Saturdays were my only opportunity to hit the duck flats.

It wasn't that I didn't hear the approach of the other hunters. Even early on in my hunting career I knew that proper hunting ethics dictated that you shouldn't crowd your neighboring hunters and infringe on their space, especially if they had been first on the scene. My only consolation was that perhaps my too-close and too-early-to-shoot hunting compatriots were as unaware of my presence as I was of theirs. A new strategy was needed if I was to continue duck hunting from inside the perimeter of what was becoming a virtual shooting gallery.

I came up with what I called my lighthouse strategy. Rather than sit tight and camouflaged when I heard the approach of other hunters, whether by paddle splash, oarlock creak, or noisy two-cycle outboard motor exhaust, I stood up in my canoe, flicked on my six-volt lantern flashlight, and held it high above my head to illuminate the surrounding reeds. The light's powerful beam let anyone approaching know that someone else had arrived before them.

It worked. Apparently my fellow hunters still possessed enough ethics to respect the presence and personal hunting space of another hunter in their midst. From that time on it was rare to be caught off guard by an unexpected shotgun blast just 50 yards or so away. Not so, however, for my other duck-hunting nemesis, the ICBM blaster.

ICBM blaster was the name I gave to the hunters that believed their shotguns could hit ducks and geese a continent away. As I sat in my canoe I would see a distant flock of ducks or geese approaching from on high. I'd wait patiently for their approach, watch as they'd circle back, indicating that they found my decoys or my calling tempting, and get myself ready for their descent to the water's surface and within my shooting range. Now a quarter mile away. Now 300 yards. Now 200. Now...Bang! Bang! Bang! Followed by still more volleys. And the entire flock would fly off completely unscathed, probably wondering what the loud ruckus was below.

I'll never understand why some hunters think a load of birdshot has the same range and accuracy as a round from a sniper rifle. Perhaps they just want to make sure that if they can't bring down one of those high flying birds, no one else is going to either. Maybe they're PETA activists performing their misguided roles as protectors of all things winged. In any case, it always seemed that there would be at least one of these hunters somewhere nearby that thought his 12 gauge had the range of a Minuteman missile. Many a mallard and Canada goose owes his life to these very much overly optimistic shooters.

My waterfowl hunting days are memories now, but I hope to make new ones. Career, family, and other obligations took precedence and hauling the canoe and decoys off to the waterways long before daybreak became more than I could manage. Recently, I bought a dozen new decoys and hope to resume that aspect of bird hunting soon. I also have a new shotgun that shoots three-and-a-half-inch magnum shells. At least I'm not going to be outgunned. Now I've got my own ICBM blaster.

Hooked on pheasants

About 15 years ago, a hunting and fishing buddy introduced me to pheasant hunting. Of course, in addition to a new set of hunting skills, this required new clothes, a new shotgun, and most of all, a new best friend, a bird dog.

For a couple years I tagged along with my hunting buddy, John, on pheasant hunts. We shared the use of his wire-haired pointing griffon dog, Molly. (Is it a coincidence that my wife's name is also Molly?) We tried hunting at the local wildlife management areas which tended to be fairly crowded with other local hunters. It seemed that any time a pheasant was roused from its cover, it had to run a gauntlet of inexperienced marksmen, myself included, until it ultimately, and typically, reached safety.

Then I joined the Swift River Sportsman's Club in Belchertown, Massachusetts. In addition to having 400 acres of private fields and forests, the club raised its own pheasants and would set out about 20 or 25 birds every Saturday morning during pheasant season for club members to hunt. I eventually bagged my first pheasant and I vividly recall the experience in every detail.

John and I were in some fairly open hardwoods beside one of the fields with Molly working between us. She went on point and John and I positioned ourselves on either side of her. When the bird flushed, it rose nearly straight in the air towards the canopy of oak and maple leaves. Just before it reached safety in the high leafy branches, I let go with my Browning and watched the cock pheasant plummet to the ground. It had all seemed to happen in slow motion and every detail became etched in my memory. I was hooked on pheasants.

However, I still needed to sharpen my understanding of the rules of pheasant hunting. One day John suggested that he and I bring along a friend of his, Ken, to hunt with us. John proposed that we let Ken take the first bird since he had never shot a pheasant before. I agreed. With only one dog among the three of us, John was positioned in the center with Ken and me on either side as we marched through the field.

In short order, the dog went on point. A few seconds later the pheasant, a nice hefty rooster, burst from cover and started flying off. True to my promise, I waited for Ken to take the shot and never even raised my shotgun. Bang! The pheasant plummeted to the ground, but it was John that had taken the shot and not Ken. The explanation John gave was that he couldn't help himself, but that Ken could take the next bird. OK, I guess.

Shortly, the dog went on point again. Once more, I kept my gun by my side. The pheasant flushed and just as before, John immediately raised his gun and knocked the pheasant from the sky. Now I became expert on the rules. Every man for himself.

A dog of my own

Eventually I got my own pheasant dog, also a griffon, and named him Diesel. Next to my wife, but not too far behind her, Diesel is the best friend I could ever have. He was easy to train and his instincts alone were probably 90 percent responsible for that training. When we're afield, he typically works fairly close and often glances over his shoulder to make sure I'm not too far behind. If I am, he patiently waits for me to close the distance. If I knock down a pheasant, he eagerly retrieves it and responds enthusiastically to my praise. If I miss a shot, he looks at me with eyes full of simultaneous sadness and reproach.

Diesel and I maintain a close relationship and I work hard to keep it on the best of terms. The fat and lumbering pen-raised pheasants at the sportsman's club help me in this effort. They are not all that difficult to shoot. Late in the season, after being liberally fed all year, they look more like jumbo jets struggling to get airborne, not at all like their speedy partridge and woodcock cousins who take flight as if shot from steam catapults.

Since I enjoy eating the birds I shoot, I often wait to get a bit of distance between them and me before pulling the trigger. Not only does this do less birdshot damage to the bird, but it also tends to slow down the whole shooting experience into more of a choreographed and finely timed sequence of events involving me, the dog, and the pheasant. Sometimes it just comes together perfectly.

One of Diesel's best attributes has nothing at all to do with hunting. The simple fact is my wife adores him. When I first approached her with the idea of getting a hunting dog she was not exactly thrilled. In spite of my assurances to the contrary, I think she had the notion that a hunting dog lacked personality and was just some form of four-legged killing machine. I explained that while I wanted a good hunting companion, I also wanted an animal that would be a suitable house pet. Everything I'd read about griffons and had personally experienced matched that description. My wife eventually relented just a bit and I seized the moment and came home one day with the ugliest, most homely puppy you can imagine. With my wife having a soft spot for the underappreciated, she was drawn to Diesel at first sight. (Maybe that underappreciated thing is why she married me? I might need to think about that some more.)

Now, nearing senior citizen status, Diesel still loves and expects to hunt, but also craves the attention that my wife liberally bestows on him. My advice to any hunter wanting to get his first hunting dog? Let your wife become the dog's best friend at home while you become his best hunting companion afield. All three of you will be exceptionally happy.

New land. New birds.

Before I headed out on one of my caribou hunts, I was told I might want to bring along a shotgun for ptarmigan hunting. I knew what a ptarmigan was from watching TV hunting shows, but had never imagined I'd get the opportunity to hunt for them. Basically, ptarmigan is an arctic partridge that turns pure white in the winter like snowshoe hares do in New England. When the opportunity to hunt them presented itself, I didn't pass it up.

It was the best of all bird hunting worlds. Ptarmigan hunting doesn't require a dog. You just wander aimlessly (something I'm good at) through the tundra brush until you hear cackling. The birds tend to hold tight and then burst into flight much like partridge. Since the tundra is so open, you typically see where they land and can go after them again if you miss.

The birds were midway in their conversion to their white plumage when I hunted them. Their wings were white and their bodies were still a mottled gray and brown blend of color. One of the ptarmigan I shot was mounted by a taxidermist and graced a bookshelf in my office for several years. It reminded me of those tundra wanderings every time I looked at it.

I hope to continue bird hunting for many more seasons. It's a great excuse for a walk in the fields or woods. I've had a lot of fun at it, both when everything has come together perfectly, as well as when the whole experience was more akin to a comedy of errors. And there's another reason to continue bird hunting. I've yet to shoot, cook, and eat that crow. Soon, Molly. Soon.

"Hey Ruben, you're on fire! Again."

Ruben and I were trolling for salmon and trout on Lower Richardson Lake, one of the Rangeley chain of lakes north of Andover, Maine. We'd been there many times before. This day, like many others on Richardson, had a pretty good breeze coming straight down the lake from the north.

A couple minutes before, Ruben, an avid pipe smoker, had pulled his denim jacket up over his head teepee style as a windbreak and struck a match within its confines to relight his pipe. The billowing cloud of smoke from the neck hole where his head should have been indicated that he'd been successful in the effort. Now, with his jacket back on his shoulders, his pipe firmly clenched in his teeth, and fishing rod in hand, Ruben resumed his perennial quest for "the big one."

From my seat in the stern of the boat, I could see not only the billowing clouds of smoke from the glowing bowl of Ruben's pipe filled with his favorite Mixture #79 tobacco, but also several additional wisps of smoke emanating from the front of his flannel shirt. He calmly batted out the stray embers and the new holes in his shirt joined the couple dozen others already there. We continued serenely fishing as if nothing unusual at all had happened. And if you knew Ruben as I did, indeed, nothing unusual had happened.

Hard water fishing

At that time, I'd known Ruben for about 30 years. He was the father of a high school classmate and during high school and later, I spent a lot of time at his house. It was at his dining room table I learned how to play pitch and cribbage, and also heard stories about his fishing exploits in Maine and ice fishing trips on the local river that ran through town just a short way from his back door. Later, I started to accompany Ruben and his neighbor, Jeff, on those ice fishing expeditions. It seemed like I did most of the chopping with the ice chisel for the tip-ups and jigging holes, but that didn't matter to me. I was young and exuberant. And we did catch fish, including some pretty respectable pickerel, largemouth bass, yellow perch, and other lesser species.

We'd typically bring hot dogs with us and cook them over the small bonfires we'd have on the ice. On colder days, the fires also served to restore warmth to frozen fingers and toes. As we got older, we might take along a beer or two or maybe a snort of whiskey. Sometimes seagulls, which Ruben called "white eagles," would swoop down to the ice and make off with a bluegill or two. In between running to sprung flags on the tip-ups, I'd hear Ruben's assortment of 1930s and 1940s witticisms, nearly all of which would not pass a political correctness test today. I'd laugh just as hard the twentieth time I heard one of those stories as I did the first time.

One summer we came up with a scheme to improve the quality of our winter ice fishing. We took two old bedspring frames and stretched sheets of plastic across their lengths. Then we transported the frames by canoe to our favorite fishing cove and carefully sank them into the weed beds. Once that was accomplished, we carried buckets of sand to the submerged frames and poured the sand onto the plastic-covered frames, creating our own private fishing "honey holes." The following winter, and for several more after that, we caught some really hefty largemouth bass off those bed springs. But regardless of whether or not we caught fish, or if the temperature was 30 above or 10 below zero, we always had a good and memorable time.

A journey to Lake Chesuncook

On one occasion, Ruben asked if I wanted to accompany him and Jeff on a week-long combined fishing and camping trip to Lake Chesuncook in Maine. Thinking back on the experience, I wonder if the fact that I had access to Dad's 12-foot boat and 9 ½ horsepower outboard might have had something to do with the invitation. No matter. This was my opportunity to graduate to the big leagues. I was on my way to fabled 22-mile-long Lake Chesuncook, north of Moosehead Lake and really in the midst of Maine's Big Woods country. For me, this was high adventure. It turned out to be more adventurous than I could have anticipated.

Like Ruben, Jeff was the son of Finnish immigrants and maybe that had an influence on the love of the outdoors they both shared. Another thing they had in common was a propensity to get into unusual if not outright dangerous situations. Ruben told me of just such a case that involved the two of them.

It seemed they'd been on another fishing trip to Lake Chesuncook some years before and had been trolling down the center of the lake when a wind and rain storm broke over them. As the height of the waves increased in proportion to the wind's velocity, their one-and-a half horsepower Elgin outboard motor, affectionately known as the "one-lunger," began to sputter and finally cut out completely. Jeff manned the oars while Ruben tinkered with the motor and yanked on the pull cord.

After some time at this routine and with whitecaps foaming around them, they spotted an approaching speedboat. It was large enough to effectively handle the waves and had sufficient power to navigate adequately in the storm. The boat slowed and pulled alongside. Its passenger hollered over and asked if they needed assistance. According to Ruben, and to his significant dismay, Jeff calmly called back saying they were fine and waved the boat off. Somehow they eventually made it to shore and safety. Certainly no such misadventure would befall my own trip with Ruben and Jeff.

By the time we left Massachusetts and headed for Chesuncook it must have been about 9:00 or 10:00 p.m. and well after dark. We were quite a sight on the highway. Jeff was behind the wheel of his vintage early 1960s VW bus. Ruben was sitting on a makeshift bunk bed in the back and I was in the front passenger seat. Dad's aluminum boat was inverted and lashed to the top of the VW. Inside the van we had enough food, camping, and fishing gear for a month-long expedition, never mind the week to ten days we planned to be away. Not noted for its horsepower even when empty, the overloaded VW van chugged northward along the Maine Turnpike significantly below the 70 MPH posted speed limit.

After a stop at the first Howard Johnson's rest stop (they were HoJos in those days, not Burger Kings.), Jeff and I switched seats and I drove while he navigated. The slab-sided VW van was bucking the strong crosswind that tried continuously to send us into the breakdown lane. And the aluminum boat on the roof only served as a sail, catching even more air in its effort to drive us sideways.

Suddenly, at about 2:00 a.m. and somewhere south of Bangor, the van started pulling violently in the opposite direction towards the passing lane. Worse yet, the interior of the van was filling with dense smoke that wreaked of burnt rubber. Ruben, who'd been dozing on the bunk in the back, woke up just as I managed to force the van to the breakdown lane on the right and come to a stop. We all piled out to investigate.

The entire driver's side rear wheel assembly had detached from the axle and become trapped inside the wheel well. As it rubbed on the inside of the wheel well, the friction created the smoke from the heated tire rubber. To make matters even more serious, when the wheel slipped from the axle it had sheared off the brake line as well.

How could such a thing have happened? Let's just say that Jeff's backyard mechanic skills were a bit suspect. He considered belting a stubborn-fitting part with a hammer as finesse. Older VW vans had their rear wheels attached to the axle by a single large nut threaded onto the axle and held in place by a cotter pin. The nut was missing and who knew how many miles earlier it had come off so searching in the dark for it was out of the question. And even if we had found it, as it turned out, the threads on the axle had been damaged by the detached wheel.

While we were pondering our predicament, a tractor-trailer rig pulled to a stop beside us. Salvation seemed at hand. The driver cranked down the passenger-side window and hollered down to us, "You guys need some help?" Jeff immediately responded, "Nope, we're all set." With that, the driver shrugged and he and his big rig set off again into the black desolation of the nighttime Maine Turnpike. Shades of Ruben's and Jeff's storm-tossed adventure on Lake Chesuncook all over again. And we weren't even anywhere close to our yet-to-be-realized destination.

But Jeff did have a solution to our dilemma, of sorts. We jacked up the van and removed the wheel from the wheel well. The good news was that the tire was still inflated, though badly chaffed. The bad news was the answer to a multi-choice question with the correct answer being "all of the above." Missing retaining nut, lost cotter pin, broken brake line, stripped threads on the axle, no replacement parts, and, of course, standing alone as a group without help beside the road on a deserted section of the Maine Turnpike at 2:00 a.m. in the morning.

First, Jeff fashioned a wooden plug from a roadside tree branch and jammed it into the broken brake fluid line. He then further secured the plug with several wraps of electricians tape. Jeff found a hacksaw blade and we took turns using it to somewhat restore the threads on the axle shaft. Why we did this I'm not quite sure since we didn't have a nut to thread back on the axle anyway. We remounted the wheel assembly onto the axle and used something, I don't recall what, to try to secure the wheel in place. We lowered the van from the jack to test our Rube Goldberg repair.

We rolled about 10 feet forward and the wheel promptly fell off the axle again. Back to jury rigging. After jacking up the van again, re-remounting the wheel, and cleaning up the threads a second time, Jeff used the hacksaw blade to cut off the thick wire handle of a barbeque grill. By straightening out both sides of the handle he now had a piece of pliable steel wire about an eighth inch thick and a foot and a half long. He inserted one end into the hole in the end of the axle where the cotter pin normally went and bent the remaining wire several times around the axle to secure the wheel in place.

It wasn't a pretty fix and certainly not in any repair manual, but it worked. We limped along at no more than 30 miles per hour for about an hour all the way to Bangor and found a VW dealership. We parked in the lot and slept until the shop opened after daybreak. After a couple hours in the shop and a replacement tire (I thought we should have purchased two) and a repaired brake line, we resumed our journey northward.

A special lakeside dessert

We eventually arrived at the foot of Lake Chesuncook and set about preparing to embark on the camping and fishing portion of our expedition. The goal was to travel about halfway up the western shoreline and set up camp at a spot called Sandy Point and use that as our fishing base of operations. Our logistics could have used some better planning.

It turns out that if you take one 12-foot boat and load it down with an outboard motor, extra fuel, three grown adults and all their food, camping, and fishing supplies for a week, you run out of space on that boat, to say nothing of freeboard, pretty quickly. To lighten the load, we began unpacking some of the less essential gear. Half our clothing, some of our food, my portable radio, extra fuel, a tool box, and many other items went back into the van. Once underway on the water we maintained about two inches of freeboard. Thankfully there was no wind and shifting position once seated in the boat was definitely out of the question. Nevertheless we pressed on and for safety sake, kept as close to the shore as we could.

Upon arrival at Sandy Point and after setting up our tents and getting our campsite squared away, we tried some fishing. Apparently the fish didn't get the notice concerning our arrival. Instead we settled for a carried-in dinner. Jeff had taken care of the menu planning so whatever we ate was going to be a complete surprise. It was steak and it was delicious. Even better, Jeff had promised a special dessert after dinner. Ruben and I cleared the plates and watched as Jeff dug through his duffle bag and produced two restaurant-size cans of stewed tomatoes. I had a flashback to some of the "non-essential" items we left back in the van in favor of those stewed tomatoes. I would have been happier just listening to my radio.

In spite of Jeff's special dessert, we had a great time at Sandy Point. Lake Chesuncook was one of the last remaining sites in Maine where pulp wood was still boomed across the water for eventual delivery to the paper mills. The booms were formed by chaining a long line of huge tree-length logs together and then bringing both ends together to form a loop. The center of the loop was filled with thousands of four-foot-length pieces of pulp wood and the whole self-contained boom was then towed by a tugboat from one end of a lake to the other. At that point the pulp logs were sluiced by flumes and rivers to the next lake and ultimately to the paper mills. Many of the lakes in northern Maine were either formed or deepened by dams to facilitate the process of moving pulp wood to the mills. Today the process is handled entirely by motorized trucks.

As we dined that first night we watched a tug in the center of the lake moving almost imperceptibly along with a huge mile-long boom of logs in tow. Even though the tug was a mile or two out on the lake, we clearly heard the steady thrum thrum thumming of its massive engine straining against the resistance of the boom. We went to bed that evening to the sight and sound of the tug and awoke the next day with it still in front of our campsite, chugging along and having only made minimal progress during the entire night.

That next day we trolled up to, and all the way around, Gero Island. Then, as well as today, Gero Island is a wildlife sanctuary, but back in the days when logging was done using teams of horses and oxen to haul the logs, Gero Island was the site where hay was grown and harvested as food and bedding for the draft animals.

Despite the miles of dragging our lures through the depths of Chesuncook, we caught no fish that day, or, for that matter, any other day we spent at Sandy Point. After several days we broke camp and departed Chesuncook. We visited, fished, or stayed at many other storied spots such as the Big Eddy, the Little Eddy, and Ripogenus Dam. The Penobscot River was full of pulp wood on its way to the downstream mills and that provided a convenient scapegoat for our lack of fishing success.

The trip back to Massachusetts was significantly less dramatic than the process of getting to northern Maine the week before. However, Jeff did manage to inject a couple memorable moments. Once, on a local two-lane Maine road, we passed another semi-ancient vehicle and Jeff and the other occupant recognized each other. Both vehicles stopped and backed up towards one another. Jeff rolled down his window and called out to the other driver, "Any grog up the line?" Such are the roadside pleasantries when long-lost friends meet in the Maine North Woods.

Another memory was a bit less tasteful, but equally memorable. Jeff had a rather nasty habit of every so often rolling down the driver's-side window and letting loose with a huge wad of spit. Naturally, this was accompanied by all the appropriate sound effects. This might not seem worth mentioning except for the time he did it while we were heading south on the turnpike just as a car with two middle-aged ladies was passing us. The horrified look on both their faces is something that is impossible to erase from my mind. I hope their windshield washer reservoir was full at the time.

I don't recall catching a single fish during the entire Chesuncook experience, but I wouldn't have traded the adventure of it all for anything. More than forty years later I still remember it like it was yesterday.

Further adventures with Ruben

Ruben and I shared additional fishing adventures. A year after the trip to Chesuncook, we spent a week camping and fishing on Lobster Lake in Maine. We even managed to catch a few salmon on that trip. Mishaps were few, though I did shrivel a pair of old leather army boots when I left them too near the fire to dry out one evening. And we learned that hanging a Coleman lantern inside the tent just below the crossed fiberglass ridge poles has a distinct tendency to cause those poles to develop a permanent bend.

We also continued our wintertime ice fishing excursions and I'm certain the tendonitis in my elbows today is a direct consequence of chopping all those holes for the tip-ups and jigging sticks. When Ruben retired from his job he boasted that he went ice fishing for the next 30 consecutive days. I have no doubt that he actually did.

As Ruben got a little older, he developed an illness called macular degeneration, a disease that causes progressive loss of straight-ahead vision while still maintaining some peripheral sight. Ruben was declared legally blind and was no longer able to drive a car. After some initial setbacks, he came to accept his situation and we continued our adventures. Sometimes he'd come with me and we'd fish Lower Richardson Lake and sometimes I'd drive him to Maine and drop him off at his son's house in Rumford. If we were out fishing, I'd have to tie the knots in his line for him.

Even Ruben's blindness had its lighter moments. For example, if we came to an intersection while driving and had to stop, Ruben would look to his right and declare, "It's OK to go. No one is coming." I'd reply, "But Ruben, you're blind." To this Ruben would state that he didn't see any cars approaching. For safety sake, I'd take a good look anyway.

Another ritual was the stop at the "chapel" on the way home from Maine. The chapel was Ruben's name for the New Hampshire State Liquor Store. We always stopped at the chapel and my job was to read the prices of the various whiskies so Ruben could judge which brand was the best value. After making his purchase and getting back in the car, Ruben would irreverently make the sign of the cross and we'd resume our southward pilgrimage. I'll admit to sharing many a "higgo" (Ruben-ese for a whiskey highball) at his dining room table.

Glowing embers

One year in late May, Ruben and I joined two of my friends and went to a camp one of them owned in Palermo, Maine. We

35

fished on Branch Pond the first day and caught a few trout. I'd been to the camp once before with Ruben and the camp's owner for ice fishing over a New Year's weekend. That trip was relatively uneventful except for getting rousted out of bed a bit after midnight by a fire started inside the wall behind the wood stove. Barefoot, we dashed outside into the snow, ripped boards off the side of the camp, and threw snow on the flames to extinguish them. As I said, it was a relatively uneventful trip.

We were having a great time during the May trip, but Ruben didn't seem quite himself. Late the second night, Ruben woke me up and said he was in severe pain. It was so bad we immediately realized that he needed some serious medical attention and we quickly packed up and headed for home. After several doctor's visits, batteries of tests, and some exploratory surgery, Ruben matter-of-factly announced to his family, and later to me, that he had cancer and it wasn't curable.

Initially, while talking to him, you'd never imagine he was dying. We still played cribbage and shared a few higgos. Ruben resumed smoking his beloved pipe, which he had given up a few years before. As time progressed, the disease took more of a toll. It was terrible to see him failing. By November, Ruben was gone. I'd lost my closest friend.

It took some time, but slowly the pain of missing my friend has subsided. After twenty-five years it's been overshadowed by the memories of the great adventures, as well as the misadventures, we shared together. I still miss my friend, but every time I think of him, pass by the New Hampshire State Liquor Store, or chop an ice fishing hole in the frozen river, I can't help but remember Ruben and smile. He's still with me, puffing on that pipe and shooting its glowing embers high into the sky.

First Deer

I stalked him through the thickets and spruce trees. Sometimes his tracks were in the snow and sometimes in the mud. Up one side of a mountain and down the other. Crossing a stream and over my boot tops. From just before sun-up until last legal light. From my teenage years to middle age. And still he eluded me.

The whole truth

OK, so it took me a really long time to take my first deer. Like 27 years long. Now the truth is out there. And it wasn't a big, hulking, heavy-antlered buck. It was an average-size doe. And I didn't stalk it silently through the woods for hours. I'd barely left my truck when the doe stepped into the skidder road in front of me and paused long enough for me to make the shot. But I really paid my dues for that doe. Really.

Today, I watch outdoor TV shows and see parents or other adults taking their sons, daughters, or other young children into the field for their first deer hunting experience. Then it's right there on video. Bang! The youngster brings down a fat ten-pointer with one shot and everyone is all smiles and high fives. My reality was quite different.

Dad was a good fisherman and took me fishing often and taught me a great deal about the sport. However, he didn't hunt. The only firearm he owned was a souvenir World War II Japanese rifle he brought home after his U.S. army service ended in 1945. He had a friend who was the range safety officer at a local sportsmen's club who took my brother and me to that club to practice safe shooting. Eventually, I was given my own .22 rifle and as I got older I graduated from shooting Campbell's soup tin cans at 100 yards to clobbering woodchucks at a nearby farm. I honestly don't know where it came from, but in my late teens I developed a desire to go deer hunting. Maybe it was from exposure to Dad's *Outdoor Life* magazines.

First deer hunt

Dad had another friend in a neighboring town and his backyard abutted some public woodland. I made arrangements with the friend and showed up one December Saturday with my newly acquired shotgun. The friend, named MacMillan (I never learned his first name), lived in what can only be described as an underground bunker. His home had concrete walls and was mounded on the sides and roof with soil. Only the front door and windows on either side of it were exposed to the open. While a bit on the dark side, Mac's home was surprisingly comfortable. Dad suggested that I make a gift of some Polish kielbasa as a thank you for the privilege of being allowed to hunt, and I dutifully presented the sausage to Mac. He was quite pleased with the gift.

Then I set off into the woods alone for my first deer hunt. Talk about a babe in the woods. I had no idea what I was doing. I recall slowly walking through those woods for most of the day and seeing nothing. As I was returning to my car I walked over the crest of a small wooded ridge and saw a nice buck standing amid the trees. We stared at each other for a couple seconds. I was in disbelief. Then, the buck quickly bolted. I never even raised my gun. So much for my first deer hunt. Others soon followed.

After purchasing my camp in Andover, Maine, I tried my luck solo hunting for a couple years and saw and shot nothing. Dad tried to help again. An employee of his, Bill, was a deer hunter and we arranged a week-long trip for Dad, Bill, and me at the camp. We covered a lot of ground that week and once Bill had to face down a bull moose that I spooked towards him. We had a lot of fun that week and ate a lot of good food. But still no deer. Bill even invited me to join him in subsequent years to a hunting destination he frequented on an island off the coast of Maine. The scenery was unique, the experience was great, but the results were the same. No venison.

A brother's luck

I'm one of those people that reads up on something and tries to follow the advice of the experts. My brother, Andy, is not. While I tried for expertise, Andy trusted to dumb luck. I recall a brook trout fishing trip where I tried to neatly float my worm delicately into just the right spot in the eddy of the stream. Andy flung his worm into the air. It wrapped itself around a small alder twig and hung suspended about six inches above the water. A 14-inch brook trout immediately launched itself at the worm and hooked himself. The trout was even considerate enough to stay on the hook until Andy could retrieve him. I caught nothing.

Once when we were on a family deep-sea fishing trip, I managed to hook and boat my biggest-ever cod fish. It weighed about 45 pounds. Less than 30 minutes later, Andy boated a 50 pounder. It seemed he always managed to outdo me.

Andy and I developed a hunting style we called leapfrogging. One of us would slowly still-hunt along a logging road for 30 minutes and then sit. After 30 minutes, the person at the starting point would slowly walk to where the first person was sitting and then move ahead for the next 30 minutes, and so on. In this way we were double-covering a significant section of hunting territory. The first year we tried this strategy, I was sitting and heard a gunshot ahead of me and knew it had to be Andy who made it.

At the time, Andy didn't have the best of hunting weapons. He was using Dad's old 7.7 mm souvenir Japanese army rifle. He'd spotted a nice buck walking parallel to him through the woods when buck fever took hold. He raised and lowered the rifle three separate times. The first two times he said he couldn't see the sights on the rifle. By the third try, the buck had spotted him and headed for the deep thickets. Andy got off a shot and we found where it had bored a neat hole through a birch tree. His luck changed the following year when he bought a secondhand Winchester .30-30.

We were both sitting on ground stands where we thought deer might cross a logging road. Within a short time I saw a buck sneaking through the beech trees in my direction. If he kept coming I'd have an easy shot. But just before he got into the clear, he reversed direction and headed off to where Andy was sitting. Bang! Andy had taken an offhand 80-yard shot, through the trees, with iron sights, and put the .30-30 bullet through both of the deer's lungs. Field-dressed, the deer weighed 181 pounds.

Bear and moose first

My luck was about to change. The next year Andy and I tried again. We'd hiked towards the summit of a mountain on a new logging road and had seen nothing except tracks. We were returning to the truck and walking side by side and talking when a black bear walked into the middle of the road in front of us and stopped broadside. All three of us momentarily froze. I raised my rifle and quickly aimed just behind the front shoulder. Just as I pulled the trigger, the bear pivoted away and took a half step. However, it was still directly in line with my sights and the bullet went through the left haunch and lodged just beneath the hide in the opposite front shoulder. It ran about 40 yards, let out a last bawl, and died in the middle of a stream. It wasn't a deer, but I was happy. This was my first-ever big game animal.

About this time, Maine had begun permit-only moose hunting through a lottery system. Only one thousand permits were available and of those, only 100 were offered for non-residents like me. I applied anyway and Andy was my sub-permitee. I'd completely forgotten about the lottery and was very surprised when I received a phone call stating that I was the third alternate. If only three non-residents decided not to pay the fee for their permits, I'd get my chance. And that's just what happened.

Andy and I made the choice to self-guide our hunt. Our designated hunting area was Zone One in the far northwest corner of Maine. We found a campsite at a river crossing and set up our tent. It took us until Thursday, but I eventually took an 800-pound bull moose. It was some of the most delicious meat, wild or store-bought, I've ever eaten. But it still wasn't a deer.

A new rifle, a mirror, and better luck

I went back to my solo hunts in the Andover, Maine, area. Maine became a bucks-only state and no longer permitted any-deer hunting. As if it hadn't been tough enough for me just trying to see any deer, now, I had to be certain the deer had antlers before I shot.

I recall hiking up a mountain logging road early one morning and being surprised as three does burst from the freshly cut area below me. I had my rifle up, but didn't see any antlers. Then another doe followed, and then another. I desperately looked for antler points, but to no avail. By the time the parade was over, I counted eleven does, but not a single buck in the bunch.

A couple more years of hunting by myself yielded the same result. Nothing. It's fortunate that I enjoy just being out in the woods all day. A hunter or a fisherman has to be an eternal optimist, otherwise they'd give up during the dry spells. But by this time, my dry spell was about 27 years long. Something had to change.

On one northbound trip during the summer, I stopped at the Kittery Trading Post and spotted in the used gun rack a Marlin .44 magnum semi-automatic carbine with peep sights. I liked the little carbine immediately and it fit my budget. Even better, I found that I was deadly accurate with it, at least at the rifle range. The gun weighed so little that it was a joy to carry. Its only drawback was that for such a small firearm, it packed a disproportionately large recoil due to its light weight. No problem. I could handle that. The carbine would become my new deer rifle.

That November, early one morning, just as I was passing the end of the pavement and about to enter the gravel logging roads for a day's hunt, I spotted something lying in the rubble of an old collapsed camp. It was a small rectangular mirror in a wooden frame. They say that a broken mirror brings bad luck. Maybe the opposite would be true with an unbroken mirror. While I'm not normally superstitious, I picked up the mirror and put it behind the front seat of my truck and continued into the logging country.

My destination that day was a freshly cut road that ran beside Mosquito Brook. The brook emptied into Upper Richardson Lake and the road headed into some thick flat timber land before rising sharply up the mountain slopes. I parked off the main logging road and began walking slowly and quietly along the brook road.

I was armed with two items that day, other than my 27 years of dogged determination. The first was my little .44 magnum carbine and the second was a doe permit that I was fortunate enough to draw for the area I hunted.

I hiked about a quarter mile in and was just past the deck area where the loggers loaded their trucks earlier in the season. Ahead of me was a skidder path used to drag logs to the deck. Eighty yards away, a whitetail doe stepped into the middle of the path with its body turned so that its backside was facing directly towards me. However, it had its head turned to look back over its body in my direction. I was sure the doe would bolt into the woods at any moment. My only ethical shot was at the doe's neck. I raised the carbine and took careful but quick aim and pulled the trigger.

To my amazement, the doe dropped in its tracks. It wasn't a trophy buck, or even a big doe, but it *was* a deer. My first. At that moment, I couldn't have been happier. I was able to back my truck to within about 100 yards of the doe and loaded her in the back after first taking care of the field dressing chore. My 27-year quest for my first deer was over. On my way home I stopped at Dad's house. He was almost as happy as me.

Since bagging that first deer, I've taken about a dozen more, including some bucks, in places as varied as Maine, Massachusetts, Tennessee, and Anticosti Island, Canada. Even though it took me 27 years to get the first one, in retrospect, I wouldn't change history at all. During those 27 years I met some interesting characters, made some good friends, successfully hunted for and harvested a bear and a moose, and had many memorable experiences. That good-luck mirror that I found that morning by the roadside on the way to Mosquito Brook? Today it's hanging on the wall inside my Andover, Maine, camp. It still reflects a pretty decent smile.

Part Two : The Loincloth Fits

Again alluding to Cornel Wilde's movie persona, I gradually honed my sportsman skills. Rather than constantly having my environment take charge over me, I slowly but surely gained confidence and took control of it. Not without setbacks. Nothing makes you more aware of your vulnerability than being dropped off in the middle of the Maine woods with no hope of pick up for at least half a day and then having an intense rain storm break out. And the temperature is hovering just above freezing.

But when your guide eventually shows up and casually mentions that he didn't think you could take that kind of exposure to the elements and you actually did, it reinforces your spirit and encourages further expansion of your frontiers.

Part two's chapters cover my expanding universe of outdoor challenges and experiences. I'm no longer completely naked, but still have a lot to learn.

Rollie and My Caribou

When my hunting partner, Charlie Wade, and I first arrived in the caribou hunting camp and sat down for our first meal, I thanked our native Newfoundland guide, Rollie Burry, for passing me the sugar for my coffee. Rollie smiled and said he preferred we not thank each other for anything until we'd taken our animals. Then, he would thank us. Over the next couple days I learned to comply with his odd request, but only after a few slip-ups.

Welcome to Justin Lake, Labrador

Wednesday morning, the third day of our trip, was clear, cool, and windy. The 40-degree temperature felt more like half that. I'd been awake since sunrise, fishing from the shore of the Justin Lake campsite for arctic char. A couple fish followed my spinning lure in, but only a small one dared to take a bite at it and for its reward, I set it free to get bigger and wiser. Mostly, I was just passing a little time before breakfast and setting out for the day's caribou hunt.

Justin Lake is located at the base of the Torngat Mountains, just above 58 degrees north latitude, near Hebron, an abandoned Moravian mission at the northern tip of Labrador and about a mile inland from the Atlantic Ocean and Sagalak Bay. The area is home to the Koroc caribou, a small, non-migratory herd spread over northern Labrador and eastern Quebec and known for its large-sized, heavy-antlered animals.

Charlie and I selected Justin Lake as our destination because it promised everything we wanted: arctic char fishing, the possibility of a barren-ground black bear, and most of all, a chance for an impressive caribou. We also wanted to get as far north as we could, well above tree line and into some truly remote country. Since this was the first guided hunting expedition for either of us, it was to be as much of an adventure as it was a hunting and fishing trip. Justin Lake met all our requirements. We'd planned the trip for months and now it was finally happening.

The campsite was primitive, but more than adequate for our needs. And it certainly qualified as remote. We were probably the only human beings within a hundred miles. There were two tents set on wooden platforms. Charlie's and mine was unheated and plenty big enough for all our gear and us. Even with early September's nighttime temperatures in the 30s and low 40s, we managed to stay quite comfortable. Our bunks consisted of sheets of plywood nailed to two-by-four frames with four-inch thick foam pads for mattresses which were surprisingly comfortable. Whenever we got thirsty, it was a simple matter to walk out the front of the tent and take a dipper of water right out of the lake. I don't think I've ever tasted finer water.

The second tent, serving as Rollie's home, supply shack, and kitchen and dining room, was located just behind ours. It also functioned as the meeting hall and had a small kerosene heater for warmth. It contained a full-size propane gas range and oven, a big dining table and chairs, a battery-powered two-way radio on which we listened to the optimistic and successful hunting reports from other camps, and an assortment of tools and storage bins. The camp was all the more impressive since everything had been flown in by float plane.

The only other man-made structures at Justin Lake camp were the 20-foot trimmed spruce poles that suspended the radio antenna, the screened-in meat shack where we hoped to hang our caribou quarters, and the outhouse, respectfully and appropriately located a hundred yards or so uphill and away from the tents.

The outhouse was a site to behold. It was only about four and a half feet tall and so small that maneuvering in and out of it required a fair amount of dexterity. We nicknamed it the mansion. Its only redeeming feature was that whenever you paid it a visit, the view of the lake made the trip up the hill more than worth the hike.

One other aspect of the camp facilities was somewhat noteworthy. Shortly after arriving in camp we noticed that the canvas of the cook tent had been ripped down the side and roughly sewn back together. The same was true of its screened entrance. When asked what had happened, Rollie told us that about two weeks before, a black bear had come into camp when no one was around and tore things up looking for food. In addition to the damage to the tent, the bear had also flattened the meat shed and the outhouse. Rollie had patched things up admirably, but warned us to be on the lookout for any black bears and that if we saw one, shoot it. He said the bear had come back once again and he'd scared it off by heaving a frying pan at it. I noticed an old rifle lying on the ground and from its apparent condition, the frying pan was probably more lethal. I wasn't sure either weapon would have been much use had a stray polar bear come into camp, something Rollie mentioned was a possibility and that neither Charlie nor I was eager to experience.

As it turned out, the marauding black bear did return to camp later in the week while Charlie and Rollie were there. For the bear, it represented a fatal error in judgment. For Charlie, it represented a new bearskin rug.

Incredible sights and sounds

The land and views around the camp were breathtaking. The campsite was at one end of the three-mile-long lake that was nearly encircled by steep mountains. When the wind was calm, it was difficult to distinguish the reflection on the lake from the sky and land surrounding it. Sunrises and sunsets were magic times of day. There wasn't a single tree anywhere to give perspective to distance or size. Boulders that appeared to be the size of a small automobile turned out to be closer to that of a three-story house.

To the north, rock walls rose steeply with cascades of water running down their sides, providing a soothing background sound whenever the wind was still. Straight ahead were more mountains with flat plateaus between them and the shoreline. The land to the south was a combination of more flats and rock ridges arranged in tiers and gradually rising to another set of peaks. The North Atlantic Ocean was behind the camp and about a mile away behind a small ridge. The outlet of Justin Lake flowed into the sea and served as the highway for the arctic char entering and leaving the lake. While standing on the ridge behind the campsite, you could see the cold blue ocean water and an occasional iceberg drift past between the coast and some rocky offshore islands. Seals were daily visitors at the lake's outlet, preying on the char as they followed their migratory journeys up the stream.

Other sights and sounds were equally exciting. We could hear wolves howling to one another late at night in the distance. I'd heard eastern coyotes many times, but this was a much more eerie and primitive sound. There was no mistaking it for anything else. The northern lights filled the night sky from horizon to horizon with a shimmering glow that continually changed in color, shape, and intensity. During the day the ground was a blaze of color in its own right. It was as if you were in a plane circling 10,000 feet above autumn foliage in New England. The difference was that here I was only five feet above it and the "foliage" consisted of inch-high mosses, lichen, and berry bushes. The blues, yellows, oranges, reds, and greens all blended together with the gray granite rocks to form a spectacular quilt of color covering the entire landscape. I'd expected the tundra to be mostly barren. Instead, it amazed me with the variety and richness of its beauty.

Master of the tundra

A few things were apparent about Rollie even if we didn't yet know him well. He knew the tundra and was completely comfortable there. We learned that he had been at the Justin Lake site for about a month with several different hunting parties and had declined a trip back to Shefferville, Quebec, for a rest. He was also physically fit. Even at 10 years my senior, he bounded across the rocks and streams as if they were level ground. But perhaps the most unique thing about Rollie was his speech. By that I mean, it was difficult at first to understand his Newfie dialect. It was English, but with expressions and pronunciations that took a bit of getting used to. For example, if Rollie asked me how I was doing, he'd say "'Ow ye doin', me b'y?" And the letter "H" got added to and dropped from words for no apparent reason. To this day, when Rollie gives me a telephone call it takes me a minute or so to get the gist of what he's saying.

My stomach called me back from my fishing and daydreaming and I could hear Rollie stirring in the cook tent. He was doing double duty, also serving as unofficial cook until the regular cook arrived in camp. So far we'd eaten fresh-caught char and some caribou back-strap steaks left by the previous week's hunters for our evening meals. Rollie, somewhat apologetically, called it "rough grub." Charlie and I called it delicious.

I walked back to the cook tent after a few more casts for some breakfast and warmth. The kerosene heater with its warm glow was just sufficient to take off the early morning chill and dampness. Charlie joined us and we sat down for hot tea and coffee, bacon and eggs, and stories. Charlie and I still weren't familiar enough with Rollie to tell which of his stories were true, which were fiction, and which—maybe most—were a combination of the two. It didn't really matter. They were all great listening and were adding much to the enjoyment of our trip. Every meal at Justin Lake was hearty and filled both the stomach and imagination with nourishment.

Time to hunt

Charlie and I had been hunting for the last day and a half, getting the feel of the land and plotting our strategies. We'd seen a few caribou, but nothing trophy-class or close by. I told Charlie that I was now wearing my lucky shirt, the one that my wife kept threatening to throw in the trash. Taking a look in my direction, Charlie said he could understand why. The faded green chamois shirt had holes in the sleeves and beside the pockets, a couple bloodstains, and the collar was worn to a tatter. I'd been wearing it when I'd taken three or four deer over the years as well as a moose so it had a place of honor in my hunting wardrobe. I'd be too embarrassed to be seen in it publicly at home, but in the Maine woods or here in northern Labrador's sub-arctic tundra, it was warm and comfortable. It just might help me find my caribou today. And that day, I *did* feel lucky.

As we collected our rifles and packs after breakfast and went up the hill behind the tents, I told Charlie that I was going to head south and sit on the ridge from which the previous week's hunters had shot two caribou and a large black bear. According to Rollie, the bear wasn't the same one that had previously torn up the camp. The remains of all three carcasses were still on the ground. I was hoping that maybe some more caribou would funnel through the gap between the ridges, or another bear might decide its breakfast was waiting to be served. Charlie and I wished each other good luck and he headed east for the boulder-strewn bowl at the base of some peaks. Rollie said he'd look in on us.

I had rested on this same ridge the previous day to get the lay of the land. For some reason I looked down at my feet and spotted two things that didn't belong there. One was a spent silver Remington .300 UltraMag rifle cartridge. It was probably left from the shot that killed the bear. The second item was pink in color and about the size of the end of my little finger. I bent over and picked up what turned out to be a hearing aide. I could imagine the scenario. The elderly hunter shot the bear with the potent UltraMag and the jarring recoil had knocked the hearing aid from his ear. I later returned the hearing aide to Rollie who said he'd get it back to its owner. I'll bet that hunter never expected to see it again. I kept the empty cartridge casing.

I made my way to the ridge in about 45 minutes and settled in for whatever might pass below me. My plan was to sit and watch for as long as I could take the cold and blustery wind and then climb down and walk along "the road." The road was the name I'd given to a straight, three-mile-long natural cut through the granite. It was paved with grass and flowers gone to seed and looked like Mother Nature's bulldozer had carved its way through the rock with the higher mountains on the left and the tundra sloping gently to the lakeshore on the right. If anything crossed the road, I'd be able to quickly spot it from my perch.

I was pretty exposed to the weather on the ridge, and the fierce wind was picking up even stronger. I put on my rain suit as a wind break, wrapped a scarf around my neck, and put on mittens, but after about two hours the cold got to me and I'd had enough. It was time to get to lower ground, out of the wind, and follow the rest of my strategy for the day. I planned to walk the road along the south shore of the lake. I descended and skirted around the caribou and bear carcasses and walked along one side of the gap.

Once out of the wind and moving, I immediately started to feel warmer and started looking for another place to sit and watch for animals. Something made me look back up the ridge to where I had been sitting and there stood Rollie. I waved, but I could tell he hadn't seen me in my camouflage rain suit against the backdrop of rock and he went back along the ridge in the opposite direction and out of sight. I felt he had to have been looking for me for a reason. After only a couple minutes Rollie reappeared on the ridge and this time I moved away from the granite wall and waved as I silhouetted myself against a grassy background. It worked. Rollie spotted me immediately and motioned that I should join him back on the ridge. He seemed excited. Ten minutes later I was by his side.

Rollie brought me some food: a raspberry square pastry, two big oatmeal cookies, and a big slice of delicious, fresh-baked raisin pie. I devoured the pastry and put the cookies in my pocket for later. Rollie also brought me something else. He told me that when he first topped the ridge he had seen a large caribou stag cross the road going toward the lake about a mile or so away and well beyond where I was walking. He suggested we go after it and I didn't need to be coaxed. Once again I descended the ridge and headed up the road, this time with Rollie in the lead.

After about a half mile, Rollie borrowed my binoculars, though it seemed he used them just for confirmation of what his eyes had already told him. He scanned the ridges on the left and spotted two caribou grazing on the slopes and pointed them out to me. Both were fairly small animals, probably females, but at least we knew there were some caribou in the area. A short ways farther on he spotted another one high on the ridges and this one looked a little larger. He thought he saw something else beside it, but said it might just be a rock. I looked and thought for sure it was a rock. Rollie took one more look and this time the rock moved. It was a larger, light-colored caribou stag. We couldn't tell how large the antlers were from that distance, but decided this was an animal at least worth getting a closer look at. We started to climb the slope.

A caribou materializes

Before we left our starting point, Rollie had warned me to keep an eye to our back trail. He explained that because of the terrain and with caribou continually moving and bedding down, it was entirely possible that one might cross behind us after we passed an area.

We'd been climbing for only a few minutes when I looked behind us and off towards the lake. About 500 yards away in an open area of vegetation I spotted a magnificent caribou. It was angling away from us and moving slowly ahead towards the shore of the lake. I could tell this was a prize animal even at that distance. I could see the pure white mane encircling its neck and its large size. It was much larger than the caribou we had been glassing on the slopes above us.

Most of all, I noticed the antlers. They were tall and spread wide apart, deeply palmed at the tops and with a broad double bez in front. I could also see at least a single large shovel above the caribou's nose. And unlike most of the animals we'd seen so far, this one had shed nearly all of its velvet and the light brown antlers reflected the morning's sunlight. This animal was the epitome of my mind's-eye image of what a trophy caribou should look like and I wanted none other.

I called ahead to Rollie. At the second call, he turned and I pointed off to the right. He saw the caribou too and we both immediately descended the ridge and headed up the road to try to get ahead of the animal. We were well below the caribou's line of sight while on the road so we could move fast and unobserved.

On the way, Rollie said he wasn't sure if this was the biggest animal around or if it had a double shovel, making it a truly trophy-class animal. It didn't matter to me. I had gotten a good look at it and told Rollie, "That's the one I want." I was certain. "Then let's go get 'im," was Rollie's reply.

We spent some time climbing small rises and looking for the caribou, but had lost sight of it in the rolling rocky ridges. It might have doubled back or bedded down behind a hill. I told Rollie that I didn't see how it could have gotten ahead of us so we kept moving forward, angling closer towards the shore of the lake. About 15 minutes had passed since we'd last seen him. We entered a long rolling area of short vegetation that flowed down to the shoreline, about 200 to 250 yards distant.

Seemingly from nowhere, the caribou, *my caribou*, materialized. He was still slowly walking along parallel and near the shore, grazing as he went. Rollie said he'd probably stayed next to the lake the whole time, that being the reason we hadn't seen him sooner. He appeared even more magnificent than when we'd first seen him.

Rollie and I crouched and noted there was a small rise between the caribou and us. By keeping low, we were able to move fairly quickly and cut the distance by about 100 yards. We were now well within good shooting range.

The two of us crawled on all fours and I could feel my heart pounding with excitement. We were about 100 yards away when I decided to get into a sitting position for a shot. I sat up and put my eye to the scope, but could only see antlers above the grass. We'd have to crawl closer. I didn't want to stand up for fear of spooking the animal.

We crawled some more and at about 80 yards I got ready for another attempt at a shot. Rollie told me we could crawl perhaps another 10 yards, but I said I was fine. I remember thinking that this was the culmination of the whole trip and the months of anticipation. I was focused only on the caribou in front of me. Nothing else distracted me.

I chambered a round. The scope on my Remington 7mm magnum was turned down to four power and when I looked through it, the animal was almost broadside to us and filled the eyepiece. I eased off the safety, put the cross hairs just behind the left shoulder, and slowly squeezed the trigger.

I only half-heard the sound of the rifle and its echo off the mountains and barely felt its recoil. The caribou arched its head to the sky while its rear quarters sank to the ground. Then the front half slowly lowered as well. It fell where it had stood, a good clean shot.

After my caribou went down and we were walking towards it, I recalled Rollie's admonition that we should not thank each other for anything until we'd taken our animals. Now Rollie looked at me, smiled, shook my hand, and quietly said "thank you." I did the same in return. We celebrated by sharing the oatmeal cookies I'd stuffed in my pocket earlier. My smile lasted the entire two-mile walk back to camp, even with the heavy set of antlers and cape spread across my shoulders. I hardly felt the weight. I had my caribou and an adventure I'd have with me forever. (The caribou unofficially scored 376 2/8 points, Safari Club scoring, qualifying it for record book status. To this day, it's the most impressive of my several caribou trophies.)

Justin Lake postscript

There is quite a bit more to tell about our trip to Justin Lake, but it doesn't all fit neatly into the context of the narrative above. The following covers those aspects of the trip.

Hunting and fishing were not our only adventures during our stay at Justin Lake. A tragic event happened while we were there. We had arrived on September 9, 2001. The whole world knows what happened on September 11, 2001.

Charlie and I had been away from camp and hunting that fateful day and completely oblivious to world events. Rollie turned on his shortwave radio that evening and was met with a barrage of confusing chatter on what had transpired in New York City and elsewhere. One story we heard was that 50,000 people had been killed and that the United States was at war with someone. We didn't know who. We were told that all air traffic in North America was grounded until further notice. Even if we had wanted to leave, we couldn't.

Eventually we got a story that was closer to the truth of what had happened. We both called our wives on the satellite phone and reassured them that we were OK. It was a scary time to be so far away from home.

Rollie, Charlie, and I were fairly pragmatic about the situation and resolved that there was absolutely nothing we could do except to continue hunting and fishing, which we did, but not without an awareness that the outside world had changed while we were away.

How to filet a caribou

The next day, September 12, was the day I took my caribou. A comedy of errors ensued once it was down. Rollie asked me for my camera to take some photos. I was travelling light that day and confessed that I had left it in camp. No problem. We could take pictures back at camp. However, preparing the caribou for transport back to camp was a different matter.

It seemed Rollie was also travelling somewhat less than fully prepared that day. He said he had not brought his knife along and needed mine in order to cape and quarter the caribou. I was well equipped for this, or so I thought. First, I produced my Shrade Old Timer pocket knife. Rollie asked if I had something a bit more substantial. I then brought out my Leatherman tool and opened the blade on it. This was met with a grimace. Time for the heavy artillery. I then unsheathed my Rapala fish filet knife with its slender 10-inch blade. In a style similar to that of the movie character Mick Dundee played by actor Paul Hogan in the movie *Crocodile Dundee*, Rollie laughed and said, "That's not a knife." It wasn't what he expected, but Rollie made do.

Knife notwithstanding, I was enthralled with how Rollie butchered the caribou. Each quarter was neatly severed from the torso with minimal blood and cutting. Once that was accomplished, Rollie peeled back the hide from the spine and exposed the back straps. He deftly removed these in two long pieces. Then he counted down a specific number of vertebrae and severed the spine. After cutting through a couple ribs on each side, he bent back the spine and exposed the inner tenderloin filets, the tenderest parts of the caribou. Finally, Rollie used that filet knife to cape the head and remove it and the attached hide for later mounting. The whole process took only a short time and never required opening up the animal. Rollie joked that this was the first time he'd ever fileted a caribou. From that moment on, my nickname was "Filet." I consider it a well-earned badge of honor.

We found some pieces of plywood beside the lake shore once the butchering was completed. We put all the meat on the wood and then covered it with an emergency metalized mylar survival blanket and put more wood and heavy rocks on that. This was to keep the meat protected from the flies and wolves. Rollie knew that the float plane was due in camp in a day or two (assuming air traffic resumed post-9/11) and the meat could be easily picked up rather than carried back to camp. The cool temperatures would prevent spoilage.

Paying attention while watching Rollie butcher that caribou had its benefits. Charlie shot his own caribou a couple days later and, as luck would have it, Rollie was not with us at the time. Now equipped with a proper knife, Charlie and I duplicated Rollie's procedures on this caribou and while it took us longer, we achieved the same end result. I've since seen this form of caribou dismemberment accomplished several times and am continually amazed at its simplicity and efficiency. It's so much easier than the traditional gutting of a deer or other similar creature, though some meat is lost in the process.

After I returned home from Justin Lake, I decided to send a small gift to Rollie in appreciation of both his guiding expertise and his tolerance of a complete neophyte to the tundra. I purchased a new Rapala filet knife and had it engraved with the words. "Rollie's caribou filet knife." Rollie called me after receiving it and we both had a great laugh.

The hunting trip to Justin Lake had one final surprise in store for us. When departure day arrived, we were grounded. Not only that, but we were isolated for an additional four days. Frankly, I viewed this as a bonus. We were in beautiful remote country. We could still fish for arctic char. And the food, rough grub or not, wasn't about to run out. We had two whole caribou to eat if it came to that.

Eventually the weather cleared and the float plane set off from Shefferville to retrieve us. We ran into low clouds on the return flight and as we flew low over the Torngat Mountains I reflexively pulled my legs up to my chin. We went through a mountain pass so low that I could see small pebbles on the ground.

Another trip with Rollie

I had expected my trip to Justin Lake to be my one and only trip-of-a-lifetime, caribou-hunting adventure. However, the tundra bug had bitten me and even today I'm still seriously infected. Two years after Justin Lake I found myself again in Shefferville, Quebec, and on my way farther north. This trip was with the same outfitter and I had specifically asked to again have Rollie as my guide.

I had no idea upon arrival, at a different campsite this time, whether or not my request had been honored. But when the float plane's cabin door opened, there was Rollie at dockside. Not only that, but his wife Ruby was present as well and did the honors as camp cook. Rollie was an excellent cook at Justin Lake, but Ruby was even better. Ruby made a point of being surprised at the amount of pickled beets I ate at camp that week. Little did she know that as the grandson of a Russian immigrant I was very used to eating beets, fresh or pickled, at many a meal. To this day I enclose a label from a jar of pickled beets in every card or letter I mail to them in their Gander, Newfoundland, home.

I took both my caribou during the first day of hunting on this second trip with Rollie. Neither was as magnificent as the one I shot on my trip to Justin Lake. While taking my limit of caribou on day one left a lot of free time at camp, it also allowed me to just relax and completely enjoy the trip and Rollie and Ruby's company. On this trip, I learned that sometimes the wild animal trophies you bring home are less significant than the memories you take back with you.

Tundra Perfection

"I don't want to see any trees."

"There are no trees," Carroll replied.

"Are you sure? Can you prove it?"

"I'll send you a couple photographs," was Carroll's final answer.

I heard Carroll's words, but based on my experience two years earlier, I was more than a bit skeptical. If I was to make another significant investment in a hunting adventure to the barren arctic tundra only to feel cheated and disappointed when it was over, I didn't want to be, once again, kicking myself in the butt for being misled.

No trees. A promise kept

Four years before, I'd gone on a remote caribou hunt to Labrador, my first outfitter hunt ever, and I'd had a wonderful time, one beyond my wildest expectations. Two years later, I booked the exact same trip with the same outfitter and while the trip was successful by the definition of shooting caribou, it was quite a letdown in terms of what was promised and paid for versus what was delivered. It left me knowing the outfitter was little better than a conniving used car salesman and I had been his mark. I didn't want it to happen again and I was performing my due diligence.

That second caribou hunt was supposed to go to the same Labrador location as my first trip. In reality, once my hunting partner and I arrived in Shefferville, Quebec, to depart by float plane for Labrador on our last leg of travel, we were surprised to learn that our final destination was just 70 or 80 miles away in Quebec. Not only were we not hunting the Koroc caribou herd as we'd been promised, and at the premium rate we'd already paid, but we were to be hunting the local George River herd in scrub tundra woodlands barely a stone's throw from civilization. In fact, from the air we saw dirt roads leading most of the way to the cabins at the lake where we were to stay. We made the best of it, but the bad taste in my mouth remained long after the trip was over.

For this third trip, I did some Internet research that eventually lead me to the firm of Fins and Furs Adventures in Skowhegan, Maine. Fins and Furs Adventures is an agency that books hunting, fishing, and other outdoor adventures with prescreened outfitters worldwide. One of the owners, Carroll Ware, and I connected by phone. I informed him of my objective and of my past disappointing experience and he assured me that I would have a happy outcome this time. In a show of honesty, Carroll sent me the promised photographs of the intended destination and true to his word, there were no trees to be seen. Better yet, Carroll would be going on the trip too so that if anything was not to my liking, I had a customer service representative ready at my side.

Leaf River Lodge was to be my destination. It was situated on the river of the same name and roughly halfway between Ungava Bay and the northern end of Hudson Bay, just south of the Arctic Ocean. Not only were we to hunt caribou, but two caribou at that as compared to the single animal limit in Labrador. There were also the prospects of barren ground black bear, ptarmigan hunting, and fishing for lake trout, brook trout, and Atlantic salmon. My toughest challenge was likely going to be getting all my gear for the various hunting and fishing opportunities picked out and packed and still under the 70-pound baggage weight limit.

My hunt on the Labrador tundra four years previous had been extremely remote. We'd stayed in unheated platform tents, did without electricity, used a ramshackle outhouse, and bathing consisted of dipping a washcloth into the lake beside the tent. Not so at Leaf River Lodge. While we were certainly going to be geographically remote, we were going to have to "endure" a few creature comforts. Each pair of hunters would have their own small heated cabin. There was a central bathhouse with flush toilets and hot showers. Electricity would be provided by a generator. And a central dining room offered first-class meals and even wine with every dinner. I was quite sure I could handle the "sacrifice" and learn to live with the amenities.

Departure day finally arrived. We drove to Montreal and spent a comfortable night in the Holiday Inn after enjoying a great steakhouse meal hosted by Carroll. Then, except for a few souls that sought additional camaraderie and sustenance provided by the hotel bar, it was off to bed for our last night south of the tundra.

The plane is older than me!
Well, maybe not quite older, but almost.

After weighing them in and turning our duffels over to the outfitter's staff, we boarded the bus for Montreal's Duval airport. And there was our plane, a 1950s vintage Convair 580 twin-engine turboprop. I assured myself that despite the old air bird's age, it was probably rugged enough to take on anything the tundra could dish out and still ask for more.

I was in for another surprise once inside the Convair. All the seats in the front of the passenger cabin had been ripped out and all our duffel bags and gun cases were piled on both sides of the center aisle and held in place by cargo webbing. Thirty-two seats remained in the rear of the cabin for me and the other hunters heading north. While the regular airlines had instituted strict post-9/11 security measures, our rules were a bit more relaxed. Most of us carried knives on our belts and maybe a box or two of rifle cartridges in our pockets. No security personnel bothered to check us out and I saw no metal detectors in use. In short, we were armed to the teeth. Woe to any hijacker that tried to take on this flight.

After a short run on the taxiway, the plane pulled itself into the air with the aid of the venerable turboprop engines and we slowly gained altitude. While the sparse interior did little to dampen the engine noise, the view from the windows was spectacular. We quickly left Montreal behind and flew over a landscape dotted by lakes and sliced by rivers. Ultimately, we reached our first stop, Lac Pau, where we landed on a packed gravel runway.

Lac Pau exists only by the grace of man. It's a massive lake formed by manmade dams to help create a huge hydroelectric project in remote Quebec. The runway was built for the sole purpose of shuttling in equipment and workers for the construction job and the project's subsequent operation and maintenance. There is no terminal as such, no radar that I could see, and not much in the way of amenities. In fact, for those of us that needed immediate use of a restroom upon landing, we were directed to the nearest growth of underbrush, men and women alike.

In relatively short order, we were transported to the shore of the lake where a fleet of several float planes were waiting to take groups of hunters to their final destinations. Each plane accommodated six or seven passengers plus the pilot. In addition to us hunters and our baggage, the planes also held cargo in the passenger cabin. While some hunters had their partner seated next to them, others had a 55-gallon fuel drum as their traveling companion. Lunch was a sandwich picked out of a cardboard box. No choice. Just take what was handed to you. That day it was baloney and mustard.

On the final leg of the flight to Leaf River Lodge, we flew over some of the most beautiful country I've ever seen. Few trees. Hundreds of sparkling lakes and ponds. A myriad of colors that spanned the entire spectrum. And, with a hint of what was to come, hundreds of pathways worn deeply into the tundra by the hoofs of thousands of generations of migrating caribou.

Our plane circled the camp and touched down smoothly on a wide section of the river and taxied to the dock. Staff, mostly the guides, helped us off the plane and we quickly assembled at the central meeting hall where snacks and the owner, Alain Tardif, awaited us. Alain went over camp policies and procedures, solicited and answered questions, and assigned cabins. After unpacking and obtaining licenses, we checked the accuracy of our rifles and were soon enjoying the first of many delicious dinners in the dining hall. The carafes of both red and white wine on the tables were a nice and welcome touch. Hunting was to start first thing in the morning.

I woke up once during the night and needed to use the bathroom. Rather than journey all the way to the bathhouse, I opted to go out behind the cabin. While standing there in the dark doing my business, I noticed something light-colored walking back and forth just a few yards away. I thought it might possibly be a caribou and flicked on my flashlight. Rather than a caribou, I saw a wolf. His eyes glowed from the beam of my flashlight and despite his constant motion, he never took those eyes off me. After a minute or so of our mutual observation of one another, I went back in the cabin and left the wolf to his patrolling. I'd heard wolves before on a previous caribou hunt, but this was the first time I'd ever seen one.

Hunting according to a plan

Leaf River Lodge has a well-planned methodology to their hunting. They have exclusive hunting rights to approximately 80 miles of the Leaf River and each day a pair of hunters and their guide travel by boat to their designated area. Once reaching their site for the day, the hunters can cruise the river and go ashore if they spot caribou from the water or land their boat and hike inland a bit to seek out the animals. No one else hunts that area that day. The next day, hunters and guides are assigned to a different section of the river. As hunters tag out on their caribou, natural progression dictates that the hottest hunting areas along the river are available to anyone that has not yet filled their tags. It's extremely rare that anyone doesn't get their quota of two caribou during the week.

The boat ride is spectacular all by itself. The boats are equipped with jet drive outboards since propellers would have a high likelihood of banging on submerged rocks. At several pinch points in the river the current gets quite fast, especially if you're going upstream which was the case with us, and there are standing waves a couple feet high that must be negotiated. While not quite

63

heart-stopping, these spots do get your adrenalin pumping and thinking about what to grab first in case of capsizing. We managed the waves and rapids without incident and eventually made it to our assigned hunting area.

Our guide, Jacques, brought the boat to the shore and suggested we head inland a bit. Our boat was crewed by Jacques, myself, and my assigned partner, Mark, as well as Carroll who was accompanying us, since as host for the trip, he had no assigned hunting partner. We walked inland and were soon over a rise and out of sight of the river. I'd won the flip of the coin and had first crack at a caribou.

In fairly short order, Jacques spotted a small herd of caribou heading in our general direction. It was only a question of whether they'd come on our side of a small bunch of scrub spruces in a gully or stay more distant on the other side. As luck would have it, they chose the other side and we had to scramble to get within range when they came out. We dropped our packs and I learned how slow and tiring running over rough tundra ground can be while weighed down with layers of clothes, ammo, heavy rubber boots, and a rifle.

Gasping for breath, I'm sure my first two shots landed somewhere in Quebec, but without having first passed through a caribou. I settled down a bit and my third shot put the animal down. Instead of hitting the heart-lung area where I'd been aiming, a spine shot in the lower neck still did the trick. As Carroll later mentioned to me, "Dead is dead." The caribou turned out to be a very respectable bull with a nice double shovel set of antlers. I was happy.

Later that afternoon I sat on a knoll while Mark went after a bedded caribou on a facing hillside. His stalk, mostly out of sight from my vantage point, seemed to take forever. After about 45 minutes I saw a small group of caribou rise from their bedded position and then watched as one of them slumped back to the ground. Only then did I hear the crack of Mark's .30-06 rifle, confirming that he was the reason for that particular caribou's return to its prone position. First day and two caribou in the boat and headed back to the lodge. Life was good.

Over the course of the next two days, Mark, Carroll, and I managed to take four more nice bulls. Both of mine were double-shoveled and I couldn't have been happier. We ambushed one of Carroll's bulls at a narrow river crossing. I recall peering into the water beneath the boat and seeing the bottom littered with antlers. There's no telling how many caribou had met their demise at the hands of Mother Nature in the swift waters of the Leaf River at that particular choke point. Certainly it was many more than what we hunters were responsible for. All tolled during the week, we probably saw in excess of 5,000 caribou and this wasn't even the height of the migration.

Another vision that sticks in my head from those first three days of the hunt was of the white hillsides that often surrounded us. But they weren't white from early snow. As we watched one white slope, it began to slowly lift into the air and then we heard a rising crescendo of sound as thousands upon thousands of snow geese took off to resume their southward migration. The sound wasn't just their calls. It was also their wings beating the air. If we'd been goose hunters, we'd have filled our limits in seconds.

Limited out on caribou, what's next?

Three days into our hunt and Mark, Carroll, and I had tagged two caribou each and were done hunting land animals. Time to bring out the shotguns and find some arctic ptarmigan. On Thursday we once again headed out onto the river and looked for some rolling land that might hold ptarmigan. We had our rifles in the boat as well, just in case we came across a barren ground black bear.

Earlier that day, Carroll and I had tromped through some of the scrub growth behind the lodge and managed to take several birds. Arctic ptarmigan are similar to New England partridge, or as some call them, roughed grouse, except that in the arctic, the birds' plumage turns completely white in the winter and their feet have feathers all the way down to their toes. At this time of year, mid-September, these birds were midway into their transition and while their bodies still sported their scenery-blending mottled brown colors, their wings and feet were already pure white, making them extremely visible when spooked into flight. And they seldom travelled alone. If you located one, chances are there were others nearby.

We did a lot of walking that day with each of us taking turns as the "bird dog" to flush out ptarmigan. They flew fast and close to the ground and always made a distinctive clucking sound just before and after they took flight. They also tended not to fly too far so that if you didn't take a bird on your first attempt, you were likely to get a second chance. We arrived back at camp that evening fully exhausted, but also completely exhilarated. The pressure of the hunt for caribou was off, if pressure was indeed what it could have been called, and we were just at ease with our surroundings and the beauty of the place. Even the weather had been perfect and treated us to several nights of spectacular displays of the northern lights. Could it possibly get any better than this? In a word, yes.

Land, air, and now water

Day five, Friday, and our last full day at Leaf River had arrived. We'd taken our caribou and shot a bunch of ptarmigan, so the only logical choice that remained was fishing. And to make the situation even better, Carroll had requested that Jacques prepare a shore lunch for us that day. No baloney sandwiches and pastry for us. We were going to have, the fishing gods willing, riverside, pan-fried brook trout filets. All we had to do was catch our lunch in order to turn desire into reality. Just to ensure that we were going to be well fed regardless of what the fishing gods had to say about the matter, Jacques had brought along some caribou tenderloin, sliced potatoes, and several fresh ptarmigan breasts from the preceding day.

Again, into the boats and off to one of Jacques' favorite spots. At our first stop and after only a few casts, I was certain I'd snagged the bottom. My spinning rod with its 12-pound test line would not budge. But strangely, the rod tip seemed to bob up and down a bit. Maybe it was a submerged log or just the effects of the strong current? No, the line was now slowly travelling upstream in the current. Impossible, unless it was really a fish. After several minutes of guessing and encouragement by Carroll to persevere, I saw a humped back breach the surface. It wasn't Moby Dick, but it might as well have been.

My sunken log turned out to be a massive Atlantic salmon. The current was swift and my tackle was light. If I got this fish to shore I'd certainly have to have luck on my side. Roughly 45 minutes later, luck did prevail. With Carroll's and Jacques' encouragement I was able to bring the fish into an eddy and hoist him up for some photographs. He was a 46-inch, 30-pound Atlantic salmon, by far the largest fresh-water fish I'd ever caught. Carroll informed me that many fishermen fished their whole lives and never took such a fish. I wasn't just honored, I was sincerely humbled. And after measuring the fish and taking several "for-the-record" photographs, I carefully revived the fish and released him back into the river and felt great about doing so.

We fished some more that Friday and caught several more brook trout and even a few smaller salmon that were released. We kept several of the trout and added them to the menu for lunch. Jacques cut some brush, lit a small fire, and heated peanut oil in a frying pan. We ate fried potatoes, fresh brook trout filets, sautéed ptarmigan breast, and fried caribou tenderloin.

In my marketing job in the high tech sector, I'd once eaten a five-course meal at an industry awards dinner on the coast of the Mediterranean Sea in Monte Carlo in Europe. There, I ate Beef Wellington, trout in some sort of rich cream sauce, a different wine with every course, and a dessert I can't even begin to pronounce. It was all delicious, but it didn't come close in comparison to that shore lunch on the banks of the Leaf River in Quebec.

Saturday dawned and we packed to head home. I was regretting departure and wistfully asked myself what it might be like to spend the winter there on the shores of the Leaf River. Of course that was not possible, but it was still fun to think about. I said good-bye to Jacques and tipped him with what I hoped was a generous amount.

As the float plane headed back to Lac Pau, and from there via the Convair back to Montreal, I watched the tundra slip in and out of sight through the clouds as snow squalls blotted out the land below. I could see flocks of snow geese bucking the headwinds as they purposely continued south towards a warmer climate. And in the gaps between the clouds, the snow squalls, and flocks of snow geese, there was nary a tree in sight, just as I'd been promised.

Leaf River postscript

Since that first trip to Leaf River Lodge I've been back twice more and have yet a third trip currently on the calendar. The staff has changed somewhat over the years, but the quality of the operation has remained constant and excellent. If anything, it's gotten even better.

I keep hoping for a black bear to cross my path, but that has yet to happen. Black bears have been taken in each of the three weeks I've been there, including one of about 500 pounds so the possibility is real. The fishing has remained superb and I've had a couple more incredible shore lunches. Remi Laprise, my guide on my 2013 trip, happened to mention that he had been taught to cook as part of his guide training. It showed. And finally, I've even managed to spot and photograph a small herd of musk ox at Leaf River. That was a real and rare treat.

One other constant at Leaf River, as well as elsewhere on my trips, has been the quality and character of the other hunters. Sometimes hunters get a bad and undeserved rap as being low-class, knuckle-dragging Neanderthals. I've yet to see that and doubt that I will.

Towards the end of the week during my most recent trip to Leaf River, one of the other hunters in our group took me aside and quietly asked why I was always smiling and seemed to be enjoying every single minute of my experience. My simple answer to him was, "How could I not?" I was with a great bunch of people, having the time of my life, yet again, and eagerly looking forward to what the next minute, hour, and day would bring. Hunters and fishermen, whether successful or not in taking their quarry, experience this feeling often. I think that's a pretty good way to live.

Leaf River Redemption

With one final surge of power, the eight-pound, football-shaped landlocked salmon shot two feet out of the water and hung suspended in the air for a moment with the sun glistening from its silvery scales. Then, with a twist of its head, it snapped the line connecting it to my Gray Ghost streamer and plunged back into the depths of Lower Richardson Lake—taking with it my chance for a fish of a lifetime.

A haunting memory

That was about ten years ago and the memory still haunts me. For more than 35 years I've been trolling the waters of Lower Richardson every spring in hope of netting a salmon big enough to brag about. For me, there's no finer fighting—or tasting—fresh water game fish than Maine's landlocked salmon. I've caught my share of smaller salmon, even a couple in the three-pound range, but nothing of "wall-hanger" caliber. And now, after a 20-minute fight filled with aerial acrobatics, my son, Matthew, and I had just witnessed what I fully expected was my one shot at personal fishing glory, disappear in a watery splash. The fact that it happened within net's reach of the boat only added to my disappointment and misery.

I should have been using new line. Or a different rod with less wear on the guides. Or played the fish even more patiently. No matter. Second guessing myself wouldn't put the salmon in the net. We just put away the rods and headed back to the camp for the rest of the day. Lunch was pretty subdued. I consoled myself—not quite successfully—that at least I'd had the opportunity to match my skills against such a fish and almost came out the winner.

Every year since then, Matthew and I talk about "the fish" on our annual fishing trips to Lower Richardson. We tease one another about how big that salmon must be by now.

A chance at redemption

Another of my passions, in addition to landlocked salmon fishing, is caribou hunting in Canada. I booked a hunt to Leaf River Lodge in northern Quebec in 2006. Along with fall caribou hunting, Leaf River offers the secondary sports of ptarmigan hunting and fishing for brook trout, lake trout, and Atlantic salmon. I wanted to be prepared for as much hunting and fishing as could be packed into the week-long trip so it was a bit of a challenge to get my rifle, shotgun, and fishing tackle—to say nothing of warm clothing for late September's unpredictable weather—all packed and under the 70-pound baggage weight limit.

During the first four days of the trip, my hunting partners, Carroll and Mark, and I had tagged out on our caribou with two nice bulls apiece. Carroll and I had also seen some fast and challenging shooting action with the ptarmigan. Several of the cackling and acrobatic arctic birds, halfway into their white-phase plumage, fell to our shotguns. Day five, our last full day in camp, was reserved for fishing.

After loading ourselves and our gear aboard our boat, our guide, Jacques, quickly had us headed a few miles upriver to try our luck for some brook trout. We were told to expect mostly brook trout up to three pounds and maybe even an occasional five pounder. I was taking my first cast into the current within minutes of the boat landing and anticipating that tell-tale tug on the line.

On only the fifth or sixth cast my line pulled tight and I hollered, "Fish on!" But the line didn't move and the bend in the rod remained constant. I was starting to feel a bit embarrassed by my premature exuberance since I now figured I was securely hooked onto the riverbed. Then, ever so slightly, I noticed the rod tip take a couple slow dips downward and I felt the tension on it increase. I thought maybe I was snagged on the end of a sunken log that was bobbing in the current.

When the "log" moved sideways and then a bit upstream I knew I was hooked to neither the bottom nor a log. It had to be a fish, but what brook trout could be so large as to resist almost any attempt to budge it? Carroll said he suspected I had hooked onto a large lake trout and commented that it just hadn't yet realized that it was hooked. With only 12-pound test line on my reel I knew I couldn't put too much pressure on the still-unseen fish or else the line would snap. (Unpleasant memories from Lower Richardson Lake were starting to resurface.) The slow-motion duel with my mystery fish went on for another several minutes. Then things changed dramatically.

"Jesus Christ!"

Fifty feet from shore a huge Atlantic salmon rose from the depths and its body arched above the water's surface. It looked like one of those video clips of a nuclear submarine lunging into the air from the sea and then crashing down again with a huge splash. All I could muster was a "Jesus Christ!" bellowed about half a dozen times and which is probably still echoing across the tundra. This exclamation was all the more amazing since I'm not a very religious person. Maybe I should start believing in miracles. Wasn't the apostle Peter a fisherman?

For the next eternity, or more accurately, maybe 30 minutes, it was a contest to see who would come out ahead. The river's current was swift and every attempt to bring the salmon closer to shore only seemed to make it drive farther out into the river. Would my second chance at a fish of a lifetime redeem my previous close-but-no-cigar experience, or would fate again frustrate me and intervene on the fish's behalf?

Eventually, and with considerable encouragement and advice from Carroll and Jacques, I was able to turn the salmon into some calmer water and slowly bring him close to shore. Only when Jacques slipped the net under his head—not all of his length would fit in the net—did I dare breathe a sigh of relief and fully realize what had just happened.

I'd landed a monster hook-jawed, male Atlantic salmon. He measured 46-inches long and weighed 30 pounds (estimated by the taxidermist based on the photographs and measurements we took). And best of all, after the high fives, the measurements, and photographic proof, we revived the salmon from his ordeal and released him back into the river. With a powerful thrust of his tail, he was free again to swim wherever he chose.

I believe every fisherman dreams of one day catching that one huge, trophy-class fish that serves as the highlight of his life's fishing experience. I've been lucky enough (so far) to have had two such experiences. The first ended in a crushing disappointment. However, my Leaf River redemption has lessened the pain considerably and taught me an unforgettable lesson in fishing appreciation. My second experience ended in pure exhilaration.

Next spring, like every spring, I'll once again be trolling on Lower Richardson Lake and looking for that same trophy landlocked salmon. And I'm also going back to the shores of the Leaf River. I know where a couple of large salmon are cruising beneath the surface of both those bodies of water—and they're growing even bigger.

P.D.

P.D. (Paul David) Malone was one of those people who constantly found ways to surprise you. It seemed he could do or had done virtually anything he set his mind to. Hunting, fishing, archery, reloading, parachute jumping, championship swimming, extreme skiing, knife making, leather tooling, drawing, and rubbing elbows with sports and movie celebrities. He even managed to surprise me the night I found him dead.

Making an impression

I first met P.D. through his daughter, whom I had recently begun dating. While it wasn't going to be the typical nervous-teenage-boy-meets-the-father-of-the-girl introduction, after all, Molly and I were both in our mid-40s and had each been married before, I was still a little apprehensive. But I had a plan.

Molly had told me enough about her Dad that I knew, like me, he was also passionate about hunting and fishing. At age 80, however, and with the infirmities of age catching up with him, P.D.'s days in the outdoor wilds were behind him. Now, his past adventures, and my more recent ones, could provide the fodder for conversation starters. My entry point was going to be through a photograph.

A few years previous, I'd managed to catch a fairly respectable three-pound landlocked salmon on Lower Richardson Lake in Maine. In those days, and for quite a few years, Lower Richardson had suffered from over-fishing and the annual taking of smelt in the springtime. Smelt were the salmon's primary food source and reducing their population not only limited the number of salmon the lake could support, but also diminished their size through slower growth. As a consequence, the quality of the fishing had suffered and it was relatively rare to catch a fish, let alone one of legal size. All things considered, my three-pound salmon was not bad and I had a photograph in my shirt pocket to show to P.D. I was hoping to impress him, at least a little bit.

I don't recall exactly what I expected to see the first time I met P.D., but it was probably someone at least as physically big as his history. When the door to his home opened I was greeted by a slightly built, balding man, not much over five feet tall and who might have tipped the scales at 110 pounds if he was soaking wet. We exchanged pleasantries and small talk as I waited for the proper moment to pull the photograph out of my pocket.

The opportunity presented itself and I showed P.D. the pride of my recent fishing experience. He held the photo, looked it over a bit, and didn't seem all that much impressed. In fact, he really didn't respond to it at all other than to ask me to wait while he went to retrieve a fishing photograph of his own. He went upstairs, my photo still in hand, and returned in a minute or two.

"Here's a photograph of a fish I caught," he quietly said with a bit of a sly smile on his face. I took the photo from his hand and stared in disbelief. There was P.D. standing beside a fish held aloft by a rope suspended from a dockside pole and the fish was taller than him. The fish was an alligator gar that P.D. had shot with an arrow somewhere in his home state of Missouri. Not only that, the gentleman standing beside P.D. was Ben Pearson, a noted archer in his day. P.D. added that he and Ben had been quite good friends. Being a minor-league archer myself, I knew who Ben Pearson was and had often seen his son, Wayne, on various outdoor hunting TV shows. I humbly asked P.D. to hand my picture back and I returned it to its hiding place in my shirt pocket. Not only had P.D. outdone my prize fish by a mile, he had also given me my first hint of his affinity for rubbing shoulders with people of some notoriety. Score one for P.D.

In another conversation, I mentioned to P.D. that as a boy I'd once seen Ted Williams give a fly casting demonstration at a Boston sportsman show in the 1950s. Ted put the fly dead center into a floating circular ring time after time at a considerable distance from where he stood. P.D. responded with, "The last time I spoke with Ted…" I don't recall what P.D. said after those first few words. All I knew at the time was that the man speaking to me had actually met and spoken with the person I regarded as the greatest baseball slugger that ever lived. P.D. 2, Pete 0.

Maybe talking about hiking in the mountains would work. I told P.D. about my hiking experience in the White Mountains of New Hampshire and my several hikes to the summit of Mount Washington and of watching people ski in Tuckerman Ravine in the springtime. Again, P.D. topped me. He calmly explained how he had once skied *over the headwall* of Tuckerman Ravine and then on down through it. Even more impressive was the fact that he'd done it on old-fashioned wooden skis bound to his feet with leather straps. P.D. 3, Pete still 0. Obviously my efforts at impressing P.D. with my feeble attempts at outdoor prowess were doomed to failure from the outset. A new strategy was called for.

Better off listening

I fell back onto what works so well in many of life's situations: just listening. And I had my ears and brain filled. For example, P.D. had been a championship swimmer in high school in Missouri and as a result, won an athletic scholarship to college. Related to swimming, he casually mentioned that he'd once met Johnny Weissmuller, the Olympic champion swimmer and movie actor who played Tarzan in many films. By this time, I was not surprised at this newest revelation.

Another of P.D.'s acquaintances was Bradford Washburn, or as P.D. new him, Brad. P.D. and Brad were good friends and often exchanged phone calls and mail. While the name Bradford Washburn might not mean much to most people, to those of us who recall the first successful ascent of Mt. Everest by Sir Edmund Hilary in 1953, we remember Washburn as the person who created the most detailed maps ever of Everest before the era of satellite navigation and GPS positioning. Brad Washburn has an entire wing named after him in Boston's Museum of Science. He and P.D. maintained a friendship for much of their lives and Washburn sent his personal condolences when he was unable to attend P.D.'s funeral service due to his own failing health.

P.D. was also a bit of a golfer, though apparently not one of any significant notoriety. (At least I could take some solace in the fact that he didn't excel at *everything* he tried.) But somehow he'd managed to meet and talk to Arnold Palmer, so even at this, he still maintained a lofty stature. A few years after I met P.D. I managed to get a pair of tickets for him to the Ryder Cup matches when they were held in Brookline, Massachusetts. Unfortunately, by that time P.D.'s health was declining and he was unable to put the tickets to use.

I learned more of P.D.'s early years. For example, he told me of the time he and a boyhood friend were canoeing and fishing in some Missouri river backwater and realized they were near the site of an illegal moonshiner. When they approached too close for the bootlegger's liking, the moonshiner tossed a couple lit sticks of dynamite in their direction to discourage their further incursion. With the stern, not to mention, loud message received, P.D. and his friend quickly left the area.

Over the ensuing months, P.D. gave me the cook's tour of his home. By profession, he'd been a medical illustrator of quite some notoriety. However, by avocation, he was a master of many more skills.

P.D. showed me rifle and pistol reloading machinery with which he prepared his own custom cartridge loads. He possessed leather tooling equipment that he had used to make and decorate knife sheaths, belts, and other leather goods. Of course, he had made the knives themselves as well. He opened the cover of a monthly outdoor hunting magazine and there was a photo of P.D. wearing buckskins he'd made himself from deer he'd shot himself. The photos were an accompaniment to an archery hunting article he'd written. He showed me a surplus parachute he'd purchased and had used just to prove he could jump out of a plane and survive. It seemed as though P.D. could not only do almost anything, but could make almost anything as well.

Denizens in the basement

The basement of his home had its resident denizens. There was a stuffed bobcat that had certainly seen better days. Many years earlier it had probably looked quite fierce. Now it seemed more fearful than fearsome. There was the snout of an alligator gar, perhaps the one from the photo I'd seen when we first met. It was posed as if breaching the surface of a concrete slab. The slab was painted to look like the surface of a lake and the gar was poking its head above the surface in a particularly menacing pose. There was also an assortment of various bones and antlers from which P.D. had fashioned knife handles, buttons for clothing, and who knew what else. One of those knife handles was particularly interesting to me.

At birthdays or for Christmas, P.D. would always give me a gift. Sometimes it was a check, making sure that the one he gave to his daughter was always slightly larger, and rightfully so. At other times, the gift was something from his inventory of no-longer-used outdoor equipment. One such item was a very nice buck-style knife that he had made himself. It came covered in a protective coating of grease so it was as good as new and with one of his handmade leather sheaths. I took special note of a piece of white bone in its handle. When I asked P.D. what it was made from, his only answer was, "those medical students were always giving me things." I knew enough not to enquire further, but when I was helping clean out P.D.'s house after his death, I did find a paper bag in the basement floor joists that held what I took to be human forearm and hand bones with some pieces missing. The remaining bones and pieces, which I nicknamed "Lefty," were summarily cremated.

As mentioned earlier, due to his advanced age and physical infirmities, P.D.'s daredevil days were behind him and I could tell he especially missed hunting and fishing. Here was where I could score some points. A gift of some frozen venison steaks brought a twinkle to his eye. As did the large, fresh trout I once brought to his home. The fish was big enough to provide a good meal for

P.D., Molly, and me. Additional gift entrées included caribou meat, pheasant breasts, and more venison.

While we never asked for his consent, P.D. seemed quite happy when Molly and I got married. We visited him fairly often and frequently brought more frozen surprises from our freezer. He also thoroughly enjoyed "babysitting" for our Newfoundland dog, Sampson, though it was questionable just who was taking who for their walks.

Care not needed

As P.D. neared his ninetieth birthday, his health deteriorated more rapidly. He was no longer able to properly take care of the large home he lived in alone since his wife had passed away some 20 years before. His son, who lived in a neighboring state, and I, took turns mowing his lawn and grocery shopping. We tried to get P.D. to consider moving to an assisted-living facility, but his one meeting with an elder affairs representative on the subject didn't go well at all, at least not as far as the representative was concerned.

P.D. and the representative sat down for a chat in his living room. P.D. made it clear that he knew everyone was concerned that he was no longer able to take care of himself. He assured the representative that he could and to prove his point, calmly mentioned to the woman that he had three loaded pistols all within arm's reach even as he sat and talked with her. The astonished woman immediately got up, left, and announced she would not be returning until the firearms were gone. That return visit never happened.

We shouldn't have been surprised. P.D. was quite used to taking care of himself. Once, when he'd been bitten on the neck by the family dog, he put his medical background to use. He had calmly taken a needle and thread, stood in front of a mirror, and proceeded to stitch himself up. He didn't view this as anything exceptional. It was just how he was.

P.D.

Winter arrived and true to his independent nature, P.D. refused neighbors' offers to shovel the snow from his stairs and walkways. He would stubbornly insist on doing it himself and even climbed the stairs to the third-story flat roof of his home to clear snow from the drains.

His son and I continued alternating on the weekly grocery shopping visits. One evening, after a particularly cold spell lasting several days and with a half foot of newly fallen snow on the ground, I pulled up to P.D.'s home for my turn at the grocery run. First, I took the snow shovel from the back of my truck and cleared the walkways and stairs. I finished shoveling and knocked at the front door. I tried several more times and still got no response. I tried calling on my cell phone to no avail. I knew P.D. had to be home, but since I did not have a key to the house, there was no way for me to get in unless P.D. came to the door, as he always had.

Fearing the worst, I peeked through a window and saw P.D. lying on the floor several feet inside the front door. I called the police from my phone and they were able to eventually force open a door and we confirmed that P.D. was beyond help. He had a wound on his head and from the evidence, it seemed that what had happened was that he had tried to do some shoveling outside, had a heart attack, and fell and hit his head. He'd managed to return inside and, rather than use the phone to call for help, he apparently laid down on the sofa and then got up some time later, walked a few steps, and collapsed where we found him.

After the coroner's people took P.D. away, and after the police left, it was up to me to secure his home. I nailed shut the door we had forced open and proceeded to look for any valuables that should be removed for safekeeping. Lastly, I looked for firearms. In an upstairs closet I found several rifles and a shotgun and locked them in my truck. Then, before leaving, I decided to check the chair where P.D. had told the elder affairs person he could easily defend himself. Sure enough. In the bookcase on one side was a .22 caliber semiautomatic pistol. On the other side of the chair was another pistol, this one a .357 magnum revolver.

And underneath the seat cushion was a third small caliber semiautomatic. Every one of them was fully loaded and ready to fire.

I would have liked to have heard many more of P.D.'s stories. Unfortunately, he ran out of life before he could personally tell me more of them. Even as his life came to an end, P.D. still had stories to tell and surprises to deliver.

The T13 R14 Moose

I'd won the lottery! I hadn't gotten the official notification yet, but I knew the prize, if I could claim it, was going to be big. Really big.

No, it wasn't Powerball. Not Mega Millions. Not even Tri-State Megabucks. But the odds of winning were just about as steep. It was the 1990 Maine moose lottery and making the thrill of winning even sweeter, I'd won one of only 100 coveted non-resident permits. Actually I was the third alternate, but the Maine Inland Fisheries and Wildlife person that called assured me that there would be enough people in the first 100 that would decline their spots that I was sure to make the final list. The prediction turned out to be true and soon enough I was sending in my permit fee and reading the material IF&W sent in the mail. Now what?

Until this point in my hunting experience, the only animal larger than a woodchuck that I'd taken was a Maine black bear when our paths crossed while I'd been deer hunting the year before. And my sub-permittee, my brother Andy, wasn't much better off, having taken just one deer in his hunting career. At that time, my only rifle larger than a .22 was my .308 Browning iron-sights-equipped, lever-action BLR. Andy's firearm was a .30-30 Winchester. We were going to be babes in the Big North Woods of Maine on our moose hunt. But that wasn't going to stop us. The hunt was on.

You *can* get there from here

Andy and I settled on a do-it-yourself moose hunt. Our designated wildlife management zone was Zone One in Aroostook County, about as far north in Maine as you can get and well beyond commuting distance from either my camp in Andover, Maine, or Andy's second home in Bryant Pond. We were going to camp in a tent, fix our own meals, and do our own guiding. We had no idea what we were in for. We'd travel to Zone One in Andy's Chevy Suburban and take a large snowmobile trailer with us for extra hauling capacity. The Saturday before opening day we loaded all our camping gear, coolers, ice, food, fuel, firearms, and anything else we thought we might need and headed north. Our plan was to find a campsite somewhere in Zone One and set ourselves up for the week. Five hundred thirty-five miles later we arrived. We located a small campsite at the junction of the Big Black and St. John Rivers in the unorganized township of T15 R13 WELS.

Maine has a naming system for the less populated, unorganized areas of the state and it's based loosely on a grid pattern and similar to a checkerboard. When viewed on a map, T15 means "Tract" 15 (a vertical column of sections of land and water), while R13 refers to "Row" 13 (the horizontal component of the grid). WELS means West of the East Line of the State, referring to the easternmost boundary of Maine. It's much simpler just to say that we stayed at a campsite where the Big Black and St. John Rivers met.

The weather cooperated and we set up a pretty snug camp. Andy's large tent provided for sleeping quarters and gear storage and a covered picnic table served for cooking and eating meals regardless of the week's weather. With no one else staying at the site, we brought a second picnic table under the wooden canopy and had all the room we could wish for. A small fire pit contained our evening camp fires and also offered a way to dispose of burnable trash. After a Saturday of driving and camp set up, we settled in for a night of anticipation and a Sunday of scouting.

A simple plan

Sunday we drove. A lot. We covered all of the logging roads in the immediate area and checked out several bogs shown on topographic maps to come up with a plan for where we might hunt on Monday morning. We also saw how other hunters were far better prepared than us. Some had mobile campers that offered luxury accommodations compared to our canvas-roofed bivouac. More than once we saw pickup trucks with small observation towers built into their beds to allow an elevated view of clear cuts and a significantly wider field of vision than we had at ground level. No matter. We were sure that come Monday morning a large bull moose would step out from the bushes as we cruised the gravel roads and pose for us while we collected our wits, loaded our rifles, and took him down.

I'd read one account of the previous year's hunt, where a hunter spotted a nice bull before legal hunting time on opening day and just sat and waited until the designated hour, loaded his rifle, and ended his freezer-filling quest moments later. If the goal was just moose meat, then I guess he succeeded, but Andy and I wanted more from our adventure.

We drove many miles on Monday and never saw a moose. None on the roads, none beside the roads, and none in the bogs. But no worries. Hunting success rates in those early years of Maine's reinstated moose season were roughly 90 percent. We were sure all we had to do was keep driving and looking for moose. Sooner or later a bullwinkle would fall into our laps. Unfortunately for us, the local moose population didn't see things in quite the same light.

Accompanied by coyotes howling during the night and lumber trucks rumbling over the nearby bridge in the pre-dawn hours, we started Tuesday with the same high level of anticipation we had on Monday. Again, we slowly drove over as many miles of dirt road as we could cover. It was astonishing how many "moose" turned out to be uprooted tree stumps several hundred yards away in the clear cuts. Late in the day, just before legal hunting time ended, we did catch a fleeting glimpse of a small bull moose as he bolted from the road and into the thick alders. By the time we got to the spot, he was nowhere to be seen or heard, but at least we had seen a moose and knew we weren't on just a wild goose chase. Late Tuesday night, Andy woke to hear some large animal in the bushes outside the tent. Neither of us ventured outside so we'll never know if it was a moose or a bear, the latter of which we had also spotted near our camp.

Call of the wild French moose

Wednesday was a new day and also a day to refuel. We filled the Suburban and all our extra gas cans before leaving Ashland, Maine, and heading into the woods. But a full day of scouting and two long days of road hunting left us starting to run low on fuel. St. Pamphile, Quebec, was significantly closer than Ashland, Maine, so we headed for Canada. In those days, you didn't need a passport. While loading up on gas might seem hardly worth mentioning, the day did provide two rather interesting anecdotes and examples of how things have changed in just a few short years.

When we reached the border station and were giving our information to the Canadian customs official, I casually mentioned that I had an unloaded .22 caliber pistol in the glove compartment. Looking back, I don't know why I brought it except that the thought was to use it if it became necessary to efficiently dispatch a downed moose without ruining a lot of prime moose meat in the process. Andy and I were quickly greeted with a great many French words from the agent, most of them loud, and none of which we understood. However, we eventually grasped the idea that bringing a handgun onto Canadian soil was not conducive to friendly cross-border personal or international relations and that if we left it with the customs official we could claim it upon our return. We complied. Who knew that Canadians were so touchy about handguns? Obviously not us.

The other incident on the Canadian side of the border concerned our purchase of an instructional moose-calling cassette tape. (CDs didn't yet exist.) We'd brought along a portable radio for entertainment at the campsite. Just something to listen to while we sipped on a beer or two by the evening campfire. The radio came equipped with dual cassette decks and the thought occurred to us that we might be able to turn up the volume and play the sounds of an amorous cow moose at an appropriate time and place in order to lure a like-minded bull into shooting range. All we had to do was find such a recording.

While in St. Pamphile, we located a sporting goods store and through animated gestures and broken English, made the storekeeper aware of our desire to purchase a cassette of moose calls. He produced just such a tape and we bought it. With cassette in hand, we headed back to camp to try out our new purchase.

While the cassette did indeed contain many moose calls, it primarily contained detailed verbal instructions, in French of course, on how to mimic those sounds, and probably what their meaning was in moose-to-moose lingo. Andy and I will never know. We tried dubbing just the calling portions of the tape onto another cassette, but to my recollection, that was as far as our moose calling lessons got. We never used the tape.

Time running out

By Thursday, I was getting concerned. We hit the road again and while we did spot one small yearling calf, we had still not seen a decent-size shootable moose. We even tried driving the bulky Suburban down a very wet corduroy road of spruce trunks. We hoped to reach a remote swamp, but ultimately turned around and returned to more solid ground rather than risk being mired up to the axles in muck.

About noon we were parked beside the road wondering what to try next. A lumber truck pulled up and stopped beside us. We'd seen and kept out of the way of the massive lumber trucks all week, and the fact that one had come to a halt beside us seemed unusual. Out of the cab jumped a slightly built man dressed in work clothes and boots and with an excited expression on his face. He spoke a mix of French and English, but in the end, we understood what he was trying to tell us. Just a short way down a nearby road he'd just seen a bull moose feeding and he was willing to take us to the place. We didn't need to be asked twice.

Andy and I led the way while the truck driver followed closely behind. Within five minutes we spotted the moose. It was instantly apparent that while he wasn't a giant, he was certainly big enough. Andy and I piled out of the Suburban and I inserted the clip into the Browning. I immediately slipped on a fallen tree and did a face plant into the mossy ground. I quickly recovered and then, moving more cautiously, continued walking through the slashing and blow downs in the recently cut woods and got to within about 100 yards of the bull. When it became evident the moose was on to our intentions, I raised the rifle and fired.

I recall seeing air escaping from both sides of the moose, indicating a double-lung shot, and then he went down. But he was immediately back up on all fours, staggered a bit, and started to walk away. A second shot to the lung area put him down again and a final close-up shot ended it. Smiles and high-fives between Andy and me and the truck driver followed. Now the real work started.

How to move a moose

We brought a come-along and lots of rope with us, but the moose had dropped a couple hundred yards from the edge of the road. Getting him to the road and ultimately onto the trailer was going to be no small feat. It looked like we might have to quarter the moose in order to get him back to camp. However, the truck driver and I had a different plan in mind.

I'd read where it was not uncommon to approach someone in a nearby lumbering operation and hire a log skidder to drag a downed moose to the roadside. I had a crisp $50 bill in my wallet for just such an eventuality. Even without me mentioning this, the truck driver said that if we busied ourselves with gutting the moose, he would return with equipment to help us bring the moose out of the cutting. So while Andy and I took on the chore of disemboweling such a large animal, the driver headed off in his rig with a promise to return.

We were just about finished with the task, when we heard rumbling on the road. Up drove the same truck driver, but instead of the log skidder we expected, he had a huge bucket shovel on the flatbed low-boy trailer he was towing. And apparently he was in a hurry. Instead of lowering a ramp to get the shovel off the trailer, he simply drove it off the side on its metal tracks. He quickly covered the distance from the road to the moose and in the process deftly picked up and flicked to the side whole fallen trees as if they were toothpicks.

Once he and his machine arrived at the moose, we just tied a rope around the moose's antlers and wrapped the other end around the lowered bucket. He raised the bucket and there, suspended with all four legs well off the ground, hung our moose, dangling in mid-air. In short order, the driver retraced his tracks back to the side of the road and lowered the bull. We untied the rope and he quickly drove the machine back onto the lowboy, again not bothering with ramps.

Before he drove off, the truck driver and I shook hands again and I happily handed over the $50 bill. In addition to thanking me for the cash, he asked if I planned to do anything with the moose's heart. To be honest, I hadn't thought that far ahead, but said that if he wanted it, he was welcome to it. We got out a big plastic bag and dropped the soccer-ball-sized heart into it and tied off the opening. I asked the driver what he planned to do with it. He rubbed his stomach and said that his mother would slice the top off, stuff it, and bake it in the oven. I'm not sure which made him happier, the $50 or the moose heart, but I know that truck driver drove away a very happy man.

Our moose gets a speeding ticket

After the truck driver left, I stayed with the moose while Andy drove the Suburban back to the campsite to retrieve the trailer. When he returned we ran a rope through the front of the trailer and around the moose's horns and, with the help of the Suburban and some other hunters, dragged the entire animal onto the trailer. From there we drove back to the campsite and filled the moose's body cavity with plastic milk jugs containing blocks of ice to cool the carcass as rapidly as possible. The next day, Friday, we planned to get the moose tagged and hoped to find a processor to handle the butchering chores and then we'd be on our way home.

Imagine our amazement on Friday morning when we heard the moose "breathing." We were both pretty sure that a dead moose, especially one that had been dead for the better part of a day, couldn't breathe. It turned out that because of the manner in which the moose was positioned on the trailer, and even though all his internal organs had been removed, expanding air in his throat was audibly being expelled through his mouth every couple of minutes.

After packing up and departing the campsite, repairing a flat tire on the trailer, registering the moose at the tagging station and getting an estimated weight of 800 pounds, we looked for a processor. We made a stop at the Ashland, Maine, IGA supermarket and arrived at an agreement with the butcher who did private game processing on the side. The only hitch was that it was going to take him a couple days to complete the task. Even here, fortune smiled on us.

If we paid an extra $100, he would be willing to have a friend drive the butchered meat all the way to Massachusetts for us. We immediately agreed. That $100 was going to get me home at least two days early and save a day-long 950-mile round trip to come back and pick up the processed meat. We delivered the moose to the butcher's residence and then began the long trek home.

A couple days later, I received a call from the Maine State Police at 3:00 a.m. I was asked if I was expecting a shipment of certain unnamed goods and could I identify those goods. I said I could and gave the officer the tag number associated with my moose. Apparently that was the answer he needed to hear. He proceeded to allow the driver he'd stopped for speeding on the Maine Turnpike to continue his southward trip to Massachusetts. The driver even helped Dad load the meat into his freezer.

Today the shoulder mount of that moose shot in the T13 R14 WELS section of Maine graces the hallway of my home. I also brought home one other souvenir of the adventure.

Sometime shortly before we arrived at our campsite, the state of Maine replaced many of the marker posts that separated the unorganized townships from one another. They put up the new markers, but just left the old ones lying on the ground beside the road. That old T13 R14 marker, now repainted, also has an honored place in my home and serves as another reminder of a memorable experience in the Big North Woods of Maine.

Long Island Luxury

This was way over the top compared to what I was accustomed to. A resort chef. Twin lobsters. Succulent scallops and other equally delicious seafood side dishes. Thick and juicy filet mignon steaks. Scenic seaside vistas. After-dinner cocktails by the fire. All the guests in their most stylish attire. Cost? Just $40 each. No, not for the meal. For the meal *and* the whole week's stay! I should mention, this wasn't Long Island, New York. It wasn't the Hamptons. It was better. I was on Long Island, Maine, in deer hunting camp, just offshore from Blue Hill. And the trip started a year earlier in Andover, Maine.

An offer I couldn't refuse

A year before, Dad and I had taken a week-long November trip to my newly purchased camp in Andover, Maine, for deer hunting. While Dad was not a hunter, a friend of his, who was also his part-time employee, was. We invited him along as a guest. Bill was older than me, about Dad's age, and an experienced hunter. He'd been on many hunts in Maine and taken several deer over the years. Maybe some of his luck would rub off on me. We brought along a Thanksgiving turkey to cook and lots of other food and drink. If nothing else, we were going to eat well.

Bill and I hunted hard all week. We trekked up the sides of mountains and through forests and swamps. The closest we came to excitement was when we were walking towards each other from opposite sides of a bog and I heard loud crashing and ice breaking. Shortly thereafter I met up with Bill and he was still a bit rattled. Apparently, I'd startled a bull moose from my end of the bog and it had charged off in Bill's direction. As he told me when we met up, "All I saw was this big brown animal with huge antlers and red in his eyes coming right at me. I had my rifle raised in self-defense if it became necessary, but at the last second, the moose veered to the side and off into the timber."

We never even saw a deer, but the three of us still had a great time and I added a bit more to my hunting skills from someone who had more experience. There was one other thing I gained. Bill extended an invitation to accompany him the following year to one of his hunting destinations. He'd been going to a camp on Long Island, Maine, as a guest of the camp's owners for several years. Now Bill was asking me and Dad if we would go there with him the following year. We didn't need to be asked twice. November of the following year took an awfully long time to arrive.

A Long Island welcome

Dad and I had no idea what to expect. We showed up with Bill at the appointed day and time on the shore of the mainland in Blue Hill, Maine. Long Island was just two or three miles offshore. At the time, Long Island was uninhabited except for a couple seasonal camps. It's about a mile-and-a-half long and about a half mile wide and mostly forested with some wild blueberry fields interspersed among the trees.

After a short wait we saw a lobster boat approaching and it eventually pulled up to the dock. A slightly rotund guy bounded off the boat and shook hands with Bill and introduced himself to Dad and me as Wayne. He was the camp's owner and the lobster boat was our ferry to the island.

Mainers take a lot of kidding about their Down East speech accent. Even though I've lived in New England my entire life and have a bit of an accent of my own, I'm not going to say that the ribbing placed on those dyed-in-the-wool Mainers isn't well deserved. It took about three days before I was able to fully understand Wayne when he spoke. To hear him, you wouldn't think he had the benefit of much education or business savvy. Nothing could have been further from reality. I later learned that Wayne had several businesses and was actually a millionaire several times over. We loaded our gear on the boat and shoved off for the island. Louie, another guest, was also onboard and greeted us like we were long-lost cousins. It was obvious that Louie had been sampling a fair amount of some Long Island iced tea, otherwise known as Old Grand Dad.

We slowed down as we neared the island while we were still a considerable distance from the shore. It was explained that the dock at the island had been damaged by sea ice the previous winter and it would be necessary to transfer to a small open boat for the last hundred yards or so to shore. Bill, Dad, and I and all our gear safely switched boats and then Louie tried. It was classic slapstick humor. Louie had one foot in our small boat while the other was still in the lobster boat, and the two boats were drifting apart. The whole event happened in slow motion. The separation of the boats became too great and Louie dropped into the ocean. Just before he took the plunge, I was able to grab his collar and prevent him from going completely under. Bill and I hauled him into our boat where Louie just laughed and acted like nothing had happened. I'm not sure he was even able to feel that cold November ocean water.

Later in the week Louie told me how he'd once shot himself with his .30-06 deer rifle that he had carried loaded into camp. He showed me the entrance and exit wound scars in his side. Somehow I wasn't surprised.

Roughing it

Bill, Dad, and I arrived at Long Island on Saturday. Most of the other guests were locals and so could hunt while we, as non-residents, had to wait until Monday to begin hunting. We used Saturday afternoon to get settled into camp.

Shortly after climbing from the shore to the camp, we were told we'd be staying in the old camp. We were the last to arrive so we got what was left in terms of bed space. While the new camp had a generator and electric lights, we had gas lanterns. New camp—flush toilet; old camp—outhouse. New camp—comfortable beds; old camp—mouse-infested bunks. New camp—propane heat; old camp—wood stove. New camp—hot and cold running water; old camp—no water. Well, except for sleeping and hunting, we'd spend the rest of our time, including meals, in the new camp. I was just happy to be there and didn't really mind at all.

Sunday was to be feast day. Someone brought in a bunch of lobsters and another local guest contributed fresh sea scallops. The cook, who did not hunt, was the chef at a resort in Florida. He asked for a volunteer to dig a bushel of clams at the shoreline. I jumped at the opportunity. A hunter in camp had taken a deer on Saturday so there was fresh venison. For dinner, we warmed up with some of the best creamy and buttery clam chowder I'd ever tasted. Bowls of steamers also graced the table. The next course was juicy venison tenderloin steaks with sea scallops and baked potatoes on the side. Lastly we had two lobsters apiece accompanied by corn on the cob. I turned down a third lobster. Even with the workout I'd gotten from digging the clams, hauling and splitting firewood, and helping with other camp chores, I still found it hard to move after such a meal.

After dinner it was time for the evening's entertainment. This consisted of playing cards and drinking. Mostly drinking. Bill and I came up short on both accounts. I was used to playing cards for nickels, dimes, and quarters and allowed myself $35 or $40 for the week. Within a couple hours I lost my bankroll and was relegated to spectator status for the rest of the week. As for the drinking, Bill and I brought a fifth of whiskey to share between us and a half gallon to contribute as camp liquor. Within that same two-hour period when I was cleaned out of my card-playing money, so too did our contribution to the camp bar get consumed. Obviously, if I had drunk a bit more my card-playing skills would have improved. Or not. Besides, it's not a good idea to get the best of one's host. We did have fun.

There were some other interesting experiences at Long Island camp. One was the outhouse. It was rustic even by backwoods Maine standards. It had a roof, four walls, a door, and a seat positioned directly over a small stream that led directly into the ocean about 100 feet away. Back in the 1970s people weren't as concerned as they are now about environmental issues. But what really made a visit to the outhouse unique was doing so when it rained. And it rained a lot during our stay on Long Island. In fact, it rained so much that it became necessary to wear knee-height boots after a storm if you wanted to avoid the foot-deep water swirling above the level of the outhouse floor. I just called it automatic flushing.

I mentioned that the old camp had other inhabitants—the mice. If we came back to camp in the middle of the day, we made ourselves a snack of hot dogs heated on the stove in a frying pan. One evening when we came back after dark and shone a flashlight inside the camp before lighting the gas lights, we spotted two beady eyes reflecting the light beam back at us. It was a mouse calmly sitting on the edge of the frying pan and munching a bit of leftover hot dog. I'm fairly certain it was the same mouse that shared my sleeping bag with me a couple nights later. At least we had developed a bit of a personal relationship by then.

A year later during another stay at Long Island, Bill and I were able to stay in the new camp. It was considerably more comfortable than that first year's stay, but still not without incident. On the first evening we had the obligatory card game and drinking session. The results were about the same as before. Several of the locals had a bit too much of the free whiskey and fell soundly asleep in short order after lights out.

About midnight it seemed like everyone woke up at the same time to a camp filled with thick choking smoke. We all bailed out of the camp and onto the deck that overlooked the ocean. We counted heads to make sure everyone was out and came up one short. A couple minutes later, Louie stumbled out of the smoke-filled door and onto the deck. He was followed a couple minutes later by someone who had gone back in with a flashlight to find the source of the smoke. The culprit? Who else but Louie. It seemed he'd removed his rifle from its plastic case and left the case too close to the downstairs fireplace. Once again, the fact that Louie had been at the center of the event was no surprise.

Elusive deer, lasting memories

I never got a deer on Long Island. I came close on several occasions. I caught fleeting glimpses of deer as I walked along rocky ridges. At the time I was still very inexperienced so it wasn't all that hard for the deer to elude me. Once I had a doe sneak behind me as I sat at the base of a large pine tree. That deer never knew I was there, but the one following behind her did and alerted the first one before I could take a shot. Other hunters in camp were able to score on their hunts, but the primary purpose seemed to be just to relax and have a good time. I didn't regret not getting to fill my tag. Or losing the majority of my hands while playing cards.

I went to Long Island three years in a row. I had a great time in each of those years. Shortly after the third trip, Bill passed away. I never heard why and didn't know about it until a few weeks after he passed. I suspect it was from lung cancer as he was a heavy smoker and had a chronic cough.

I had come to know Wayne and the other hunters at Long Island fairly well during those three years, but I was still pretty much an outsider and had been the guest of a guest. Somehow it just didn't feel right to invite myself back without Bill being there. I have many fond memories of my visits to Long Island, now nearly 40 years ago. The food, the card games, the new friends, even the mice. I even sometimes wonder how Louie is doing. I hope he survived.

On Stand

I'd been sitting motionless for several hours, alone, on a metal and fabric seat clamped firmly to a thick spruce tree, 20 feet above the ground, in the middle of the northern Maine woods, in subfreezing late November temperatures, with no prospect of being picked up by my guide until dark. And, I was enjoying every minute of it. But it wasn't always so.

Right brain vs. left brain

I'm convinced that sitting all day in a tree stand waiting for a shooter-class deer to unsuspectingly saunter on by is more of an art form rather than a discipline. Sure, it takes some right-brain thought and preparedness, but mostly it requires left-brain appreciation for the beauty of the natural world that surrounds us.

Right-brainers, those for whom reason and logic are the only true paths to success, can't muster the fortitude to last out the day in the tough conditions described above. Their only thoughts are about the creeping cold that seeps through their clothing, the insatiable need to be in some state of near-constant motion, and to be the instigator of causing something, anything, to happen. Whereas the left-brained among us, those who can get into "the zone," have learned to displace the cold and other discomforts to somewhere else in the universe, are at peace with becoming part of the forest itself, though with more concentrated senses of observation than those of nature alone. We use those senses to allow nature to come to us on its own terms.

I started out very right brained. Early on in my deer hunting efforts I was naïve enough to believe you just went into the woods in a "deer-y looking" area and popped one of the critters with a blast from any appropriate weapon of choice and that was that. To that end, one November pre-dawn morning I walked into the woods behind my camp in Andover, Maine, armed with my new

Browning lever-action rifle and a thick roll of newspapers to sit on to protect my backside from the cold of the forest floor. Within an hour I was freezing cold, fidgeting more than I thought humanly possible, and thoroughly dispirited. New tactics were required.

For years after that, I practiced still hunting. "Still hunting" is a bit of a misnomer since the hunter isn't actually sitting still at all. You walk slowly through the forest, taking care with each step not to snap a twig or brush against a bush or branch, and stopping every so often to see if you can spot a deer through the trees. The idea is to see him before he sees you. One advantage of still hunting is that you are in at least some state of motion which helps circulate your blood and supply needed warmth to your body. Though I think I was a fair-to-good still hunter, I only saw deer on rare occasions. In fairness to myself, the western mountains of Maine where I did most of my deer hunting in the early 1970s and 80s had suffered some severe winters that had depleted an already sparse deer population.

I was still trying to occasionally sit in one spot for hours on end, believing that would be a more productive strategy. I improved at it by being better mentally prepared and by outfitting myself with more appropriate clothing and equipment. But, I still couldn't just stay in one spot for more than a couple hours. Then, one day, my left brain took over.

I was slowly walking along a logging road just after dawn one day near my camp and following what looked like a game trail into the woods for a ways. I found myself on a ridge that overlooked a gully containing a stream. Better yet, the view into that gully was fairly open. Even better still, I found a natural seat formed by rocks that enabled me to comfortably sit and rest while I peered into the gully. Except for the short time it took me to find the spot that day, I spent the whole day there. I didn't see a deer, but found something even better. I found my left-brain hunting partner. Or rather, it found me.

While I sat in my natural rock chair I watched the red squirrels run up and down their highways through the trees. I saw partridges sneaking along the floor of the gully, looking for beechnuts while staying alert for foxes, coyotes, or other predators. Every once in a while I heard the leaves around me rustle and spotted a mouse searching for a seed or two for its lunch. And about once an hour or so, I even allowed myself to nod off to sleep for quick catnaps and found that any nearby noise would instantly rouse me from that nap.

The Zen of hunting

Sitting in one spot from sun-up to sun-down became easy from that day onward. It was almost a Zen-like experience. I still had to prepare properly by dressing warmly, bringing along sufficient food and drink, and especially making sure I had something comfortable to sit on. That last need was met through the use of a couple foam seat pads clipped behind me to my belt. Thus equipped, I discovered that I could spend a full day in complete harmony with nature in any weather. And, in doing so, the woods opened up to me with things I had seldom seen or heard before.

I'm blessed with 20/20 vision so even the flash of wings of a small songbird over 100 yards away was plainly visible. A pair of young does ducking in and out of a spruce thicket appeared as obvious to me as a hunter-orange coat. The slightest motion, whether a dried maple leaf fluttering across a meadow on an otherwise calm morning or the bobbing head of a partridge in a cluster of alders, became keenly apparent once I learned how to sit completely still for hours on end.

And, if my observation post was off the ground in a tree, my senses became even more acute and able to take in still more of whatever was going on. From a vantage point 20 feet or so in the air, my observation powers seemed to increase by an order of magnitude. It became not only possible to peer horizontally through the forest, but vertically as well.

I've learned a few things over the years since my hunting stand Zen revelation that I've found helpful in maintaining my ability to sit tight all day. In addition to dressing warm, bringing sufficient sustenance, and adequate seat padding, the following tips are also useful:

- Always use a safety strap or vest if you're in a tree stand or on a ladder stand. This is especially important if, like me, you're prone to occasionally nodding off.

- As you settle in to your stand, arrange your gear so as to minimize movement as you reach for those items. I like to hang my pack from the front of the chair rail in front of me, making it easy to retrieve items such as calls, binoculars, and food.

- Rather than fidgeting around in your seat every few minutes, plan to take a five-minute stretch break once an hour. It relieves the tedium and helps keep muscles from tightening up.

- Reward yourself. I reward my time on stand with a piece of candy every hour or so. Allowing myself to take a catnap is another reward. Use what works for you.

- Ease up on the coffee. I've learned that bladder capacity decreases in proportion to advancing years. And the colder the temperature is, the chore of filling the pee bottle becomes more uncomfortable and complex.

- Give yourself something to do. It may be reading a book, doing a crossword puzzle, mentally planning a task or event, or again, whatever works for you.

Things may still go awry

So, now that I can sit all day in an elevated deer stand, my dreams of bagging a big buck will certainly be answered. Right? Wrong. Not only is Murphy's Law applicable (Anything that can go wrong, will.), so is Schwartz's Law (Murphy was an optimist.).

For nearly a decade I've been a November guest at Northern Outdoors in The Forks, Maine. Northern Outdoors is a four-season resort that has more than enough activities and amenities to please almost anyone. These include snowmobile tours and rentals, whitewater rafting trips, and fishing excursions, as well as warm and cozy guest accommodations, an onsite microbrewery, a great bar and restaurant, and an outdoor hot tub. Even though she doesn't hunt, my wife enjoys the trips to Northern Outdoors too. It's the one hunting trip where she's more than happy to accompany me.

The resort is transformed into a hunting lodge every year during the month of November. Northern's guides pre-position tree stands for their clients and shuttle them back and forth to those stands. I've used the same guide, Dan, for the majority of my visits and he's done an admirable job of putting me in the right place at the right time. Dan has learned that once I'm in my stand before daylight, I won't be coming out until dark. (I do know, however, that he drives by my drop-off point during the day, looking for a piece of flagging tape that I might tie to a twig, indicating that I need his assistance.) But the deer gods have not smiled on me on these hunts.

I always seem to be looking in the wrong direction. While a tree stand affords roughly 270 degrees of vision, you still have that big tree trunk right behind you. I once had a northern Maine monster buck sneak past me to the rear. If I'd had the stand set just a few inches more to either side, that deer would be on my wall today. By the time I spotted him, he was just about to disappear behind a bunch of spruces and no last-minute calling or grunting could persuade him to come back.

Another time, I had a huge-bodied buck come out of the woods nearly below my tree. It was a squawking partridge I'd been watching that alerted me to his presence. However, in the interest of promoting the growth of a trophy-class deer resource, Northern Outdoors asks its hunters to shoot only mature bucks with curved-rack antlers. The buck below me had only one hugely thick, but scraggly antler on one side of his head and nothing on the other side. However, he was as big as an ox. By the time I had decided that this was an old mature buck that was well past his prime and probably not likely to survive the winter, he was disappearing into a thicket. I still kick myself for that one.

There were other times, in fact, many times, at Northern Outdoors that deer eluded me, and in some years I've sat in a tree stand all week and not seen a deer at all. Such are the fortunes of deer hunting in the big woods of northern Maine. But I wouldn't trade even those barren years for anything. I've witnessed otters and beavers swimming in their waterways, seen owls and hawks pluck small rodents from meadows for their meals, watched moose browse their way up a hillside only to come crashing back through the woods when something startled them, and watched countless ravens soar overhead as they croaked their language back and forth to one another. All of these things are nourishment for my left brain.

A transferable state of mind

The last several years I've expanded my hunting opportunities to encompass spring black bear hunting. While my first black bear was taken as an animal of opportunity while I was still-hunting for November deer in Maine, I've become an ardent fan of hunting bears over bait from an elevated stand. Some hunters prefer ground blinds, but sitting on the ground in the presence of food with bears roaming around after dark just doesn't appeal to me. So I've learned to apply my deer stand skills to black bear hunting.

Most recently, my outfitter of choice has been Double Buck Lodge in Stanley, New Brunswick, Canada. Owner, Conrad Rollins and his staff go out of their way to provide an enjoyable experience to their clients and they are exceptionally good at bringing bears to their baits.

Whereas, being able to sit in a deer stand from sun-up to sun-down in November has been a significant challenge, bear stand hunting is a piece of cake in comparison. Bears are most active in the evening so there's no need to spend the entire day in the stand. We typically head to our stands about 3:00 p.m. and are out of the woods by 9:30 p.m. or so. And the springtime temperatures are certainly milder than those of late fall where I once had my water bottle freeze solid inside my pack. We spend the mornings fishing, playing cards, eating, napping, reading, accompanying the guides as they check the baits, or just plain relaxing. For me, it's like a hunting vacation. But one aspect is very similar. I still spend considerable time alone with my thoughts, observing nature, and anticipating the appearance of my quarry.

Black bears do not disappoint. While you'd think that a bulky animal like a bear would go through the woods like the proverbial bull in a china shop, they are anything but. Bears are like the stealth fighters of the woods. Ninety-nine percent of the time you will see them before you hear them. Nearly every bear I've seen has just materialized in front of me. One second there's just the bait barrel in front of you and the next, there's a big black animal trying to tip it over to get at the goodies it conceals.

There are some other observations I've made over the years concerning bear hunting from a stand. Chief among them is to watch the other woodland animals. They will tell you what's happening or about to happen. Blue jays, Canada jays (also called whiskey jacks or gorbies), red squirrels, chipmunks, raccoons, and ravens are all frequent visitors to bear baits. And if they are bobbing around and acting like they don't have a care in the world, it's with good reason. That type of activity means they are feeling unthreatened. It also means there is probably not a bear destined to imminently appear.

The reverse is also often true. If whatever critter happens to be swiping a bit of old pastry from the bait site suddenly charges off at top speed, get yourself ready. While your hunting senses can be fine-tuned, they are still significantly inferior to those of the lesser creatures of the woods. If they aren't on constant alert for danger, they can become a snack for anything higher up on the food chain.

I was once watching a bait site where a raccoon was calmly reaching under the barrel, removing, and then eating bit after bit of food. This went on for about 10 or 15 minutes. Suddenly, as if it had been given an electric shock, the raccoon wheeled around and left the site at top speed. Not two minutes later, I saw a black shape slowly approaching. It turned out to be a fairly small black bear. I never heard his approach, but the raccoon had, and beat a hasty retreat.

Bears also display the same prey-predator behavior among their own species. Another time I was watching a bait site and saw a small bear tip over the bait barrel and start in consuming its contents. But instead of just sitting there and eating his fill, he would tentatively take a piece and walk away just out of sight for four or five minutes and then return and do the same thing again. In all, he went through this ritual about six times. Finally, and without warning, he bolted off into the woods. Shortly thereafter, a much larger bear took his place at the barrel. Apparently, when it comes to who has first choice at the bait barrel, size does matter. The valuable lesson I learned was that if a bear is acting nervous, and is of questionable shooting size, wait a bit and see if his larger nemesis shows up. Your patience might be well rewarded.

The long and the short of all this is that time spent on a game stand is only wasted and dreary if you make it so. It is just as easy, with the right amount of both left- and right-brain planning, and maybe a bit of perseverance, to make every minute of every hour spent observing your surroundings not only worth the effort, but also quite enriching to your hunting soul.

Part Three : Fully Clothed

OK, maybe not exactly fully clothed, but close enough. Like Mr. Wilde, I've reached my destination. I'm confident enough in my skills and abilities that I'm now willing to share them with others. I can look back with satisfaction and salute both my own efforts as well as those of the people that helped get me this far. I still have challenges, not the least of which is the one of the advancing calendar. But I can keep that one somewhat at bay for now.

It's also slowly dawned on me that no one starts out as an expert. Those television hunting and fishing personalities that I used to envy so much…well, I do still envy them. But except for the luxuries of money and sponsorships, they don't have a whole lot over me. They started out at one time with nothing as well.

The chapters in part three are my measure of how far I've come and how well I've succeeded in becoming a lifelong, dedicated outdoors sportsman. I'm no longer naked. I'm wearing red and black checked plaid with pride. And if I'm hard to spot, I'm probably wearing camo.

Diesel

No, not the Hollywood actor. And not the internal combustion engine technology either, though there is a link. Diesel is my wire-haired pointing griffon bird dog. And where most bird hunters write eulogies about their best-friend dogs after they've gone to that big field trial in the sky, Diesel is still right here beside me as I write this. I might even read it to him when I'm done to see if he concurs that it's accurate. He always has an opinion.

That's a dog?

I wanted my own bird dog from the moment I started pheasant hunting. But I had a couple obstacles to overcome. Well, actually only one…my wife. Molly had this image in her mind that a hunting dog was this cold, impersonal hunting tool with about as much personality as my Browning shotgun. I'm still reluctant to let her in on the secret that my Browning actually *does* have a personality, but that's a subject for another story at another time.

I'd even settled on a breed of dog. My bird-hunting friend, John, had had three successive griffons and I'd hunted pheasants over his dogs for several years. I knew the griffon to be not only a tenacious hunter, but also a great house pet with an endearing personality. Another trait I liked was that griffons tend to work close to their hunters and not range too far. Still another trait I'd read about was that griffons were regarded as the four-by-fours of hunting dogs. No brush pile or thicket was too much for them to burrow into in pursuit of a game bird. I'd witnessed this firsthand with John's dogs.

It was based on these capabilities of performing like a four-wheel-drive vehicle and never-ending endurance in digging for the bird that Diesel got his name, even before I found him. Diesel engines have a reputation for being rugged. To my way of thinking, that matched the griffon's reputation. Now I just had to find the dog to hang the name on.

I considered contacting the same breeder that John used, but that breeder was in Colorado and I didn't want to have the dog shipped east by an airline. An Internet search yielded the names and locations of several local griffon breeders and this led me to Green Mountain Griffons in Lyndon, Vermont. I contacted the owner and learned that he was expecting a litter in the fall and would put me on his list. One tip that he gave me was that if I wanted the dog to really bond closely with me, I should plan on picking the dog up when he was 42 days old. Not 41 days or 43 days, but 42 days exactly. The litter was born on October 2. The countdown began.

I had a deer hunting trip planned for that November on Anticosti Island in the Gulf of St. Lawrence in Canada. A quick check of the calendar showed that day 42 was exactly on the day we would be driving back from the hunt. I convinced my hunting partner to delay our arrival home by one day and make the overnight stop in Vermont. After the week on Anticosti, and with four deer in the back of the truck, we arrived in Lyndon, Vermont.

It's hard to imagine a more homely looking bunch of clumsy fur balls. There were eight pups, four males and four females. Three of the females were already spoken for, but none of the males, which was what I was looking for. They were all falling down, tripping over one another, and looking and acting like anything but skilled hunting dogs. They more closely resembled animated dust mops with legs. Making a decision on which one to bring home was going to be difficult.

I quickly concluded that I couldn't make the decision and that I would let the dogs make it for me. I'd done the same thing several years earlier when my wife and I picked up a cat at a shelter and it had worked out well. As we walked into a room filled with rescued cats and their cubby holes stacked to the ceiling, one cat jumped down and landed on my shoulder. Twenty years later, we still have that same cat, Delilah, and now at age 22 she's still going strong, though minus most of her nine lives.

After about 20 minutes of my sitting on the floor and watching the pups play, one of them kept coming over to me and showed his curiosity. That was enough for me. I now had a dog to attach to the name. I put newly christened Diesel into a pet carrier and headed back to Massachusetts. We hadn't driven more than a few miles when it became apparent that we had a choice to make. We could either put up with a whimpering puppy in the carrier on the back seat for the next several hours of driving or else I'd have to hold Diesel in my lap for the trip. I chose the latter. Diesel quickly fell asleep and never made another sound for the entire trip home.

A giant chew toy

Diesel didn't know it then, but he was in for a surprise upon arrival at his new home. Rather than seven equal-size siblings to romp and play with, he met Sampson, his new canine brother. Sampson was our 130-pound black Newfoundland and was the kindest, most gentle and laid-back dog anyone could imagine. At the time, he was about eight years old and considered close to being a senior citizen in terms of life expectancy for a Newfoundland.

Diesel had little respect for his elder. He constantly played and parried with Sampson who also seemed to relish the companionship. Sometimes the play consisted of Diesel grabbing an ear in his jaws and being dragged about the house rather than let go. The two would play for long stretches of time and Sampson would frequently even roll on his back in a sign of submission and let Diesel be the alpha male in the two-dog pack. When Sampson got tired of the play, he'd just sit on Diesel and that ended it. It's safe to say they developed an instant and enduring bond of friendship.

Their friendship extended to protecting one another. When Diesel was still a pup, Sampson would often check on him just like any parent would do with a young child. He'd make sure Diesel was where he should be and invite him to curl up with him when it was time to rest. In later years, as Sampson neared the end of his life and became slow and more feeble, a role reversal happened. Just as human children look after their aging parents, Diesel took on that responsibility with regard to Sampson. That caretaker role lasted until the end of Sampson's life. No one in the family was sadder than Diesel at Sampson's passing.

Time to get serious

In the spring of his first year, Diesel and I got serious about training. At least I did. Diesel, not so much. But determination on my part paid off. By using a starter pistol and a pheasant wing stuffed inside a paint roller I was able to teach Diesel to retrieve. I didn't have to train him to point as that aspect seemed to come very naturally to him. Finally it was time to take him on his first hunt. Disaster. All the training was forgotten in an instant.

I went quail hunting with my friend, John, who also had his griffon. His dog would lock up on point and Diesel would happily charge right past John's dog and bust the covey before we were within shooting distance. No amount of calling or discipline made any difference. To Diesel, hunting was just an excuse to play. This uncontrollable activity continued the rest of the day and the following weekend as well, in spite of more training sessions at home that seemed to go well. The third weekend proved the charm.

Diesel went scampering into the field and I expected the same undisciplined behavior as before. Suddenly, Diesel froze in mid stride. He was locked onto a bird and waited patiently until I released him. When the bird fell at my shot Diesel ran after it and returned it to my feet. I was stunned. It was as if the switch in his brain on how to properly hunt had been flipped to "on." He even honored the points of John's dog that day, something that I had not taught him. My new bird-hunting partner had finally arrived. Diesel officially became a bird dog that day.

Doctor Gentle and Mr. Killer

Since that first successful bird hunt with Diesel, we've never looked back. He's become an outstanding pointer and retriever. When we hunt, he's all business. It's as if he has a duel personality. At home he's the most loving and playful pet anyone could want. He puts up with the grandkids and roams the house with one of his ever-present squeaky toys always in his mouth. As a watch dog, no alarm system can compare. If any vehicle, person, or animal enters the yard, he sounds the alarm from his perch on a living room chair with his head resting on the back cushion. If a crow lands in the yard or a squirrel decides to run across, all hell breaks loose. The rest of the time he's Dr. Gentle.

When Diesel is hunting, or even out just for a walk in the woods with me, he turns into Mr. Killer. He constantly jogs ahead of me, from one side of our path to the other, and burrows deeply into every thicket and brush pile in search of prey. On more than one occasion when we've been bird hunting, he has not only pointed pheasants, but also managed to grab them in his mouth before they get a chance to take flight. If I wound a bird and it starts running, he'll keep after it no matter how far or where it goes and dutifully bring it back to me. When I miss a shot at a bird he's pointed and flushed, I get a look of mixed sorrow and disgust. It's like he's telling me, "Too bad you missed, Pete, but I did my part and you flubbed yours. Who's the loser?"

If Diesel had a different name it would be Tough Guy. Once, when he was done hunting and jumped into the back of the pick up before I was ready, he fell backwards and caught his foot as he tumbled. I took him to the vet to check out his lameness and was told that he just had a sprain and would quickly recover. The next weekend we went pheasant hunting again and after a while I noticed that he was limping. By the time we got back to the truck he was running on just three legs. Even at that, he was hunting and we still managed to get our limit of two pheasants. A return trip to the vet and some X-rays showed a broken bone in his foot. This time Diesel got a well-earned rest.

Other times he's hunted through bloodied feet, broken toenails, and eyes forced closed by hundreds of tangling brambles. I can't imagine what keeps him going through those times, but I'm certain he wouldn't want to be doing anything else.

The only drawback to Diesel's hunting persona is that it instantly turns on if he sees our pet cat, Delilah. While Delilah used to have free roam of the house, she now spends all her time behind the closed door of our bedroom. Diesel has gone after her a couple times and I'm certain would have extinguished what remains of her nine lives in a flash if he caught her.

Changing times

Diesel is now 12 years old and when he and I return home after several hours in the field he shows his age by arthritically limping around and spending a lot of time curled up in front of the wood stove. While he's in the field he uses every last ounce of drive he possesses, leaving nothing in his tank when he's done. Of course, I show no such signs of aging. Well, maybe just a bit. I tell my friends that 66 is still just "approaching middle age."

I think Diesel has another couple years of brush busting and bird hunting left in him, but I'm going to keep a close eye on him and not let him get too far ahead of himself. I want to have him around long enough to teach his skills to a new dog when the time comes. With that goal in mind, at the end of the recent upland game season I contacted the same breeder in Vermont where I found Diesel. Even though it's been over a decade since we last spoke, he said he remembered me because of the name Diesel. I explained to him that next year I'd be interested in another puppy and was told that I'd again be placed on his waiting list.

What I didn't tell the breeder was that, as with Diesel, I already have a name picked out. It will be interesting to see which puppy matches up to the name Muskie. No, not the fish. And not the former U.S. Senator from Maine. I plan to name the new dog after the swamp rodent. Unlike Diesel, who isn't fond of water, I see some waterfowl hunting in Muskie's future. Did I mention that we have another middle-age Newfoundland dog named Murphy?

And Delilah the cat may have to spend a few more years in bedroom exile. Life for the two-legged and four-legged members of our household is about to get considerably more interesting, again.

Diesel Postscript

Muskie may have to learn more on his own than was planned. After much testing at the vet's office, it was determined that Diesel has an illness called Cushing's disease. He has a tumor growing within his brain and it will ultimately cause his demise. But it hasn't slowed him down much yet. The new upland bird season has started and he's as tenacious as ever in his efforts to find birds for me. The vet says he could have as much as a year left. There's no way to tell. Until that sad day comes, we're making the most of every minute and doing what we both enjoy most.

The Tennessee Judge and the Black Bear

"I hope you brought some help with you," Tony called out to Vance, his guide, as he approached Tony's elevated stand after dark in the gloom of a New Brunswick, Canada, cedar swamp.

"Oh my God," thought Vance, "Tony's hurt himself." Instead of helping Tony drag a black bear out of the woods, Vance was going to be the one needing help dragging Tony out. Tony, being a man of somewhat large proportions, was going to be more than a little difficult to haul back to camp without that additional help. "What did you do? Fall? Break a leg?" Vance asked.

As it turned out, Tony and Vance really did need help—lots of help.

Settling in

Tony, his nephew Will, and I were part of a group of hunters assembled by Carroll and Lila Ware. We came to Stanley, New Brunswick, for a spring black bear hunt. Most of the hunters knew each other and had gone on bear hunts before. The one completely new face in the crowd was Anthony ("Tony") Sanders, a judge in the Tennessee court system who specialized in working with and helping the youthful citizens of his county.

While being an experienced hunter, Tony was new to black bear hunting, as well as to some of the other animals of the northeastern corner of North America. Not only was he hoping to bag a bruin, but he was also optimistic that he might catch a glimpse of that monster of the eastern woodlands, a moose.

Sunday, all the hunters settled into Double Buck Lodge bear camp. Our hosts, Conrad Rollins and his staff, made sure everyone was comfortable and well fed. After dinner, we traded hunting stories, told tall tales, bragged about our prowess at playing cribbage, got reacquainted with one another, and got to know a bit about Tony.

Monday morning, several of the group accompanied the guides as they freshened the baits and, in turn, the guides learned the hunting preferences of each hunter—whether they preferred an elevated stand or a ground blind, and whether they planned to use a firearm or archery equipment. Since this was his first bear hunt, and also in response to his southern charm and storehouse of down-home wit and humor, everyone tried to give helpful advice to Tony. One tip was that because a bear moves so silently through the timber, he would seemingly just materialize from thin air. It wasn't clear if Tony believed all we told him or if he thought that we "Yankees" were pulling his leg just a tad.

Failure and success

Monday afternoon each hunter headed out with his guide. Anticipation ran high. For my part, I was headed for a tree stand where the previous year I'd blown an opportunity at a large bear and was now hoping to redeem myself. Shortly before dark I spotted what appeared to be a shooter bear moving through the trees in my direction. Eventually he made his way toward the bait and sat on his hind legs, facing me, directly behind the barrel. With the light failing, I took the shot.

Deer hunters can experience buck fever. There's a related ailment that can afflict bear hunters—bear fever. Later examination showed that my bullet had struck a log significantly to the right of my bear and never touched hide nor hair. So much for my Monday evening hunt.

The story was a bit brighter back at camp. Will had connected on a nice bear and so had one of the other firearms hunters. Several others had seen bears. In total, nine different bears were spotted on the first evening, an auspicious start. Unfortunately, Tony wasn't among those to see a bear.

Tuesday came and went with another bear being taken, this one weighing about 250 pounds, and several others were spotted, including a sow with triplets. Again, Tony was not among the fortunate, though he did see a fisher cat to break the monotony of his evening on stand.

Wednesday was the day for my redemption. On Monday I'd forgotten that baited bears typically hang around the bait for some time and that if the hunter is just patient and waits for his adrenalin to subside, he can bide his time, wait for the best shot angle, and take a relaxed shot. When my bear came in, and after letting my heart rate settle to a more normal level, I raised my Marlin .45-70 and positioned the crosshairs just where they needed to be and squeezed the trigger. Down went the bear on the spot and my bear hunt was over. Not so for Tony.

In addition to my bear, another hunter, the fifth out of the six of us using firearms, took his bear on Wednesday. This left Tony as the only one of us yet to see, much less shoot at a bear. We could all tell he was a bit discouraged. But his luck was about to change.

Tony's turn

Thursday, Conrad made the decision to move Tony to a different stand that might be more promising. It was situated well into the woods, accessible only on foot, and right at the edge of an exceptionally thick cedar swamp—not an inviting place to track down a wounded bear if it came to that. Tony climbed into his stand and waited to see what would happen. First he had to clean a rather large pile of bear droppings from the old school bus seat that served as his stand.

A while later he spotted his second fisher cat of the trip and passed some time watching its antics. After a little more time he heard some branches snap off to the side and soon made out the silhouette of a mature bull moose passing his stand. Well, at least he'd seen his moose. But for a bear, time was running out and so was daylight.

Then, about 9:00 p.m., a bear just silently appeared from nowhere near the bait. As it approached, Tony noted both its large size and the fact that it had a side-to-side, swaggering style to its gait as it walked. He also saw that its ears were set wide apart on the sides of its head as opposed to sticking straight up on top. Both the gait and the ear position were bits of advice Tony had been given as indicators of a large bear.

Tony let the bear reach the bait and decided that this was a good bear to take. He centered the bear in the scope of his Weatherby .300 magnum and as the bear was about to touch his nose to a snack on top of the barrel, he fired. The bear crumpled in his tracks.

Tony waited a few minutes and then climbed down to look over his trophy. It looked like a big bear, but being new at this bear hunting game, he climbed back into his stand to await the arrival of Vance and a more experienced opinion.

Waiting for a verdict

Vance was much relieved to see that it was not an injured client that needed help. And when he saw the bear he knew that they both would need some significant assistance getting it back to camp. Eventually, many hands, feet, and strong backs, chief among them, nephew Will's, accomplished the task.

Sometimes bears, like many hunted animals, suffer from "ground shrinkage" when actual size back at camp turns out to be smaller than the estimated size in the field. Not so with Tony's bear. In the woods, weight estimates ranged from 325 to perhaps 350 pounds. When hung from a scale at camp, it topped out at 408 pounds, a magnificent example of a springtime New Brunswick bear with a beautiful thick and shiny black coat.

It took a little while for Tony to fully realize how fortunate he had been. Maybe a little of the "Tennessee tea" (aka: Jack Daniels whiskey) he shared with us that night helped, but we were all pretty sure he headed back home as a happy man.

Even though Tony is a judge, his word is not always final back in Tennessee. Before he left he drafted a document destined for a higher court back home and had each of us sign it. Tony petitioned his wife, Frieda, to grant an exception and allow him to put his full-size, record-class New Brunswick bear mount in his home. At last check, the jury was still deliberating.

The .45-70 Dinner Bell Bear

It's 8:00 p.m. on Tuesday. It's just the second day of my spring black bear hunt with Double Buck Lodge in Stanley, New Brunswick, Canada. And I've got the biggest black bear I've ever seen in my life lined up in the crosshairs of my scope. He's just 66 yards away and nosing at the bait barrel, completely oblivious to my presence. He's giving me a perfectly steady broadside shot. The set-up couldn't be better. My heart rate has slowed. I'm calm. The adrenalin rush has subsided. My Marlin 1895 Guide Model rifle in .45-70 is steady and solid in the fork of my shooting stick. All I have to do is pull the trigger and this bear is going back across the border to the United States with me.

Just one thing is amiss. I can't pull the trigger. I want to, but I can't. Oh, how I want to!

First night

Carroll Ware put together the trip and accompanied me to New Brunswick for the latest episode in what has become for me an annual spring black bear hunt. Conrad Rollins, owner of Double Buck Lodge, had assured us that the black bears were hitting the baits hard. He told us to be patient and the bears would come to the baits willingly. Multiple bears were being seen at several different bait sites.

Anticipation ran high both Sunday evening and Monday morning. I'd hunted before with both Carroll and Conrad and if past results were indicators of future success, I was sure to be happily pleased once again. Carroll sighted in his bow, two other hunters in camp fine-tuned their crossbows, and I checked out the accuracy of both myself and my rifle. Two more bow hunters were scheduled to join us during the week. We were literally loaded for bears.

Monday afternoon and evening I sat silently in a ladder stand and heard nothing except the drumming of a nearby partridge. A bit later, three coyotes that also must have heard the partridge trotted directly under my stand. When I leaned over a bit to get a better look at them, one turned his head, looked up at me, and without breaking stride, seemed to have an expression in his eyes that said, "What the hell are you doing up there?" Then they were gone and continued their own hunt. Three coyotes spotted, but no bears.

One of the crossbow hunters, however, connected with a nice bear that first evening. It was close to 200 pounds and the bolt from his crossbow dropped it almost on top of the bait. It was a good beginning to the hunt.

Death moan

Then came Tuesday evening. This time I sat on the ground on one side of a clearing that had been an old logging staging area. I was just inside the tree line and wearing my camo clothing and bug suit. Sixty-six yards away, on the other side of the clearing, was an upright 55-gallon drum with bear bait consisting of old, sweet pastry and some of Conrad's special bear elixir under and around it. As I was getting myself settled in, Conrad cut a shooting stick for me and later said he noticed several large piles of bear scat a few feet away and behind where I was sitting. He didn't tell me about it then for fear that it might rattle me and make me nervous. Good decision. I was edgy enough just being on the ground instead of 15 or 20 feet up a ladder which is my usual and more comfortable preference.

At 7:55 p.m. a bear cautiously approached the bait and circled the barrel a couple times. The bear looked about average size or perhaps a bit bigger than ones I'd taken in past years. After watching it for a few minutes and mentally comparing it to the bear taken the previous evening, I decided that this bear was big enough to shoot. I leveled the Marlin in the fork of my shooting stick, sighted on the bear just behind its front shoulder, and took the shot. The bear lurched forward, obviously hit hard, and disappeared behind some nearby trees. Then I heard its death moan.

If you've never heard a bear's blood-curdling death moan you can't imagine the eeriness of that sound. It's like something straight out of an old-time late-night thriller starring Boris Karloff. I've heard it once before from a bear I shot. It happens frequently, but not always. It depends on where, anatomy-wise, the bear has been hit. There were two very loud moans followed by four or five weaker ones and then silence. Carroll, who was over a mile away in his own stand, later told me that he heard the two loud moans from my bear and one of the weaker ones. That's how loud it was.

Ring the dinner bell

After the shot, I started putting my gear together in preparation to go over and see if I could find and check out the bear. I stood up, turned my back to the bait barrel, and began stuffing my gear into my pack. Then I got the surprise of my life.

Apparently, the sound of a gunshot from a big-bore rifle acts only as a dinner bell to a *really* big bear. When I turned once again toward the barrel I noticed that the opening in the trees behind it was now solid black instead of the dirt brown color it had been just a couple minutes earlier. As my eyes caught movement, they focused on the biggest black bear I'd ever seen. Most likely, he'd never heard a gunshot before. This bear looked like a swollen beer barrel, or maybe more like the 275-gallon oil storage tank that feeds fuel to a home heating system if its sides were bulging from being overfilled with an extra hundred gallons of oil. He was huge. The bear I'd just shot was a midget in comparison.

The big bear slowly waddled over to the bait site and stood up on his hind feet to push over the barrel to get at the bait. Standing on end, the bait barrel was about three-and-a-half feet tall. When this bear stood beside it, there was about another three feet more of him that towered above the top of the barrel. I was amazed.

Over the years, I've learned it's easy to overestimate the size of a black bear. In fact, among my fellow hunters I have the dubious reputation of shooting smaller bears. But my somewhat-educated guess was that this bear was probably between 400 and 500 pounds in size. In the fall, after fattening up all summer, such a bear could easily weigh upwards of 600 pounds. Five-hundred-plus-pound bears had been shot and weighed previously in the spring in this same area by Double Buck Lodge hunters. I was certain this one was at least as big as the 408 pounder that one of the hunters in our group shot the year before.

I sat back down in my seat and watched the big guy for several minutes, not quite grasping the magnitude of what my eyes were taking in. Even with the large rocks placed on top of it, he knocked over the barrel like it was a Tinker Toy. When he walked, his whole body and head lolled from side to side. His front legs bowed outwards, kind of like a mammoth-size version of an English bulldog. His ears looked like they were stuck to the sides of his head almost like afterthoughts, another sign of a really big bear. And his whole demeanor said, "I'm the boss here. All others are unwelcome. Leave now!" I know he saw me moving about, but that didn't seem to faze him in the least. Not very comforting.

I put my rifle scope on him to get a better look. After I watched the bruiser for about five minutes, he waddled off in the same direction as the bear I shot only minutes before. The thought crossed my mind that maybe he'd see my dead bear as an hors d'oeuvre, devour it, and therefore give me a chance at shooting him as well. But such was not the case, and anyway, I pride myself in following both the spirit and the letter of wildlife laws. One bear per hunter per season.

Seeing the giant leave in the direction he chose made up my mind for me. Instead of going to check out the bear I had shot, I decided to head for the road and see if Conrad might be coming back anytime soon. I knew he was probably miles away with other hunters and would only come back to pick me up well after dark. I didn't want to be on the ground in the dark with dead meat in the vicinity and a monster black bear nearby, possibly craving an evening snack. And my Marlin .45-70 somehow didn't seem quite as powerful as it had just a short time before.

Eventually, Conrad came by and we went back to the clearing together to find my bear. It was just behind the trees, about 40 feet from the barrel and stone dead. The big guy must have walked right past it as he left the area. My bear weighed about 150 pounds, about average size, and had a beautiful white chevron emblazoned on its chest. It will make a great addition to my collection and, even better, my wife has already given approval for the spot on the wall where it will go.

As it turned out, not only was I successful on Tuesday evening, but so too were Carroll and the other crossbow hunter. Each of us took bears on the same evening and they were all within five pounds of one another. In celebration of our success, I broke out one of my remaining bottles of Jim Beam bourbon that had been collecting dust since the 1970s. Dad ran a bar back then and saved the empty collector edition bottles. Mixed in with the empties were just a few unopened full bottles. It's fair to say that an additional 40 years of aging to bourbon that's already 12 years old when bottled in no way impairs its flavor.

Later in the week, the other two compound bow hunters scored on nice bears as well, one of them approaching 300 pounds. Six hunters, six bears. But none even close to the size of my .45-70 dinner bell bear.

I'm already signed up to go back to Double Buck Lodge again next year. I hope that big guy doesn't mind too much that I'll be chowing down on one of his relatives in the interim. I like bear meat even more than venison. Double Buck Lodge has exclusive rights to hundreds of square miles of prime bear hunting land so chances are good that bear will still be wandering the spruce thickets next year. I hope so. Now I know what a really big bear looks like and I'd more than welcome his appearance the next time the dinner bell sounds.

The Three Bears

Not the children's fairy tale. This is the tale of the three bears that owe their continued existence to my restraint, curiosity, and perhaps a bit of indecision.

The goal of most hunting trips is to take an animal. And for many hunters, that's the measure of success. If the animal happens to be a superior example of whatever species is being hunted, so much the better. But what if the hunter fails to take an animal? What if circumstances conspire against him? Is the hunting trip a failure? The answer to those questions lies in a recent bear hunting adventure.

New outfitter, new goal

My goal was simple for this particular spring black bear hunt. I wanted to take a BIG black bear. Something well over 200 pounds and hopefully nearer to 300 pounds. I've already shot five average-size bears in the 125 to 150 pound class and didn't fancy shooting another. I've had my chances at big bears in the past, but the fates have ruled against me and in favor of the bears at the moment of truth. However, New Brunswick was providing me with a bonus this year. Instead of the past one-bear-per-hunter-per-year bag limit, I could purchase a second tag if I wished and take two bears. Two chances to take that big bear.

This year I'd switched outfitters and was at Taxis River Outfitters in Boistown, New Brunswick. Our hosts and owners were Larry and Bonnie Davidson. They've run the lodge for over 30 years and know what they're doing, both as far as finding bears goes, as well as taking good care of their clients. As with many of my previous hunts, the trip had been arranged by Carroll Ware and Fins and Furs Adventures. Our group consisted of 10 other hunters, including several retirees like myself, business people, and two youngsters, both high school students and accompanied by their dads on the trip. One of the teens was a young man and the other a young woman with aspirations to become a Maine game warden. Sunday evening, anticipation ran high as we all settled into the lodge. Some of us renewed acquaintances from past hunts while newcomers introduced themselves to the group. We might have even sampled a few "recreational beverages."

While the sleeping accommodations were fairly spartan, though quite comfortable, with everyone in private separate cabins, the lodge was spectacular. The spacious main room had large windows on two sides, warm wood paneling up the walls and across the high ceiling, and an assortment of animal trophies on those walls that would have been impressive at any hunting tradeshow. Dining tables, sofas, and cable TV completed the décor. A fully equipped kitchen where Bonnie worked her magic, staff sleeping quarters, and two full baths rounded out the lodge building. Outside, a deck area provided an overlook of the grounds. Hummingbirds were constant visitors to a feeder.

A fire pit and surrounding benches offered relaxed seating where hunting tales could be swapped and embellished above and beyond any semblance of actual reality. Several large stacks of moose antler sheds, picked up during bear baiting operations, provided ample evidence of the size and healthy status of the local moose population. (Taxis River Outfitters also offers moose and whitetail deer hunts in the fall.) Perhaps best of all the exterior amenities was the Taxis River itself. It flows literally within a short stone's throw from the main lodge building and comes complete with a population of colorful sea-run brook trout. A game pole fitted with multiple hoists was also present and awaited our bruin offerings.

Rainy days and Mondays

On Monday we got our hunting licenses and guide assignments. Dale, a seasoned veteran, was to be Carroll's and my guide. We also got our first real taste of Bonnie's cooking. We'd had some delicious beef stew on Sunday evening as the stew was most appropriate for our group's separate and unpredictable arrival times, but Monday was our group's first planned sit-down meal. I've experienced hunting lodge meals of varying levels of culinary expertise in the past. Bonnie's were second to none and were as good as or better than some meals I've had at lodges that also had attached restaurants. During our stay at Taxis River we ate steaks, pork loin, chicken, smoked shoulder ham, and even generously sized steamed lobsters. Delicious homemade desserts accompanied every meal. Upon returning home I found I'd gained six pounds in six days. Put simply, we ate exceptionally well.

Less welcome than those meals were the wind and the rain. Both Monday and Tuesday it rained heavily most of the day. Even wearing rain gear, by the time Dale picked me up about 9:45 p.m. from my elevated stand, I was pretty much soaked to the skin on both days. The only unexpected event of Monday evening was the unseen but very audible crashing of a tree in the woods. Since I was present when it happened, I don't know if it would have made a sound if I hadn't been there. (No chance to debunk or prove the myth.) Several of us, myself included, were allowed to use the lodge's clothes dryer Monday evening and the next morning. I saw no bears those first two evenings. A couple other hunters had shots at bears from their stands, but none were taken. We blamed the weather. Wednesday would be different.

On Wednesday the weather improved. We still had a bit of rain, but the wind had subsided and the temperature was somewhat warmer. Dale suggested I continue using the same stand and I agreed. The bait had been hit by bears both evenings and I was sure it was just a matter of time before the bear's and my schedules coincided for my gain and his loss.

As we drove towards the stand along the fogged-in lumber road, I was scanning the road ahead in hopes of spotting a bear. A dark shape materialized ahead of us after we rounded a turn and I quickly called to Dale to stop the truck. Silhouetted against the fog-shrouded backdrop was a black bear. Since everything else was invisible in the murk, it was difficult to judge the bear's size. I piled out of the truck, put a shell in my .45-70 rifle, and took aim through the scope. I figured I had only seconds to make up my mind whether to shoot or not before the bear charged off into the thick underbrush. The bear had other ideas.

Rather than running off as quickly as possible, the bear began rapidly trotting towards us on the road. As he got closer it became apparent that this was not a large bear and weighed maybe 100 pounds or maybe slightly more. I unloaded my rifle and got back in the truck. The bear kept coming. Looking back, I don't know what could have been going through his mind. Perhaps he thought the big dark object in the road was a moose. Bears will kill and feed on moose calves in the spring, as well as deer fawns.

When the bear got to within about 10 yards of the truck, he stopped in the middle of the road and reared up on his hind feet to get a better look at us. Still not certain of what we were, he moved first to one side of the road and then to the other, each time standing up to get a better view. Eventually he wandered off, probably thinking that Dale's Toyota Tundra might be a bit more to take on than he was willing to tackle. We resumed our trip to my bear stand. I'd just passed up my first bear of the trip.

Croaking frogs, roaring bears

The stand was about 12 feet off the ground and set against a spruce tree about 20 yards from the bait. I was able to see only a few feet into the thick woods beyond the bait. Directly behind me was a beaver pond, complete with its resident beaver, several ducks, splashing brook trout, and an assembled chorus of bullfrogs and their very vocal amphibious backup singers. By about 8:00 p.m. I'd still seen nothing from my stand. The evening sun was warm and my full bug suit was doing its job of keeping the mosquitos and black flies at bay so I did what I often do on game stands...I took a few brief catnaps.

Awaking from one such nap, I spied a small branch twitching in the woods behind the bait and momentarily a bear appeared. He rather timidly approached the bait barrel, leading me to believe he was likely not the dominant bear at the site. Through my rifle scope he looked to be about the same size as the bear we'd seen earlier on the lumber road and therefore safe from my trigger finger. After a short visit and a pastry snack from the bait site, he quietly ambled back into the woods, only to reappear about 10 minutes later and repeat the same sequence of events. This time he left and did not return. I'd passed again on my second easy opportunity to take a bear.

Dale picked me up later and I told him what I'd seen as well as what I'd heard. While it had sounded somewhat similar to the many loud frogs in the pond, there was one sound that stood out as a cross between a bullfrog and the muffled roar of a lion and it seemed to be coming from the woods well behind the bait. Dale explained that it was likely a male bear bellowing. Bears mate in the springtime and the males call the females to them by means of this sound. Perhaps with bears, he who has the biggest bellow wins the paw of the lady?

Hunting had been better for some of the rest of our party. Two bears were taken and one was just a tad under 200 pounds, not a big bear, but certainly respectable. Several other bears had also been spotted. With the improvement in the weather, the bears were becoming more active; a promising sign.

Dead beaver, live bear

Thursday dawned with nine of eleven hunters still not having shot a bear. Time was running out. Several hunters, myself included, decided that Thursday was a good day to shoot a bear. Armed with this optimistic bravado, and after a sumptuous steamed lobster feed, we headed out once more to the bait sites. I was bound again for the same bait site as the three previous evenings. On the ride there we encountered one of the most torrential downpours of rain I've ever experienced. We learned later that golf-ball-size hail fell just a short distance away and damaged many automobiles.

Fortunately the rain let up quickly and the sun returned to the sky as we arrived at the site. While I climbed into the stand, Dale fastened a beaver carcass to a tree adjacent to the bait as an additional enticement for the bears. I gave Dale the "thumbs up" sign and was once again left waiting and watching for a big bear to show up.

Just a couple minutes before legal shooting time ended a bear silently walked out of the woods and approached the bait. He was obviously bigger than the two bears I'd already passed on, but in the dim light I wasn't certain just how much bigger. Through my rifle scope I tried to gauge his size as compared to the bait barrel, but rather than coming right to it, he headed for the beaver attached to the tree and began tugging on it with his teeth to pull it free. Should I shoot or not? In the end, a combination of uncertainty, failing light, and the second night of roaring from the woods, possibly indicating the presence of even bigger bears, yet again kept me from pulling the trigger. I had passed up my third opportunity at a bear.

Dale arrived a short time later and once more I told him what had transpired. We discussed what I had seen and decided that maybe I should have shot. Of course this was a moot point now, but I resolved that if the same bear showed up on Friday evening I would take the shot. Back at the lodge we found that two more of our group had connected and the count of bears taken was now up to four.

Friday evening found me back at the same stand once more. I'd spent the whole week and close to 24 total hours sitting in one spot, virtually motionless, often in a rainstorm, amid a swarm of mosquitos and voracious black flies, in hopes of seeing and shooting a large black bear. By this point I'd learned that I could tell time merely by when each species of frog began its unique song. I knew which dark shadows were trying to fool me into believing that a bear was approaching. I'd pretty much perfected my quick catnap technique. And I no longer had any doubts about the sound of the bears roaring in the forest. I could pick that sound out from the background noise instantly. But the bear from the previous evening never showed himself and neither did any of his roaring lovelorn friends. The only critter I saw was an owl that glided past my face to presumably pounce on a mouse or red squirrel for its dinner.

We met up with the other vehicles and their guides and hunters and learned that a total of four bears had been taken on Friday with one ultimately weighing 270 pounds. Happily, the two young hunters in our group were each successful. By the time we got all the bears and ourselves back to camp and properly taken care of it was close to 2:00 a.m. Everyone was happy. Including me. A few more recreational beverages were consumed.

It's not always necessary to take an animal to have a successful hunt. On this particular adventure I renewed some old acquaintances, made new friends, ate incredible meals, laughed until my sides ached, and watched, heard, and appreciated nature more closely than is typical. I'd call that a pretty successful hunt. Besides, those same three bears will still be there next year...and so will I.

The Many Deer of Hurricane Mills

BANG! The instant I pulled the trigger I knew the sad truth. The bullet from my Remington 7mm magnum rifle had gone about a foot under the belly of the big eight-point whitetail buck and found a resting place deep in the dirt of a field in Hurricane Mills, Tennessee, home of country legends Loretta Lynn and Davey Crockett. Before I could cycle the bolt, the buck fired up his afterburners and made it to the edge of the field and safely into the thick oak and hickory timber.

Moments before, I spotted the buck out of the corner of my left eye, coming slowly up from the shallow gulley, about 125 yards out and slightly downhill from my ground blind. The light rain wasn't a factor and all I had to do was settle the crosshairs behind his shoulder and he would have been mine. He would have been the most impressive buck I'd ever shot. I already had him mounted and on the wall at home. Would have…except for my errant shot. Davey would not have approved of my marksmanship.

But, instead of kicking myself in the rear end and bemoaning my misfortune, all I could muster was an audible chuckle and a broad grin on my face. If any serious hunter had been there to witness the scene they'd surely be searching for a reason for the humor in the situation. It started about two weeks beforehand.

Oh deer

Like every year for the previous seven, my wife and I went the third week of November to the Northern Outdoors lodge at The Forks off highway 201 in Maine. I was to spend the week as one of the lodge's semi-guided hunters, sitting all day in a tree stand or ground blind for the week, often in sub-freezing cold, waiting for a big buck to cross my line of sight. My wife, being of what she believes sounder mind, spent her days enjoying the lodge's warmth and many amenities.

Though I've yet to take a wall hanger at The Forks, I've had my chances. Somehow I always seem to be facing in the wrong direction at the critical moment or been otherwise outwitted by the deer hunting gremlins in Maine. This year was no exception. However, in 2011, I doubled up on my chances. In addition to the trip to Maine, I booked a trophy deer trip to CCW Outfitters in Marion, Kentucky, with Carroll Ware and a couple of his other clients.

CCW promotes only trophy-class deer hunting. Deer with antlers scoring 130 inches or better (three and a half years old or older) are the only ones to be taken. For any animal shot below these limits, while still a nice deer by most standards, a financial penalty can be assessed to the hunter based on the difference between the minimum score and the deer taken. In other words, think carefully and apply your antler-judging skills before you pull the trigger or release an arrow if you're a bow hunter.

Deer hunting, southern style

In a week at CCW, I saw many, many deer. And a number of them were what I would consider trophy-class, at least in my league. However, did they measure up to CCW's standards? Especially the buck that, on the last day of the hunt, walked 100 yards the length of a field before stopping broadside in front of my blind at 30 yards? I had the scope on him, my finger on the safety, and was ready to end the mystery, but, in the end, decided I wasn't certain enough of his size and lowered my rifle and watched him walk away. That was difficult. If I had it to do over today, I'd pull the trigger. So a second consecutive week of deer hunting ended without bringing home a trophy or some venison. Fortunately, I had one final chance.

Will Sanders, whom I'd met on a couple previous trips with Carroll, had invited Carroll and me to join him on his property in Hurricane Mills, Tennessee, for three and a half days of deer hunting before we flew back to New England. Tennessee has a very liberal policy on tag limits with three bucks per season and three does *per day* as the regulation. Will had assured us that he knew the location of the deer. So, after Carroll's wife, Lila, flew down from Maine to join us, we settled into a warm and comfortable farmhouse on Will's property with high expectations.

Will showed me a nice ground blind that afforded a 100-yard view up-slope to the right and over 200 yards down-slope to the left. Compared to the spruce thickets of Maine, this was like what I'd imagined prairie land hunting to be. And the first evening, while not taking a deer, I did spot two does, a spike horn, and a really nice buck. My hopes ran high for the next day.

Just before sunset the next day, the first full day of my Tennessee hunting adventure, I managed to take a nice doe. And while I was getting her ready for the haul back to the farmhouse, two other does twice came to investigate what was going on. Unfortunately, I couldn't drop what I was doing and grab my rifle quick enough to give either of them an up-close demonstration. That night, I half-jokingly informed Carroll and Lila that I was through fooling around, though I might have used somewhat more colorful language. I said that if I was lucky enough the next day to shoot another deer, I might postpone the necessary after-shot field-dressing chores to wait and see what else might transpire.

So now, the third day, and second full day of hunting at Hurricane Mills, was about to begin. Legal hunting began about 6:05 a.m. I was in the same ground blind and the same cold rain that had beset us since the first evening was falling. At least I already knew I was going home with some venison.

Fool me once, but not twice

At 6:35 a.m. I caught movement to my right. A doe was walking through the sage grass. Kneeling in the mud, I brought the scope to bear and slowly squeezed the trigger. The doe dropped on the spot at the gunshot. Wow, two days and two does. And after two weeks of nothing. Tennessee was agreeing with me.

True to my word, instead of going out to inspect this deer, which I could see was clearly dead on the ground, I stayed on alert in the blind. Just 40 minutes later, at 7:15 a.m., I saw another doe moving on my left. Having ranged the distances the day before with my rangefinder, I knew this one was considerably farther away than the first. Once again, taking careful aim, the Remington rang out. The doe ran about 30 yards and went nose first into the ground. I left the blind to confirm the obvious on this second deer and also checked on the first. Then I returned again to the blind. Was it yet possible to take my third doe of the day?

At 7:45 a.m., just 30 minutes after doe number two hit the ground, I watched as still another doe emerged from the woods below me. Again, it was a relatively long shot. Once more, the Remington did what was asked of it and this third doe dropped in its tracks. An hour and ten minutes and three does down at 110, 220, and 180 yards, respectively. I'd never had such a day of deer hunting in my life. But was it still possible to take the one-buck-per-day that Tennessee allowed?

The plan that day was to meet back at the farmhouse at 10:00 a.m. After checking out the third doe, it was still only about 8:00 a.m., so once again I settled into the blind. While sitting there, I couldn't believe my good fortune. First, I'd shot four deer in the last 15 hours. There would be plenty of venison in the freezer for my own needs as well as to share with friends and family. Next, I was having the time of my life with three good friends, Carroll, Lila, and Will. The evenings of good-natured ribbing, cribbage games, and judiciously consumed liquid refreshments were making the trip all the more special. And lastly, I was simply having fun.

So at 9:15 a.m. when that big eight-pointer strutted onto the field, it might be at least a bit understandable why I lost my concentration and some of my composure and completely blew the shot and fired underneath him. My exuberance had simply gotten the better of me. I was just having too good a time. Even missing the biggest buck I'd ever had a chance at couldn't take that away.

In the end, the measure of success or failure of a deer hunt isn't measured in inches of antler or field-dressed pounds of venison. It's judged by smiles on faces, laughter that reaches an aching point, and the unselfish hospitality and generosity of friends. At least that's the measurement of success for me.

Going Awry

The spinning rod slowly slid down the embankment. Carroll and I just stood in silent amazement. Helpless, frozen immobility gripped us as it plopped into the pond and disappeared below the murky surface. Only the spreading ripples remained.

We'd had a little time to kill before heading out for the evening's effort at spring black bear hunting in New Brunswick. Fishing seemed like a good way to pass the time, so Carroll Ware and I had been trying our luck on the bank of the small stocked trout pond at Double Buck Lodge. Shortly after the rod made its break for freedom, a fat rainbow trout started leaping out of the water, trailing a length of monofilament line from its jaw. The only solace in this particular event was that this time, it hadn't happened to me. The submerged rod and its attached acrobatic trout belonged to Carroll. Better him than me.

Eventually we retrieved the errant rod by tying the head of a garden rake to a rope, tossing it into the water as a grappling hook, and dragging the bottom of the pond until we snagged the line. The rod was pulled to shore and a bit of cranking on Carroll's part even managed to land the trout which then received a well-deserved release.

The above is just one example of how things can go awry in the outdoors whether you're hunting, fishing, or simply taking a walk in the woods. Of course there are much more sinister and tragic things that can happen when we least expect them. But I'll leave those tales to their survivors or next of kin. What follows are some of my own hard-earned and humbling experiences.

Bear fever

I wish I could say I was famous for my black bear hunts. Instead, I'm a bit infamous, at least to myself and those who have hunted with me. While I have taken my share of bears, I've also had some close encounters of the weird kind.

I do well on average-size bears. Every bear I've taken has been in the 130 to 150 pound range. Good average bears, but certainly nothing spectacular. I have had several chances at significantly bigger bears. My problem comes from the fact that while some deer hunters suffer from buck fever, I'm afflicted with bear fever. It seems that whenever I get a truly big bear in my sights, I lose all sense of hunting skill and reasoning. For example, last year I had two chances in the same evening at the same big bear and came away with nothing.

The first evening of my hunt found me in a ladder stand overlooking a bait barrel about 25 yards away. Before long a nice bear of maybe 150 pounds or so came to the bait and proceeded to eat his fill. Since I was after a larger bear, I never even raised my rifle on this one. It was great fun just to watch the bear. Since I had no intention of shooting him I was able to concentrate more on his actions and movements. He had a swagger to his gait and walked with slightly bowed legs like a bulldog. In two or three more years he would certainly make a nice trophy, but not yet. Eventually he left the bait. No other bears showed up that evening.

The next evening I was back at the same stand and bait. I learned that more than one bear was hitting the bait and my hope was that I'd see a big shooter bear on this evening. I'd been in the stand for an hour or two when I heard something behind me. The sound was of some animal moving through the muck of the swampy land. As the squishing noises got closer, I readied myself for whatever would come from behind me and into view. It might be a bigger bear or it might just be a wandering moose. I kept staring straight ahead.

Then, I both heard and felt scratching on the ladder that secured my stand to its tree. Sneaking a peek downward I spotted two yearling bear cubs clawing at the ladder. I didn't mind the cubs, but knew that momma bear had to be close by. She was. I tried to shoo the cubs away and immediately spotted their mother about 20 yards to the side. She started angrily popping her teeth at me and both she and the cubs made repeated bluff charges at the stand. This went on for over an hour. Finally, the cubs figured out that they could go around my stand to get to the bait. They did this, ate their fill, and then they and their mom waddled off into the woods. Evening number two went by. It was exciting, but no shooter bear.

Evening three was significantly different. My guide set me up in a ground blind, which is contrary to my preference of a ladder or tree stand, but my desire to take a large bear won out and I reluctantly agreed to the set-up. My blind consisted of an aluminum lawn chair set just off the side of an old logging road with a few spruce branches driven into the ground in front to break up my silhouette. The bait barrel was positioned 65 yards straight ahead of me.

The last thing my guide told me before departing was to make sure I didn't move too much "especially if the bear walked past me on the road." Great! The road was literally within arm's reach of my seat. With my innate bear anxiety, coupled with the experience of the cubs and mother bear the previous evening, these were the last words I needed or wanted to hear. Nevertheless, I sat and waited for whatever was to come my way.

A short time later a bear, a big bear, came into view from the right of the bait. Since I only had a tunnel view of the bait from my blind, I didn't see his approach until he was right at the bait. Despite my promise to myself to keep calm, let the adrenalin rush subside, and take slow, careful, and deliberate aim, I was overcome by a sudden attack of bear fever. I brought the rifle up released the safety, took quick aim through the scope, and promptly shot somewhere to the right and below the bear.

For his part, the bear looked more confused than frightened. He paused at the sound of my shot and then slowly retreated in the direction from which he'd come. Still quite rattled, I left my seat and walked to the bait where I hoped to find either blood or hair. Pretty much as I'd expected, I found neither. Dejectedly, I walked back to my blind, sat down, and replayed what had happened and all the things I'd done wrong.

The evening was still young so I resumed my vigil. I was pretty much hoping that the night would come to a close soon and I'd be back at camp where, yet again, the other hunters could good-naturedly revel in my misfortune. But a second chance came my way instead.

About 45 minutes after my missed shot, the same bear came to the bait again, this time from the opposite direction. I couldn't believe it. I waited and tried to let my excitement pass. After what felt like several minutes, but in reality was probably 30 seconds, I again raised my rifle and proceeded to make exactly the same series of errors I'd made on the first attempt. This time the bear charged off to the right again. When my guide returned we searched for blood and hair and found only a few strands of black hair that most likely had been torn free as the bear dashed through the alders.

To add just a bit more insult to injury, the next evening I shot at an average-size bear at 25 yards and shot under him yet again. This time the bullet hit rocks below the bear and sent broken pieces ricocheting up against the bear's belly. Whether from the force of the impact or from surprise, the bear flipped onto his back with all four legs clawing the air. I had enough time to jack another shell into the chamber and missed with the second shot too. On Friday, in a cold pouring rain, I passed up a shot at an average-size bear just at last light. The week ended with me seeing a total of 10 bears, shooting at two, and coming home empty-handed.

It's not my shooting ability that's suspect. I recently dropped a caribou in his tracks at 250 yards with a single shot. It's not the rifle. At the shooting range, I hit where I aim. I have a better answer for my ineptitude at shooting big bears. It's one of two possibilities. Either I'm peeking around the scope at the bears just as I pull the trigger, or else it's perfectly timed spasms caused by my bear fever. I'm trying to work on both, but in the interim, I'm going to stick with the story I tell my hunting buddies. I'm a firm believer and practitioner of catch-and-release bear hunting.

Deerly non-departed

I've also had some interesting if not outright weird experiences while deer hunting. A case in point happened at Northern Outdoors at The Forks in Maine. The forests of northern Maine don't have high numbers of deer in them, but there are some uncommonly large bucks. In the interest of promoting large body and antler size in the local deer herd, the lodge asks its hunters to harvest only those bucks with mature, basket-shaped racks.

Over the years I've seen a fair number of deer and even a few trophy-class animals. But in the forests of northern Maine there are typically only a few moments available between the time an animal is spotted and when it vanishes back into the woods. Unless you are 100-percent ready at the critical time, your chances for success diminish rapidly. I always seem to be facing in the wrong direction at the wrong time and when I eventually collect myself, the buck has disappeared. I've consoled myself with the "that's just hunting" mantra. That is, on all except one instance.

During that particular occasion, I was in my usual situation, that being in a self-climbing tree stand in the woods near a swamp. The air was still and the only sound was that of water spilling over a nearby beaver dam. The set-up seemed perfect.

I'd been in the stand for a couple hours when I heard a partridge crash through the alders behind me and land to my right near the base of my tree. By itself, that wasn't unusual. However, the partridge kept up its nervous clucking after it landed. I snuck a peek downward and saw the bird moving along the forest floor faster than it should have been. Then I caught movement to my left of a greyish brown object. That object quickly resolved itself into a deer. Not only was it a deer, it was a huge deer, probably the largest one I'd ever seen and it was slowly advancing directly in front and below me. Keeping the lodge's big-racked-bucks-only request in mind, I looked for antlers next. And here's where my mind became dysfunctional.

I didn't see antlers. Instead, I saw antler. Singular. The buck was certainly big enough body-wise to support a huge pair of antlers, but instead he had just the one. But even this was unusual. The one antler looked as thick around as my arm with a couple gnarly twists in it and ended in a small fork of two blunt stubby tines. What to do? Shoot or don't shoot?

A more experienced hunter, or at least one with a functioning brain, might have quickly realized that the buck was probably very old and in the last year or two of its life. But those thoughts only came to me later. While my two-sided debate continued in my single brain, the deer kept walking towards some thick spruce cover. When I finally made up my mind to shoot, it was just as the deer's white tail was disappearing into the thick stuff, never to be seen again.

My consolation? Since I only shoot at what I'm willing to eat, I'm pretty sure that one-antlered giant of a buck was probably so old that it would have tasted more like my L.L. Bean boots than tender venison. At least that's what I keep telling myself, even today.

Another miscue with deer took place a few years earlier. I was sitting in a cluster of blow downs at the junction of three skidder trails in the woods near my camp in Andover, Maine. It was a very cold morning and the puddles in the road were all iced over. Just getting to the spot where I was seated was a very noisy process. Finally, I managed to get settled in and was very well hidden in the brush with my back toward the path I'd come in on.

Not long after my arrival, I heard loud continuous footsteps approaching directly behind me. I knew there were other hunters in the area and was afraid that one of them might decide to set up his own blind close to mine. Not only that, but this particular hunter was making an incredible racket by breaking all the ice on the puddles that I had so carefully tried to avoid when I walked in.

Something had to be done, both to make my presence known and to get him to be a little more discreet in his woodland stalk. I decided to let him know I was there. I poked my head up from my hunkered-down position. And there I was, twisted awkwardly around and staring eye to eye, not with a hunter, but with a big-bodied ten-point buck only 20 feet away. It was hard to decide who was more startled, the buck or me. Before I could collect my wits and get into a shooting position the buck bolted to the side and disappeared into the thick stuff. Outwitted again.

Doe says "Doh!"

Sometimes things go awry for the critters too. One time I was sitting on a rocky ridge as a blocker for three hunting companions that were involved in a deer drive. (This was in Massachusetts where drives are legal.) I'd taken a doe the year before in the same area so it was my turn to help out the other guys. While I sat on the ridge, one hunter was to bust through some thick stuff and push any deer towards the remaining two guys at the other end of the thicket. While I sat on my butt, several gray squirrels ran around me in the oak leaves gathering acorns for their winter meals. They raised quite a racket, but I quickly became used to it.

I'd been sitting for only 20 minutes and became aware of more leaf rustling directly behind me and it sounded just a bit different than what had become normal background noise. I slowly twisted my head and torso to look back and found myself staring straight into the faces of three mature does. Not only that, but the one in the lead was equally aware of my presence and stomped her foot on the ground twice. I knew they would all flee in a second or two at most. Decision time.

I spun around, still sitting on my butt, and aimed my 12 gauge at the deer as they simultaneously fled off diagonal to my position. At that stage in my hunting experience I didn't even own a proper deer hunting shotgun and was using my bird gun. It was equipped with a raised rib and a front bead sight, but I was pretty accurate with it. It took only about two seconds to empty the gun of its slug followed by two rounds of buckshot.

A few minutes later, the hunter who was the brush buster appeared on the scene as I stood over a downed doe. I was pretty happy, but not as happy as I was soon to be. Shortly after he left to find our two other companions, I looked behind me and about 30 yards to the rear lay another doe, also dead. I hadn't meant to shoot two deer. It just happened.

When the whole group reassembled and realized we had two deer and not just one, we tagged the deer appropriately since we all had doe tags and dragged them from the woods. Each of us went home that day with half a deer for our efforts.

Focus on fishing

Gone-wrong fishing incidents happen to everyone who wets a line. I've had more than my share of lost-at-the-net trout and salmon, dropped-over-the-side fishing rods in 50 feet of water, and mid-lake outboard breakdowns. Yet there is the occasional event that stands out among the others. A particular trip to Lake Memphremagog on the Vermont-Quebec border was just such a fishing trip.

Several co-workers and I travelled to Memphremagog and planned to stay at a campground on the Vermont side of the border and fish in Quebec. I'd visited the lake many years before with my parents and siblings and knew there were some substantial trout and salmon in its waters. Unlike the trip with my family when we used a good-size boat and motor that could quickly cruise from one end of the lake to the other, on this trip I had my 40-year-old Old Town boat equipped with an even older 18-horsepower Johnson outboard. When loaded with me (200 pounds), a co-worker (290 pounds), and my boss (350+ pounds), we didn't get anywhere fast on the water. Nevertheless, we made the daily one-hour-plus cruise from the Vermont campsite to the Quebec fishing grounds and returned each evening. A second boat with three more members of our group made up the rest of our fishing party.

It's worth noting that the manager of the campground warned us not to shine any lights onto the water after dark in the direction of speed boat sounds that broke the pristine wilderness silence each night. He told us that the boats were making their cross-border smuggling runs of liquor and cigarettes. If we tried to illuminate the boats with a spotlight we just might receive a bullet or two in reply. We followed the manager's instructions. I may not be very lucky, but I'm not stupid.

The western shore of the lake rose steeply from the water and blocked the view of anything except the sky directly overhead. Since the prevailing winds and any approaching weather were predominately from the West, I paid particular attention to that direction.

After fishing for several hours one afternoon, I noticed that the sky appeared to be darkening and resolved to keep a watchful eye on it. My crewmates were reluctant to stop fishing for something as minor as a bit of weather. About 30 minutes later I again looked up and saw black clouds billowing over the mountain side right on top of us. Worse, there was also the crash of thunder.

I immediately ordered everyone to reel in and we reversed course for the campground. We didn't get far. Wind, rain, thunder, and lightning were on us almost instantly. The surface of the lake went from a flat calm to wind-whipped white caps in the space of just a couple minutes. Heading back to the campground meant bucking those waves and would have meant certain swamping of the boat. The only alternative was to head for the opposite shore in the same direction the wind was blowing.

I've never felt closer to death in my life. We were roughly a mile from any shore and the highest object on the water with non-stop lightning crashing all around us. Even though I had the throttle wide open, the rollers were still moving faster than we were and with each one that went under the boat we took on water as the stern rose and then sank down in the trough between waves. I had no idea what to expect when, or if, we reached shore. We couldn't change course for fear of swamping. If the shore was rocky, which was a virtual certainty, the boat would be instantly smashed to pieces with the best case for us of being stranded.

We plodded on as fast as we could go. The added weight of having taken on several inches of water slowed our progress even further. Finally, we neared the shore and I couldn't believe my eyes. The wind had driven us dead on towards a large lakeside camp. Better than that, in the water in front of the camp was a sturdy cement pier with an extension jutting perpendicular to the lake-facing section.

When we reached the pier I quickly swung the motor sideways and pulled us in behind the extension which acted as a breakwater. I cut the motor and we tied up and hustled ourselves off to the camp. The door was unlocked, but no one was home. We went inside anyway and tried to dry off a bit. The camp looked more like a complete house and, from the quality of the furnishings, obviously belonged to someone of means. We rested for about an hour during which time the storm blew over and the lake returned to its former calm state.

We closed the doors to the camp behind us and left a note thanking the owners for the refuge it provided us. After some bailing and a few pulls on the starter cord, we headed back to the campground. Upon our arrival, our other campmates said they had wondered where we had gone and if we had noticed the storm. But mainly they wanted to know if we had caught any fish. A fisherman must always maintain his focus.

Awkward in Africa

It's bad enough that I've experienced hunting and fishing misadventures close to home, but they've also followed me on an intercontinental quest. I'm speaking of things happening that were awkward in Africa.

In 2009 I fulfilled a long-standing fantasy of experiencing a safari in Africa. The trip was to the country of South Africa with the intention of taking a list of plains game animals, including impala, blue wildebeest, warthog, nyala, zebra, and kudu. Except for the warthog, I accomplished my goal. I only failed in taking the warthog because I didn't want to take a substandard example of the species and time had just run out. With the exception of one animal at which I took an ill-advised shot and that was eventually reclaimed, my shooting was on target. Not great, but adequate enough to take every other animal with a single shot.

Then there were the animals of opportunity, those that weren't on my preplanned hit list, but presented themselves if I wanted to add them to my Africa collection. By opportunity, I now believe that word means opportunity to demonstrate my occasional lapses into ineptitude. For example, with gray duikers.

The gray duiker is a small member of the antelope family and weighs only about 30 or 35 pounds, about the size of a medium-size dog. My P.H. (professional hunter), Conroy Hallgren, pointed out several during my safari and said I might want to take one. I agreed.

My first opportunity at a gray duiker came as we were heading out one morning on a spot-and-stalk quest. We were driving atop a small ridge and noticed several duikers about 50 yards away and slightly below us. Conroy picked out the best candidate and I leveled my rifle at him, took careful aim, and fired. The duiker just looked up and quickly bounded away. Conroy and I looked at one another and smiled. I shrugged and tried to suppress my embarrassment at missing the easy shot. It was so easy a shot and such an obvious miss that I even thought I might have bumped the scope and jarred it out of alignment, but deep down, I knew it was me and not the equipment.

My next duiker opportunity came the next day. And the result was the same; another complete miss at short range. I commented to Conroy that perhaps I wasn't meant to shoot a gray duiker. I received another wry smile for my remark.

Later that same day, I got one more chance at a duiker. This was at a distance of about 100 yards and I used Conroy's shoulder as a rest as there wasn't enough time to set up the shooting sticks. Finally I connected and added the duiker to my trophy list. It proved to be the toughest animal to take on my African safari. And it was yet another example of how things can go awry.

Simple things

Hunting and fishing miscues don't have to be too involved. For example, I was fishing for salmon on a recent caribou hunt after having taken my quota of two caribou. I was casting my spinning lure as far as I could from shore to reach the spot in the river where I hoped to entice a strike from a big fish. I try to check my rod and reel fairly often to make sure things such as handles are tight and the reel is seated securely in the rod. But, sometimes I forget.

It was during one of my long-distance casts that my rod suddenly got a lot lighter. I watched as not only my lure went sailing out over the water, but so too did the upper half of my two-piece fishing rod. Fortunately the line did not break and I was able to quickly reel in both my line and the rod section. I quickly reassembled the rod and then looked around to see if anyone had witnessed my casting faux pas.

Busted! There was Carroll Ware who witnessed the whole incident. Some choice comments and mutual laughs followed. I accepted it as justified payback for my reaction to the episode of his fishing rod sliding into that trout pond.

On another caribou hunt I was helping my partner find a caribou after I'd taken mine. We spotted a small herd and got into position for a shot. My partner settled in for the shot and squeezed off a round. And another. And another. And yet another. Eventually, after maybe seven or eight shots, he exhausted his supply of ammunition. I could see through my binoculars that the caribou was slightly wounded in a front leg, but was still standing. The bullets were hitting way low.

I put down the binoculars, ran over and handed my rifle to my partner and told him to use it to finish the job. After another couple or maybe three shots, the caribou finally fell. As we walked towards it, I paced off the distance. What my buddy had thought was about 200 yards was actually about 450 yards. Lesson learned? Distances on the tundra with little in the way of reference points are very deceiving. For my next caribou hunt I brought along a range finder.

Pheasants and other birds offer all sorts of opportunities for awkward incidents. On more than one occasion I've emptied my semi-auto shotgun at a passing pheasant or duck only to spur the bird on to greater aerial acrobatics. Partridge and woodcock are even trickier.

I was pheasant hunting another time when a hen pheasant bolted from the underbrush and flew headfirst into a tree and broke its neck. I hate picking out birdshot anyway. It's comforting to know that all the bad luck doesn't happen just to me.

There was the time on my African safari when I needed to finish off a common reed buck with a killing shot. I was just two feet away. I missed. They say it takes a big man to admit his mistakes. I'm currently about ten feet tall and still growing.

Many people would view these and many other similar incidents as failures, embarrassments, or maybe just frustrating bad luck. I have a different perspective on them. They are part of the sport, whether fishing or hunting. I savor them. Sure, I'll remember the triumphs and trophies, but the awkward and accidental events that are part of these adventures are just as enduring. Maybe even more so. Please though, just not too many witnesses.

Good Bye, Old Friend

We'd known each other for more than 13 years. For that entire time, he'd never let me down. Well, maybe just once or twice. But I forgave him. He wasn't perfect. He had his flaws. And as he got older, he started to show his age. And so did I. But we looked out for each other. I made sure he got the care he deserved and saw to it that he didn't take the abuse that too many of his counterparts were subjected to. In return, he accompanied me on more adventures than I had any right to expect. But the end was still a shock. Too soon. Too sudden. Too final. And much too impersonal. It was sad.

Sure, some of his systems were breaking down. But at the end, it wasn't my friend's heart that gave out. He had more heart than me. He'd just reached the end of his life. I only hope it was relatively painless.

My duck hunting companion? Deer hunting buddy? Pheasant hunting bird dog? No, none of those. It was my pick-up truck. My Ford Ranger.

My truck, my friend

Ranger was my green 1998 Ford Ranger 4X4 XLT pick-up truck. I purchased it in 2000 and, at the time, it only had about 20,000 miles on it. Barely broken in. I took it, and it took me, everywhere. With its trailer hitch, it helped me haul my boat to the more remote lakes and ponds in Maine for many fishing adventures. It took me over quite a few hills and woodland logging roads in search of moose, deer, and bear. I asked a lot of Ranger, and it always delivered. I even took it on long hauls to Canada for some of my more remote quests. Other human travelling companions sometimes gave me a bit of scorn and ridicule, asking how fast I was pedaling. I paid little attention. Ranger, with his hearty, never-say-die, three-liter engine, just kept chugging along, no matter what.

A few years before Ranger's passing, my wife told me I deserved a newer, more modern truck. I knew she was right and I admit I was sorely tempted. But then I asked my wife, "Would you rather I had a new truck, or would you rather go on another trip or two to the Caribbean?" I've never seen my wife reverse her judgment so quickly. I'd keep Ranger and Molly and I made an extra trip or two to St. Maarten. We were all happy.

The end of my ownership, but not of Ranger, came rather suddenly. One of my sons, who'd been living in California for the previous five or six years, called one day and said he wanted to come back to New England. He didn't have airfare and wanted to bring back his belongings. He needed help. The good news was that he had a job lined up when and if he arrived. I said I'd help.

By this stage in its life, the cross-country trip would likely have been too much for Ranger. I flew to California and rented, of all things, a Buick to drive home. On arrival in Massachusetts, I agreed to the unthinkable. I told my son that I'd sell him Ranger as his commuter vehicle for $500 and, if it was still running, buy it back from him whenever he was done with it for the same $500 price. Between the time of that fateful agreement and the actual title transfer, I put about $1,000 into Ranger to make sure my old friend was as good as he could be. I guess being a parent isn't conducive to being a good negotiator. At only 284,000 miles, Ranger became the property of my son.

Ranger double take

I considered buying a new truck. Maybe a new Ranger. But Ford had decided to discontinue the model. Maybe a Toyota Tundra or Tacoma. Possibly a Ford F150. Oh, the agony of sticker shock. I didn't even consider other makes. I was lamenting all this to my mechanic when he offered an alternative. It just so happened that he had a used Ford Ranger and would sell it to me. It was his personal vehicle so I knew it was probably in good shape. What year was it? I couldn't believe my ears. It was a 1998

Ranger 4X4 XLT. The same model as my old truck. And it was even forest green, also like the older truck. It did have 95,000 miles on it, but compared to 284,000, it was just a baby. It took about five minutes to consummate the sale.

My son drove Old Ranger for three more years. Annually, at inspection time, we'd put some duct tape over the rust holes in the pick-up bed and bumpers and take off the tailgate that was nearly corroded through. I still had hopes of honoring that promise to buy it back for $500. Maybe as a plow vehicle or possibly just for parts for New Ranger. Neither was to be. The automotive fates intervened.

Dearly departed

One morning the phone rang. It was my son. The news was shattering. He'd been driving Old Ranger to work and part way down the interstate, the rear differential had seized and he'd come to a quick stop in the breakdown lane. A tow truck hauled Old Ranger back to my mechanic. He confirmed that the diagnosis was terminal. The differential was scrap metal and replacement parts alone would be in excess of $1,000 and probably closer to $1,500. That, coupled with the upcoming need for new tires and ball joints was just too much to rationalize, even when taking sentiment into account. At the ripe old mileage marker of 343,383, Old Ranger had reached the end of its road. It was time to pull its plug wires and drain its fluids.

We called a salvage operator and he agreed to pay $250 for Old Ranger. Before he showed up, my son and I removed personal belongings. My mechanic suggested that I might want to take a screwdriver and pry the blue oval Ford emblem from the tailgate as a souvenir. I declined. I couldn't deface my old friend in such a callous manner. Later, in the dark of the night, I know a wrecker showed up and ingloriously attached a cold steel hook and hauled my old friend away. I didn't stay for that. It would have been too painful. Good bye, old friend. Rust easy now. We shared some good times. Didn't we.

Pushing It

Testing limits, or "pushing it," can take many forms. Sometimes it's an effort to surpass what you believe you're capable of achieving. At other times, it might be challenging authority. And at still others, it can be merely going beyond what can be expected to have a reasonable outcome with totally unexpected results. I've experienced and witnessed all three.

Testing limits

"I can't climb that. It's too steep. It's too far. I'm too old. I'm out of shape. The rocks are too big. But what if I try? Well, maybe I can. Let's go!"

Those were the thoughts that ran through my head on the second day of hunting during my last visit to Leaf River, Quebec, on my most recent caribou quest. And climb and scramble over those rocks I did, partially encouraged by my guide, Papou, and partly by my own dogged determination.

Upon arrival at camp, I'd told Papou that while I might not move too fast, I could go all day. I didn't think he'd take my bit of brazen bravado so literally, but he did. On the first day of hunting, Papou, my hunting partner Curtis, and I headed upriver by jet-drive boat, through the churning rapids, and then stationed ourselves on a rise to glass for animals. We didn't see any, so after a couple hours we moved by water to another spot. After again sitting for a while, Papou suggested we get up and move once more, this time by land.

Curtis wanted to stay where he was which actually provided a hunting advantage by offering visual coverage of a larger area once Papou and I set out. We walked another couple miles over rolling tundra, but were able to keep Curtis in sight almost constantly.

Despite the long walk and the extended area of observation coverage, we saw few animals that first day—just a few caribou cows. For my own part, I surprised myself. I'd expected to take it easy the first day, stay close to the river, and not do much walking. Instead, I'd covered several miles of rocky tundra and, although my legs were a bit sore, it was that good kind of pain that lets you know you're capable of doing even more.

On day two I set my sights higher, literally. Once again we were seeing few animals and those we did see were cows. We hiked inland a mile or two from the river and were glassing the slopes when Papou announced that there were several caribou bedded on a high slope and that there might be a bull in the group.

Curtis and I looked wide-eyed at one another. The bedding area was probably a mile and a half distant and several hundred feet higher in elevation. In addition, the only route up was through several fields of boulders, most of which were the size of sport utility vehicles. Both Curtis and I said "no way" to one another. But then I started to wonder, what if a nice caribou bull was with those cows. There was only one way to find out.

With Curtis once again opting to wait at our current location, Papou and I began our upward trek. I did take a couple precautions first. I asked how long he thought it might take us to reach the animals. Papou said a half hour so I immediately doubled that. And I also arranged a silent hand signal with Papou. When I held up two fingers it meant I needed a two-minute rest to recover my breathing and reduce my heart rate to something less than a jackhammer staccato.

The climb was probably the most demanding I've tried in more than a decade and made all the more difficult by the rifle and pack I was carrying, as well as the heavy rubber boots and multiple layers of clothing I wore. About an hour after setting out we reached the bedding area. No caribou. Papou climbed a bit farther ahead and eventually spotted the group of animals below a small ridge. As he returned to tell me this, the caribou approached closer and I noted they were all cows. I would have gladly taken one of them as reward for our efforts, but they turned and found a safe route away from our position.

Papou and I returned to Curtis' location, taking considerably less time on the downhill journey. After that we trudged back to the boat. Two days of hunting had yielded no caribou and quite a bit of mileage under our boots. Strangely, I felt stronger than ever. We covered more ground on day two than on day one. Perhaps I had been underestimating my level of fitness and capabilities. The rest of the week would tell.

On day three Curtis and I decided that if we saw a decent cow caribou we'd take it, thus ensuring we'd go home with meat for the freezer. Both Curtis and I each have several other caribou mounts and didn't need yet another in order for the hunt to be regarded a success.

Once again we headed upriver, negotiated the rapids, and hoofed it a mile or so inland to an area where I'd taken a caribou the prior year. Eventually we spotted a group of cows heading our way and awaited their closer approach. Curtis took the first shot and all the animals remained standing. He took a second shot and a cow went down. I took a shot and watched as another cow went down. I asked Papou if I should take another shot and he told me to wait.

It turned out that Curtis had not missed on his first shot. He had taken two cows and his hunt was now over due to the two animal limit. My cow meant that there were three animals on the ground and at least a mile and a half of travel back to the boat. We joked with Papou that since he was only 23 years old and Curtis and my combined ages totaled to 140 years, naturally he would be carrying most of the load of meat to the boat. After helping Papou as much as we could with the quartering chores, Curtis and I made one trip to the shore of the river while Papou made two carrying the meat. The older I get, the more I appreciate the exuberance of youth.

Day four left us with me having one more animal to take. Curtis was a bit under the weather with a cold and decided to stay in camp. Papou and I headed upriver yet again to the same area where we'd taken the cows the day before. I told Papou that I'd be happy with another cow or a small bull. Fate and Papou had other plans for me.

When we topped the rise where we expected we might see caribou, two other hunters were there before us in an area where they were not supposed to be. Their guide was trailing some distance behind them. To make matters even more complicated, several nice caribou bulls were rapidly approaching. True to his professionalism, Papou took charge and got the other two hunters in position for shots and then motioned for me to join them. The plan was for them to shoot first and then me.

There were two nice bulls in the lead and another respectable one at the rear of the small herd. One of the other hunters fired at the lead bull and it went down. I made the assumption the second hunter would take the next bull in line so I focused on the one at the tail end of the herd. I waited until the second of the other two hunters shot and then, about five seconds later, took my shot at bull number three.

As it turned out, the second hunter had passed on bull number two and instead shot at bull number three, my animal. His shot was a killing shot, but the caribou had not gone down immediately so the animal was his. Papou helped their guide, who was now on scene, with the necessary animal-quartering chores and then he and I assessed my situation. We agreed that we'd head to a far ridge where we'd seen a lot of caribou the day before and hope for the best. We didn't have to hope for long. Almost immediately we saw several cows and a young bull. Once again I told Papou that I'd be happy with any of them. No response.

Over the four days of the hunt thus far, I'd learned that Papou was a man of few words. While we waited on that ridge, he asked me if I'd seen any caribou while glassing with my binoculars. I said I'd seen a few and he replied that he'd seen two or three hundred on a far distant skyline. That was definitely beyond walking range, but would still have provided a small adrenalin boost. Papou seemed to have other ideas on what we were to do that day.

153

As the day wore on we kept traveling farther away from the river. In the back of my mind I kept telling myself that for every step we took, we had to cross all that distance again to get back to our boat. Eventually we spotted a lake that had several caribou on its opposite shore, though they did seem to be slowly angling somewhat towards us. Papou didn't ask if I thought I could make it the couple miles to the far side of the lake. He just headed out that way with me in tow and across another tundra rock garden.

Crossing the rock garden was much more challenging than it might seem. While Papou was able to pretty much hop from one rock to another, I had to be much more conscious of my footsteps. Sixty-six-year-old bones are a lot more brittle than those only twenty-three years old. The extent of the garden was about a mile across and every rock was covered in lichen making it slippery to the step whenever it was damp, which was almost all the time. In addition, many of the rocks were precariously balanced on top of others, having been haphazardly deposited there thousands of years ago by the receding glaciers. The only way to discover which rocks were unstable was by stepping on them. Having a good sense of balance is a definite advantage to the tundra hiker.

After successfully negotiating the rock garden, we eventually reached a small group of stunted spruce trees and waited while a group of several caribou approached. There were three nice bulls and the lead animal was the best of the bunch. At about 80 yards I propped my rifle on Papou's pack frame and took the shot. Down went the caribou and, as it turned out, he was a nicer bull than either of the two that the other hunters had taken earlier in the day. I believe Papou planned it that way.

At the beginning of the hunt I'd been apprehensive of my ability to walk any significant distance. But each day, I covered more ground, and tougher terrain at that, than the previous day. Taking that final long hike back to the boat seemed a breeze. Maybe there's more life left in the old bones than I give myself credit for. Thanks, Papou, for helping me realize this. I trust my tip was a good one.

Eddie

Not everyone could get away with having a taxidermy mount in their office. I had two. One of them was Eddie. Eddie liked to challenge the establishment.

I'd always wanted to start collecting taxidermy, but my requirement was that the animals had to be either ones I'd taken while hunting or animals that I found by the side of the road; aka: road kills. Eddie was of the latter variety.

Before my retirement, my daily work commute was about 40 miles each way. One February morning I noticed something brown and furry in the snow beside the curb. Upon closer inspection the object turned out to be a fisher and other than the fact that he was dead, he seemed in relatively good condition. Fishers, sometimes called fisher cats, are large members of the weasel family and noted for their ferocity. Homeowners in fisher country often learn the hard way not to leave small dogs and cats out after dark. In addition to their taking-on-all-comers attitude, fishers have a reputation as not being finicky eaters.

After showing off the fisher, packed in snow in the bed of my pick-up truck, to coworkers later that day, the animal, much to my wife's dismay, settled in a comfortable corner in the freezer compartment of the kitchen refrigerator. Soon, though not soon enough for my wife, the fisher made its way to a taxidermist. Plans were evolving.

Eventually the fisher, now named Eddie Fisher (what else?) took up residence above a bookshelf in my office. Visitors, passersby, and even complete strangers often stuck their heads in and asked what the animal was. Rather than a cause for disgust or scorn, as might be expected in a conservative, New England-based high-technology company, Eddie sparked conversation and genuine curiosity about animals and the outdoors. Of course, he also provided often needed silent yet powerful guidance and inspiration when I was confronted with particularly challenging work-related issues. Eddie was quite the renaissance fisher.

Only once did Eddie meet with a significant challenge to his presence. Upon spying Eddie, peacefully and innocently posing on his bookcase perch, a vice president, who shall remain nameless, commented to my manager that "the taxidermy must go." To his credit, my manager just shrugged and let the comment pass. Privately, I believe that the VP was caught by her own mantra of valuing differences and to have banished Eddie would have been hypocritical. Regardless, Eddie stayed and was eventually joined by an arctic ptarmigan companion. Whenever that same vice president walked by I'm pretty certain both Eddie and the ptarmigan winked at me.

A visit to the Moosehead carwash

Sometimes, pushing it carries consequences. A case in point was a fishing trip to Moosehead Lake in Maine.

For several years I had organized an annual fishing trip with some of my office mates to various New England destinations. The criteria they requested were lots of fish, easy to catch, and luxurious accommodations. Sometimes they had to settle for less than all three.

One year we made plans to camp at the northern end of Moosehead Lake in Maine at Seboomook Wilderness Campground. Lake trout, brook trout, and landlocked salmon were to be the prizes. At the time, the campground had just tent spaces, a central bath house, and a mini general store. Our plan was to arrive as soon after ice-out as possible. Mother Nature had her own plans for us.

We departed Massachusetts early on a May morning with two vehicles and two towed boats making up our convoy. We arrived in Greenville, Maine, at the foot of Moosehead about mid-afternoon. I cautioned the other driver, Bob, and his passenger, Tom, to fill up with gas and stay close behind as we still had maybe 50 or 60 miles of gravel road to cover before we reached our campsite. I was concerned that we reach our destination before dark so we could set up our large tent while daylight still prevailed.

Instead of following my advice, Bob and Tom decided to stay in Greenville and enjoy a steak dinner at a local restaurant. They said they'd catch up with us. We passed on the steaks and headed up the road on the western shore of the lake.

After a short distance it became clear that this was not going to be an easy journey. This particular year the level of the lake was unusually high due to heavy winter snows and a rapid thaw followed by a late ice-out. We arrived at a submerged causeway that spanned a small bay in the lake and quickly determined that the water was too deep even for my GMC Suburban to cross. We retraced our route to the Great North Woods gate house and asked the attendant if there was an alternate route. He said there was and provided directions. We asked him to be on the lookout for our steak-dining friends somewhere behind us and he said he would. Again we set off.

We found the alternate route and were confronted with another causeway, again submerged. This one was more than a quarter mile long with the roadway dipping in on one side of the bay and emerging on the other. Lacking the presence of Moses to part the waters for us, and rather than chance just blindly driving across and through the murky, foot-deep water, one passenger walked ahead of the Suburban and we eventually made it to the opposite shore without mishap. There we waited for our companions. And we waited still longer.

We waited until well after sunset since Bob and Tom were in a mid-size Buick sedan and crossing the causeway would prove more of a challenge to them. Time passed but they did not show up. Eventually we decided we had waited long enough and continued on our journey. Our friends would have to fend for themselves. We arrived late at the campsite and accomplished setting up the tent despite the darkness and late hour. By the time we turned in for the night, our friends were still nowhere to be seen.

We spent a restful and comfortable night and got some much-needed sleep. A frosty dawn came, but our friends did not. So we did what all concerned fishing buddies do at such times. We drank hot coffee and ate a warm breakfast. Eventually, about 8:00 a.m., the Buick carrying Bob and Tom arrived. Seldom have I seen two more miserable souls.

After their steak dinners, followed by desserts and at least a couple Moosehead ales, they headed out on our trail at about sunset. The gate house attendant informed them of our alternate route and they followed it. However, they made one small, but significant error in judgment.

When they eventually came to the submerged causeway, they neglected to follow the exact instructions the attendant provided. As with us, he told them to stay to the left of the wooden poles stuck in the right side of the roadway. Since we had crossed in daylight, this was not an issue. Also, we had a person walk in front of the vehicle all the way across. They did neither.

Not long after descending the grade onto the causeway, the Buick pitched over the side of the roadway with its submerged headlights doing an excellent job of illuminating the murky depths of Moosehead Lake. Tom threw open the passenger door and was immediately met with an inrush of frigid lake water. Despite the flood, the engine somehow managed to keep running and Tom, now completely soaked, was able to unhook the boat trailer while Bob got the car turned around on the narrow causeway. Tom reconnected the trailer and they made their way back to the now-closed gatehouse to spend a very cold and damp night in their Buick bivouac. To this day, I don't believe Bob and Tom speak to one another.

Sometimes, pushing it just doesn't pay. Other times, whether warranted or not, it provides a taste of victory over authority. And sometimes it can even restore faith in yourself.

Confessions of a Sportsman Hoarder

I admit it. I'm a hoarder. Not the kind that has 163 non-neutered cats running around his home and only one litter box. And not the kind that saves 250,000 pounds of old newspapers to create an indoor replica of the Boston skyline. Not even the type that views their weekly visit to the local landfill as an opportunity to go shopping. No, I'm a sportsman hoarder. I hoard fishing tackle, hunting gear, and taxidermy. It's a triple whammy. And I'm pretty sure I'm not alone with this affliction.

Tackle tonnage

A case in point. My trove of fishing tackle. I still have my first fishing reel that I got when I was eight years old. I'm now 66. Not only do I have that first reel, but I also still have *every* fishing reel I've ever owned. Many of them no longer work. Some are in pieces. I don't care.

Fishing equipment has a way of finding me. I don't mean just the occasional red and white plastic bobber that I retrieve from the river's surface as it tries unsuccessfully to float past me. That's passé. I'm talking about whole fishing outfits. Over the years I've found three complete rods and reels near my camp in Maine. True, one of them had been run over by an automobile, snapping the brace that connected the reel portion to its mounting support bracket. But by drilling a couple holes, inserting a metal pin, and applying a bit of epoxy, I repaired the break and now have another spare rod and reel to add to my hoard. Could this be how surgeons get started mending broken bones? Possibly.

I once found an entire knapsack filled with fishing gear on the shoreline near a boat ramp. It contained a couple fly fishing reels, line, two folders of streamer flies, insect repellent, and other assorted odds and ends. I tried to find the owner, but with no name inside the knapsack, I resorted to leaving a note attached to a stick placed exactly where I found the gear. The note listed my phone number and stated that if the owner could identify the lost equipment I would be happy to return it. I never received a call.

I also find money when I fish. My long-time friend Ruben and I were sitting on the bank of a local trout pond one morning. We were waiting for a fish to take the weighted worms we had cast from the shore. The early morning sun was in our faces and the dry leaves on the ground offered a warm seat. I put my hand down in the leaves to help raise myself to a standing position and found a $20 bill between my fingers. I'm fairly certain I later used the cash to buy more fishing equipment.

Additions to my trove of fishing tackle don't have to include current gadgets or even be functional. I have a couple dozen broken fishing rods and pieces of others. I've rationalized that if I ever need a replacement rod tip, guide, or butt cap, I probably have the spare parts on hand. I also have a plastic jar filled with worn out streamer flies. What fisherman doesn't?

When Dad and then my father-in-law passed away I inherited much of their fishing gear. There may be collector value to some of this equipment, but that would mean I'd have to part with it. Some of it is just rusty bits of metal in creaky and corroded tackle boxes and coffee cans, but I save it all anyway. I am rather curious about one item that came from my father-in-law's collection. In case whaling ever becomes socially and environmentally acceptable again, I'm ready for that day. I have my own harpoon.

Sometimes well-meaning friends prove to be hoarding enablers rather than helpers. If they spot fishing gear at a neighborhood yard sale they call me. I'm out the door almost before I hit the disconnect button on the phone. I think I might need an intervention.

I have a theory on how I became such a fishing tackle junkie. I think it might be an inherited trait. The evidence is in a story Dad told me. He owned and operated a local bar in our home town and would often let his regular customers run a bar tab on their alcohol consumption during the week. When payday came, Dad would cash their checks and deduct the amount he was owed.

Apparently, one customer's consumption significantly outpaced his earnings. To settle the debt, the customer offered Dad an entire multi-tier tackle box full of dry flies, spinning lures, and other accessories. Dad accepted the offer and the bar tab was cleared. With Dad gone, I now have that tackle box.

It seems there is only one way to conquer my fishing tackle hoarding and that is to lose the fishing gear myself. It's painful and possibly life threatening. I don't mean the occasional spinning lure that gets irretrievably snagged on an underwater log or the hook that gets wedged between some rocks, though those events do induce traumatic spasms. I'm talking about major losses. One of these events occurred while I was trolling for salmon with my boys on Lower Richardson Lake in Maine in the early springtime.

We were putt-putting along about 50 feet from shore. My boys were dragging spinning lures behind the boat and I was using a boat rod equipped with a Penn reel, lead line, a large Davis spinner rig, and a Rapala minnow at the end of the line. One of the boys got his line tangled and I reached over to fix the problem. A momentary loss of concentration resulted in my fishing rod flipping over the side and into the depths. I briefly considered jumping in after it. If the water had been shallower or warmer I might have done so. It took all the will power I could muster that day to hold my hoarding instincts in check.

Hunting and gathering

Hunting brings its own challenge to the sportsman hoarder and shows itself in stage two of the illness. That challenge for me is manifested in my firearms. Specifically, the number of them I own. Before anyone gets the wrong idea, every firearm I own is legal and my firearms permit is current. My fingerprints and photo are on file with my local police department and not for any nefarious reason. You won't be seeing me on an evening news broadcast and described as "a doomsday prepper that was armed to the teeth and barricaded inside his blast-proof home fortress." That blast-proof part would be a little bit of an exaggeration.

Dad bought me my first rifle in 1960 when I was 12 years old. It was a Marlin .22 caliber, eight-shot, clip-fed, bolt action model. It had a four-power Weaver scope, but my shooting instructor, the range safety officer at a nearby sportsmen's club, insisted I become proficient at shooting without the use of the scope. Many thousands of rounds passed down the length of that rifle's barrel. And many of those did so back in the day when a box of 50 .22 long rifle cartridges cost all of 65 cents and the local hardware store could sell them legally to someone not long out of grade school. I'd sometimes walk the three miles along the main highway through town with my rifle under my arm to get to a farmer's field for woodchuck hunting. If I or any youngster did that today, I'm sure a SWAT team dressed in full body armor and with automatic weapons drawn would intercede. Times have changed, but I still have that same Marlin .22 rifle.

Dad also bought me my second firearm. At about age 18 I wanted to start duck hunting. This required a shotgun and Dad believed in quality. He purchased a Browning (at that time, made in Belgium) lightweight, 12-gauge autoloader. I marveled at the beauty of the shotgun, but as much as I wanted to keep it pristine, I took it into the field and marshes every chance I got. More than a few ducks and crows met their demise from its business end. I occasionally loaded it with slug rounds and tried my hand at deer hunting, but never got a chance back then to test its effectiveness on one of those critters. I still have the Browning. Today it's my go-to shotgun for pheasant hunting. With close to 50 years of synergy between us, we don't often miss.

I decided to take up deer hunting seriously in 1973 after the purchase of my camp in Maine. Browning had just come out with a new model deer rifle, the BLR (Browning Lever-action Rifle). In those days you could still purchase a firearm over the counter in Massachusetts at a department store with minimal paperwork involved. A trip to Sears resulted in my acquiring a new BLR in .308. For the next 15 years I concentrated on developing my hunting skills. Another way to state that would be that while my shooting skills were fairly sharp, my deer hunting abilities required a fair amount of polishing. I did eventually take both a black bear and a moose with the BLR, but to this day I've never shot a deer with it. That would necessitate acquiring yet another firearm.

I got married not too long after filling my arsenal with the last of these three firearms. A mortgage, putting food on the table, and babies became my major financial consumers. Any additional firearms purchases would have to wait about 20 years. Fast-forward through those years and my arsenal began to expand again. Put differently, this was when the hoarding virus revived from its dormancy and struck again with a vengeance.

The racks of used firearms at Maine's Kittery Trading Post beckoned. A sweet little .44 magnum Marlin carbine attached itself to me as I wandered the store's aisles. A co-worker had a Remington 7mm magnum rifle that he wanted to part with. I had to have it. Another offered a Ruger pistol. I bought it. I had a chance to buy a classic pre-1964 Winchester .30-30. I couldn't resist. I discovered that shotguns came in gauges other than 12. Why not. Black powder firearms too? Of course. When my father-in-law passed away, some of his firearms made their way to my gun safe. You know you're seriously infected by the hoarding bug when you have to purchase a large gun safe weighing nearly half a ton to contain them all. A couple years ago I entered a raffle to help support my sportsmen's club. The result? I won a new Mossberg model 535 pump-action shotgun with an extra barrel. It's still in its original box. The opportunities and the urges are endless and I've failed completely in reigning them in.

Only once did this new strain of the hoarding impulse let up just a bit, or so I thought. Nearly all of my firearms have been gifts, secondhand, inherited, or purchased new when prices were a small fraction of what they are today. I craved one really nice new shotgun. I fell in love with a photograph of a Beretta side-by-side Silver Hawk 12-gauge model and was determined to possess the real thing. Another trip to Kittery sealed the deal. But this time, my impulsiveness got the better of me. While the Beretta was a masterpiece of craftsmanship, I couldn't hit a thing with it.

A trip to my local gun shop demonstrated to me that the gun just didn't fit me at all. What to do?

The shop's owner posed a solution. I could trade in the Beretta for something that did fit me. The trade-in value of the Beretta was close to my original purchase price. I agreed to the deal. And what did I take in trade? Not one, but *two* new CZ shotguns. One was a nice 28-gauge side-by-side and the second was a 20-gauge over-and-under model. Even in defeat, the hoarding instinct won out. Much like my propensity to keep my entire life's accumulation of fishing tackle, with that one exception of the Beretta shotgun that never fit me in the first place, I've held onto all my firearms acquisitions. Still, I don't regard myself as armed to the teeth. Maybe just to the chin.

Taxidermy torment

Inevitably, my sportsman hoarding affliction led to its third and hopefully, final phase—taxidermy. I've always wanted lifelike animals to grace the walls of my home. I don't desire them as trophies. Rather, I just want them for their beauty. They are ever-present representations of the natural world and its many species. If they happen to also be superior specimens of those species, so much the better.

When I moved into a log house I landed in heaven. Lots of wall space. Rustic atmosphere. And most significantly, an understanding wife. However, what I didn't understand at the time was that the log house came already infected with the hoarding virus. Yes, I could grace our home's walls with both real and replica animals, but I was once again destined to quickly lose control.

It started out simply and innocently enough. I had a bearskin rug that was stored in a closet in a cardboard box. My moose trophy consisted of just the antlers mounted on a plaque. I really wanted a deer mount, but since I hadn't shot anything better than a fat doe until that time, I was out of luck. I once considered buying a deer mount at an antique store, but its ratty looking appearance and the price put me off. Besides, it wouldn't have been *my* deer. Then my fortunes, as well as any last vestiges of resistance to this particular hoarding phase, changed and not for the better.

I took a small six-point buck in Maine. It was by no means a trophy, but it was my first buck. I had a short head and neck mount made. Next I took a record-class caribou in Labrador. This called for a full shoulder mount. The next year added an eight-point whitetail from Anticosti Island. And a year after that saw another caribou shoulder mount added. I was rapidly spiraling out of control. I believe there are six or seven caribou mounts now on the walls. I sometimes lose count. It's at least a small herd.

No longer satisfied with waiting to actually hunt and harvest the animals myself, I moved on to road kills. A fisher, a mink, two gray foxes, and a muskrat now call my man cave home. I almost had a nice red fox, but not even the skilled workmanship of my taxidermist could have restored him to presentable stature after his run-in with a four-wheeled adversary. But I'm still looking. A skunk would be a nice addition. And maybe a raccoon. And a coyote too.

I picked up a small owl on the side of the road one winter day. It was dead, but otherwise intact. I knew owls are a protected species so I contacted Massachusetts wildlife officials to ask for a possession permit. No such luck. They refused. I was heartbroken. When asked what I should do with the corpse, the wildlife official told me they would accept it and likely use it for educational purposes. I put the owl in a shoebox and left it on the doorstep of a nearby fish and wildlife office. I felt like I was leaving an abandoned baby there. I hope that owl found a good adoptive home. I never asked about visitation.

I once mentioned to my taxidermist, who by this time was giving me a volume discount, that I wished I had done a full shoulder mount of my moose. No problem he said. He just happened to have an extra moose cape. Sold! And the bear rug that had been stored away in a closet finally came out to meet several of his recently fallen brethren. They formed a handsome family unit. Add in a couple pheasants, several arctic ptarmigan, and a giant Atlantic salmon replica and I was close to opening my own frozen-in-time, home-based menagerie. But it still wasn't enough. My illness was that virulent. Africa beckoned. I succumbed.

In Africa I lost all semblance of control. A kudu, nyala, blue wildebeest, blesbok, zebra, gray duiker, bush buck, red hartebeest, and impala all recently joined my glass-eyed clan. For the time being my lust has been sated. How long it will remain so is anyone's guess. I'm hoping my remission will last at least a little while longer. I'm avoiding yard and estate sales. Flea markets are off limits. Visits to gun shops are restricted to just the ammunition aisles. And, I only look at the clothing sections of Bass Pro and Cabela's catalogs.

I'm not sure these restrictions are sufficient. I sometimes awaken in a cold sweat in the middle of the night with the realization that I still don't possess a .410, 16, or 10-gauge shotgun. For the fun of it, I put together a list of the African plains game animals I don't yet have. Other times I ask myself just how many fishing tackle boxes really are too many. And when I approach another road-killed creature on the highway it's becoming increasingly difficult to keep my foot off the brake pedal. Worse yet, lately our pet dogs and cat have been eyeing me suspiciously and keeping their distance. I've tried to assure them that they're safe. At least for now.

My Naked Safari

What am I doing here? Wherever here is.

It's just before dark. I'm following two near strangers through some thick bush. I'm trying hard not to snap any twigs or rustle the dry leaves underfoot and sound the "Here I am" alert to any and all beasts within a quarter-mile radius. The dense thicket is about 20 feet high and its canopy makes the already late hour seem even later and darker. I don't want to fall behind. Or flat on my face either.

I'm also trying hard not to bump into any of the underbrush. Almost everything that grows here seems to be protected by needle-sharp thorns up to four inches in length and my hunting clothing is still store-new and rip-free. So is my skin. I want to keep them both that way for as long as possible.

I can barely see five feet ahead of me, never mind the 100 to 200 yards I anticipated. And the twilight is getting still deeper. I know there are wild animals and poisonous snakes sharing the thicket with me. I'm wondering if any of them are predators I should be concerned about.

My P.H., Conroy, is following our tracker, Peter, who says he saw a nyala earlier while we bounced along the rutted path. Peter speaks only Zulu so I depend on Conroy for the translation. Peter tells Conroy the nyala is a good one. Would I even know a run-of-the-mill nyala if I bumped into one, never mind a *good* one? I'd seen photographs, but never the real thing.

Now we're emerging from the bush into a small clearing. The grass is four feet high. There's a stream to cross. Are there crocodiles in it? The opposite embankment is invisible in the dark. The sounds of the evening, whether from insects or beasts, are almost deafening. The frantic wing beats and cackles of a surprised roost of guinea fowl are a thousand times more startling than those of any flushed partridge back in New England. I don't think my senses have ever been more alert.

The fact is, I'm ecstatic to be here!

A is for Arctic. Africa too.

In reality, I did sort of know where I was, who I was with, and just a little bit of what I was doing there. I was somewhere in the KwaZulu-Natal province of South Africa and I was following my hired professional hunter (P.H.) and his tracker. We were on the trail of an animal called a nyala that Peter had spotted in the bush, but that I had yet to see. I was on safari in Africa, a dream come true, but as far as expertise was concerned, I felt more than a little bit naked.

My African safari started a few years before and a short distance south of the Arctic Circle. Or, more accurately, a few thousand feet in the arctic air, in a vintage Convair 580 turboprop aircraft that was about the same age as me at the time...nearing 60. I was returning from a caribou hunting trip on the Ungava Peninsula in northern Quebec. Little did I realize then that the ancient air bird was carrying me on the first leg of my flight to South Africa.

Like many people who hunt wild animals and are passionate about it, my dream was to someday hunt in Africa. I'd read many of the books about safari hunting, such as those by Selous, Ruark, Capstick, and Teddy Roosevelt. I had longingly watched television shows depicting the successes of P.H.s, their clients, and the trackers who accompanied them and seemed to know where the animals were headed before they did themselves. If I ever did get to go, I wasn't interested in hunting the "Big Five" (lion, leopard, elephant, cape buffalo, and rhino) or the "Dangerous Six" (add in the hippo). As I liked to put it, I didn't want to go after anything higher up on the food chain than me. In other words, if I ever managed to hunt in Africa it would be a plains game safari. I wanted animals that I *could eat* rather than the other way around.

Though I'd hunted for whitetail deer, black bear, caribou, moose, and assorted water fowl and upland birds, two things had kept me from realizing my African dream hunt. The first was money and the second was my skill level.

In the category of money, I wasn't, and am still not, a wealthy man and I was certain that an African safari of any kind was the province of those privileged few who likely made the trek to Africa in the luxury of their private Lear jets. I didn't own custom rifles, or even those made by the premium manufacturers. Four-figure telescopic optics were the stuff of dreams to me. I had a substantial mortgage. I was driving an 11-year-old pick-up truck with over 250,000 miles on it. And, at the time, my wife and I subsisted solely on my middle-management income earned working at a high-technology company. We enjoyed the occasional vacation and I had my annual hunting trip. We were comfortable, but by no means excessively or extravagantly so.

As for skills, I'm a fair shot, but I was certain that anyone who hunted in Africa needed to be able to consistently shoot one-inch groups at 300 yards after trotting through the bush Johnny Weissmuller style. To do less was to diminish the nobility of the quarry, to say nothing of acquiring a healthy dose of personal embarrassment and scornful looks from the P.H. and the rest of the safari entourage. Besides, though I'd wanted to go on a safari, the simple truth was I had no idea how to prepare or plan for one and didn't even know where to start.

A plan comes together

During that return flight from Quebec, I struck up a conversation with Will Sanders, another of the hunters with whom I'd been friendly during the caribou hunt. I mentioned to Will my desire to go to Africa, and also my doubt that such a trip would ever be possible. Will stated that he'd gone on a safari to Africa and that the cost was surprisingly manageable. In fact, he said, on a per-animal basis, an African safari can be more economical than the caribou hunt we'd just been on. I was more interested, but still not convinced and let the subject rest.

Two years later I was waiting at the airport in Augusta, Maine, along with Carroll Ware. Carroll and I were picking up the same Will Sanders for a spring bear hunt in New Brunswick. While waiting for Will to arrive from his home in Tennessee, we bumped into two of Carroll's friends, Tim and Valerie Farren of Farren Global Adventures. They were waiting to meet one of their own clients.

Tim and Valerie were the people to whom Carroll referred his clients that were contemplating African adventures. During lunch and through some further conversation, Tim and Valerie provided me with additional information concerning safaris in Africa. Maybe it was in a moment of weakness, or perhaps a moment of bravado, but in either case, I committed to an African plains game safari before we left that Bangor, Maine, airport lunch counter. Maybe it was just the free lunch. In any case, I said I'd go.

But exactly what did that entail? What do you wear? How do you get there? How do you make the arrangements? How do you determine the animals you'd like to take? What does it cost? How and who do you pay? How do you get the animals back to the United States? What are the rules? Those were the questions, among many others, that swirled in my mind. Fortunately, Tim was able to answer most of them and a long-distance call to Conroy Hallgren, the person who was to be my safari guide, otherwise known as a professional hunter, or P.H., was able to answer most of the rest.

A trip to Cabela's solved the safari clothing issue. I was told that two sets of clothing would be sufficient as the camp staff would wash and iron each day's garments on a daily basis, something that proved to be true. I'll admit it. Wearing my newly purchased safari pants, shirt, vest, and boonie hat, all in khaki or bush green, helped me to feel that this whole adventure might actually happen. At least I'd look the part.

The conversation with Conroy confirmed that my trusty Remington 7mm magnum rifle was up to the task of taking any plains game animals I might want. His only suggestion on that point was to get the heaviest bullets I could find. Several visits to the target range and practicing from makeshift tripod sticks helped my shooting accuracy. Whether or not it was enough remained to be determined.

Then there was the anguish of how many days the safari should be. My job allowed me three weeks of vacation per year and I'd already booked two weeks of that time for other vacations and had paid the deposits. Initially I booked a one-week safari. I quickly realized that to travel all that distance and only stay a week was not very sensible. One week became 10 days. I'd figure out something with my manager at work later about the additional days. Hell, if I had to beg for the extra time anyway, why not make it worthwhile. Two weeks sounded right. And since my wife would be accompanying me on the trip, we settled on a 10-day hunt and four days of sightseeing in one of the national parks in order to see some of the animals that I wasn't hunting and to round out the whole African experience. The Farrens' travel agent set up the airline booking and the dates were set.

As it turned out, the extra time issue disappeared. Three months before departure, my company announced a layoff. As part of the layoff, they were also offering a buyout package to long-term employees such as me. I'd been preparing for retirement for many years and the buyout offer was generous. After doing the math and factoring in my age, I decided the offer was too good to turn down and accepted it. The timing was perfect. Just nine days after leaving work, I'd be winging it to South Africa. The fates were smiling on me. I was ready. Or at least as ready as I could be. The job ended and the safari began.

African immersion

Getting to South Africa from the northeast United States is a long process. The one-hour hop from Manchester, New Hampshire, to Dulles International Airport in Washington D.C. was easy. The 18-hour flight from Dulles to Johannesburg was not. After about nine hours we reached Dakar, Senegal, on the Atlantic coast of Africa, but that's only the halfway point and still well north of the Equator. In Dakar we had to stay on the plane during refueling and about an hour later took off again for Johannesburg, on another eight or nine-hour flight leg. Africa is a huge continent.

Upon arrival in Johannesburg we were taken to a fine guest house to spend the night and recover a bit from the long flight. The following day we were to complete the final leg of our journey with a short flight to Durban on the Indian Ocean coast of South Africa. That first evening in Johannesburg, or as the locals call it, Jo'berg, we were treated to an outdoor braai dinner. It was the equivalent to what Americans call a barbeque. It was also our first chance to meet other hunters beginning their own safaris.

Thinking I might glean some valuable knowledge from some hunters more experienced than me, meaning just about anyone, I struck up conversations with the other guests. It turned out the four of them were all from Scandinavia and were in South Africa to hunt elephants. So much for help in my quest for information about "small game."

In reality, some plains game animals are by no means small. In fact, some, like the eland, are as big as the largest North American moose and many others put even a bruiser whitetail deer to shame. But in comparison to the mighty African elephant, both in terms of physical size as well as trophy fee, I was going after small fry. I didn't feel inferior to these other hunters, just a member of a different hunting fraternity.

A word or two about trophy fees is appropriate. Nearly all of my experience in eastern North American hunting has been on public land where you buy your license and you then hunt for the animal of your choice. Perhaps you pay a fee, typically just a few dollars, for a separate permit specific to a certain species. It doesn't work this way in South Africa, at least not where I was hunting.

Most of the hunting is on private land called concessions, similar to our game farms or cattle ranches. Even though these concessions are fenced in, they are many thousands of acres in size. You might hunt all day and never even see a fence. The animals on the concessions are the property of the concession owners and, as such, are their cash crop. The property owners manage the size of the herds and variety of species to maintain a balance of what the land will support. Each animal, depending on species and abundance, has a price on its head called a trophy fee. If you shoot an animal, in effect, you bought it. Not only that, if you wound an animal, but do not recover it, you still bought it. It causes the hunter to think seriously and aim carefully before pulling the trigger. That bullet in the chamber costs a lot more than the price on the side of the box of ammunition.

Trophy fees vary widely depending upon the species. For example, a small grazing animal such as a duiker (an antelope about the size of a medium-size pet dog) might have an associated trophy fee of $200 while a bull elephant's trophy fee might be one hundred times higher at $20,000 or more. Definitely way out of my league.

Trophy fees are in addition to whatever the day rate is for the P.H. Generally, the more difficult or dangerous the hunt, such as for any of the Big Five or Dangerous Six animals, the higher the day rate. It was for this reason, and the high trophy fees commanded by elephant hunting, that I decided that my Scandinavian fellow guest house hunters had to be either the owners of North Sea oil wells or the founders of Ikea. Perhaps both. Thank you very much, but I was sticking to and very happy with my decision to hunt plains game animals.

The next day, Molly and I arose early and departed once more for the airport and our flight to Durban. Once there, we were met by Conroy and his assistant, Brian Kelly. Conroy had the look, to me at least, of a P.H. He was strong, rugged, and looked like he could handle himself well in any situation, whether with man or beast. He'd been born in Africa, Mozambique, I believe, and spoke the Zulu language which was prevalent in the KwaZulu-Natal section of South Africa where we were to be hunting.

Brian was quite different. While he too looked like he could manage in any type of circumstance, he had a more refined, gentlemanly air about him. If he was in England, I'd picture him as the lord of a manor house and making sure that the needs of everyone about him were attended to. And that was just how he treated us. He and Molly, who was not hunting, seemed to get along famously. With Brian's quick wit and Molly's blunt questions, there was to never be a dull moment in their friendly verbal jousts.

The camp at Spoor Safari

On the way to our first safari camp we stopped to purchase food, drink, and other essentials. I had told Conroy prior to departure that I wanted to eat as varied a diet of game meat as possible, while Molly was a bit less adventurous and preferred to stick to fish, chicken, and other less wild staples. Among the provisions were a variety of native wines and a good supply of biltong, the South African equivalent of jerky. After an auto ride of a few hours (on the "wrong side" of the road), we arrived at our first camp, Spoor Safari.

Safari accommodations can range from very primitive, such as temporary tents in the bush which many consider to be the ultimate safari experience, to luxurious lodges with all the amenities of a modern vacation resort. Spoor Safari was about in the middle.

Spoor Safari had a main lodge with a dining hall and compact, but well stocked bar. The lodge buildings were set on a hillside and the concession encompassed over 11,000 acres of scrub trees, thorn bushes, and intermittent waterways. The dining area was adorned with a variety of animal heads and birds, including an eagle. Tanned hides covered the floor and a spacious deck overlooked a valley where you could view grasslands, hills, valleys, and see for several miles in three directions and all of it was within the boundaries of the concession. A swimming pool and shaded outdoor patio area completed the main lodge facilities.

Our cottage was separate from the lodge and had the same cement walls with colorful native stone inlays and a thatched roof. There were electric lights and a small refrigerator. The bathroom was equipped with a vanity sink, a flush toilet, and a stone shower stall with just a bare copper pipe sticking out of the wall as a shower head. Hot water was provided by a wood-fired boiler behind the cottage that a staff helper fired up in the pre-dawn hours each morning. We had a large king-size bed and a loft area held three cots for larger-sized safari groups. A smaller version of the main lodge's balcony overlooked the same vista. A second cottage with similar furnishings was available if a second party of hunters was present. We had the whole place to ourselves.

I checked my rifle to make sure the sights were still on and we settled in for our first evening and dinner. We dined with the concession owner, Etienne; his wife, Leona; their son, Dillon; and daughter, Mareka; as well as with Conroy and Brian. As we walked from our cottage to the main lodge for dinner, I noticed a very young wart hog following the daughter like a puppy dog. I was told the wart hog's name was "Farqi." When I asked what the name meant, Etienne said it meant "meat." It didn't sound like Farqi was destined for a long and happy future.

The kudu and impala I dined on were both delicious, though the impala was more tender. Standing on the deck that first evening, seeing the unfamiliar country around me, hearing the strange bird and animal sounds, and inhaling the dry air, I really felt like I'd finally arrived in Africa and was definitely ready to begin my safari hunting adventure. The jackal that barked outside at sunset startled Molly, but was music to my ears.

Into the bush

In planning my safari, both Tim and Conroy had asked me what animal species I was after, as well as what quality. In other words, did I want record-caliber animals or good representations of the selected species? After some research, plus checking my budget regarding trophy fees, I settled on five fairly standard animals: impala, wart hog, zebra, blue wildebeest, and kudu. My one "exotic" animal, a sixth choice, if it should present itself, was a nyala. As far as quality went, I wasn't going to be a stickler for record-book animals. I'd learned long ago to trust my guide and here in Africa that was never a truer belief. I trusted Conroy's judgment to pick out animals for me that would be of a class that any person would be proud to have on their trophy room wall. Conroy also suggested that I might want to consider what he called "animals of opportunity." I wasn't quite sure what that meant, but it sounded good to me. With those parameters in mind, we set out on our first morning of hunting.

Just the nature of the spot-and-stalk hunting was exciting all by itself. While Brian drove the diesel-power 4WD Toyota Hilux pick-up truck (roughly equivalent to the North American Toyota Tacoma), tracker Peter, Conroy, and I stood in the bed of the truck, braced against the roll-over bars, and scanned the surrounding countryside for animals. I felt on top of the world.

What had looked relatively smooth with gentle rolling hills from the lodge proved to be anything but. The gentle stretches were frequently interrupted with gullies, stream beds (some dry and some wet), and rocky outcrops. The variety of landscape was exciting to me.

That first day, we saw a lot of animals. Among them were red hartebeest, wart hogs, ostrich, nyala, kudu, and impala. However, none were up to Conroy's standards so we just observed on day one and did not attempt any shots. Two things did become apparent to me that first day. One was that at any moment, and around any bend in the road, you might see an animal of any one of several species. To someone who's used to waiting for many hours, or even days, to possibly see just one animal, this was beyond my wildest dreams. The second observation was that I was really, *really* enjoying myself. How could I not? I was in an exotic land, hunting in an overabundance of animals, and enjoying the company of good people. I was smiling incessantly.

On that first day I was also introduced to what I can only describe as refined bush country luxury. About 10:00 a.m., after having ridden around looking for animals for several hours, Brian slowly pulled the truck to a stop for no apparent reason. Everyone piled out of the truck and the tailgate came down. Within a few minutes, Brian was serving hot tea in porcelain mugs and fresh-baked cookies. This sure beat the plastic water bottles and cold ham sandwiches that were my usual mid-morning hunting fare. Within a couple days, I eagerly anticipated our morning tea times. Day one ended with no shots fired. Day two was different.

First animal down. Exhilaration.

Day two started out about the same as day one. We drove to a new area within the Spoor Safari concession and noticed a small herd of blesbok on a bare hillside. Conroy pointed out a nice buck at the rear of the herd, separate from the others and suggested it might be a good first animal to take. He and I crept along, keeping low and below the animal's line of sight. When we thought we were within range, about 150 yards, Conroy put up the sticks and gave me the go sign. I steadied the rifle and took the shot. I saw the bullet hit in the exact area where a whitetail deer's heart would be and yet, the blesbok just stood there. A second shot, nearly in the same spot, put him down. I'd taken my first African animal.

Afterwards Conroy reminded me of something he had said earlier. African animals have their heart and lung area farther forward and lower in their bodies than their North American cousins. This was something I needed to constantly remind myself of throughout the safari. I'm used to shooting to preserve meat for eating as well as hitting the vitals area which is typically just behind the front shoulder. In Africa, the idea is to shoot for the shoulder. In doing so, you'll connect with the heart-lung area and should compensate accordingly if the animal is quartering towards or away from you. By shooting at the shoulder when possible, you also are more certain of immobilizing what are typically very tough animals.

My blesbok was down. He'd been an easy broadside shot. And while I was nervous at taking my first African animal, I'd accomplished it successfully. He was an attractive animal with white markings on his face and roughly 16-inch horns. Conroy said he thought it was an older male, past his prime for breeding, and that he'd been ousted from the herd and was now on his own. Brian made the suggestion that I take not only the front of the hide for a shoulder mount, but also a portion of the lower back hide. I could then use this, along with similar pieces of hide from my yet-to-be-taken animals to make a patchwork "quilt" of the animals I'd taken on my safari. I liked the idea and proceeded accordingly. I took several photos of the blesbok and Conroy and Brian propped him up for several others, something they did for every animal I took. They'd had practice at this. I didn't.

Later that day, in the evening, Conroy and Peter spotted a nice nyala bull as we passed through some thick bush in a low area. I never did see it, though we trailed it for upwards of an hour. As it got darker, I was wondering what else might be in the thick stuff—not only what we might be trailing, but what also might be tracking us. As we walked back to the truck, where Molly and Brian awaited, we startled a flock of guinea fowl that were roosting in a tree for the night. I'm not sure who was more on edge, me or the fowl. When we arrived back at the truck, Brian looked at Molly, winked, and said, "Well your husband's back…alive." I'm not sure Molly caught the wink.

During the day, I'd noticed many native women cutting tall grass on some hillsides. I asked Conroy what they were doing and he said they were harvesting the grass for making thatched roofs. When I asked if it was dangerous work, Conroy said that they did have the rare leopard attack. Talk about a hazardous workplace. I guess I really was in Africa.

Second animal shot. Let down.

As much as taking the blesbok was a pleasant experience, my second animal was significantly less than the same. We were cruising through some grassland and found ourselves parallel to a herd of red hartebeest. They were walking through some fairly thick scrub trees and didn't present a good shooting opportunity. Conroy signaled for the truck to stop and we waited while the herd circled from left to right in front of us. Conroy had seen a good bull in the group.

The herd began crossing the road in front of us about 100 yards out. The animals weren't stopping. Conroy told me, "There's the one" and I took a quick shot, using the front roof of the truck as a gun rest. I instantly knew I'd rushed the shot and had not made a good hit on the hartebeest. In hindsight, I should have waited for another opportunity. But hindsight wasn't doing me any good at that time. We looked a bit and didn't find any blood. We decided to head back to the lodge for lunch and resume the search later in the afternoon.

Conroy mentioned that concession owners sometimes find injured animals even after the hunter has left for home or gone to another concession and they do everything possible to see that the hunter gets his animal, even if it's after the fact. That provided at least some comfort to me.

A group of staff were assembled after lunch and we all headed out to search for the hartebeest. We beat the bushes for several hours, but to no avail. Etienne sent his security person, Marco, out to look for it while Conroy and I resumed the safari. I'll admit I was feeling pretty low at having wounded and not recovered an animal. I tried to console myself that it's one of the things that eventually happens to nearly all hunters. It didn't help me feel much better.

That night, the edge was taken off a bit by a spectacular barbecue dinner. We had steak, chicken, and ribs. I'm not sure what animals the meat was really from, but they were all absolutely delicious. Dessert was something called "pup." It consisted of a layer of grits topped with a mix of bacon pieces, corn, and tomato, and then another layer of grits. The topmost layer was basted with egg. I was told this was an especially popular dish in South Africa. It would have been tasty anywhere.

Before the evening was over, Etienne told me that his crew had spotted a red hartebeest that was limping and that maybe it was the one I'd shot. He seemed fairly confident that they'd recover it. I certainly hoped so.

Before turning in for the night I noticed the Southern Cross constellation in the sky and recognized Orion low on the horizon, although he was facing the "wrong" direction. Maybe it was the strange appearance of the night sky or, perhaps just the clarity of the pollution-free air, but the only other time I've see such a clear night sky was in the Arctic. This was just as beautiful, though even more alien looking since almost none of the stars and constellations were recognizable and the Milky Way was about twice as brilliant as it appeared in the Northern Hemisphere.

Day three. Redemption.

With thoughts of the wounded red hartebeest still haunting me, we left camp on day three. We'd seen some nyala on a steep hillside the day before, but passed on them. Conroy wanted to take another look at that hillside. Almost immediately he spotted a bush buck, an animal about the size of a whitetail deer. However, he wasn't sure if it was on the list of animals that Spoor Safari was offering to hunters so we continued on. A short time later we took another look at the same hillside and spotted three nyala near its summit. Two were females and one was a big male.

Conroy knew I was a bit upset about my previous day's poor shot so, without telling me, he set me up to regain my confidence. He pulled the truck to a stop as close as possible to the base of the hill. Then he, Brian, and Peter left me completely alone in the bed of the truck. I made a rest of my pack and vest on the truck's roof and took steady aim at the nyala. I knew my rifle was zeroed in at 100 yards so even though the distance was about 175 yards, I held the crosshairs exactly on the nyala due to the steep upward angle and slowly squeezed the trigger at the quartering away animal.

I saw the bullet hit exactly where I had aimed. The nyala hunched up, took a couple steps forward up the hill, backpedaled, and then fell downhill into some thick scrub trees. The tree branches moved for a short time and then became still.

Conroy, who had been watching a short distance away, and I both felt it was a clean kill and we set about driving around the hillside to reach its top from the less-steep backside. We first picked up five workers from the farm to assist in the nyala's recovery. I'm still amazed at the off-road capabilities of the Toyota Hilux truck. Even with eight or nine people loaded aboard, we drove up the hillside without following a road and arrived at its summit unscathed. We then scrambled down the hillside on foot a hundred yards or so to where the nyala lay, resting against a clump of trees that had kept him from tumbling farther down the slope.

I didn't know how we were going to get the nyala back up the hill, but I was certain it wasn't going to be easy. I underestimated the abilities of the local workers. In short order they had the animal out of the trees, laid him on a tarp, and were pulling him up the steep incline in time with the chorus of their chanting. Two or three melodious phases followed by a synchronized pull upward. Then the process was repeated until the crest of the hill was attained. It all seemed so easy and so appropriate for Africa.

After posing for the obligatory photos, thanking the workers for their assistance, and loading the nyala into the truck for the ride back to camp, we retraced our route back down the hill. On the road back to camp we pulled to a stop as we approached another vehicle with Etienne at the wheel. He informed us that they had found my red hartebeest from the day before lying dead. I was very much relieved at this. The animal had not become scavenger food and my embarrassment at having made a poor shot was somewhat abated. I later asked Conroy what percentage of animals were lost and not recovered. His estimate was approximately ten percent.

We were back at camp by 8:30 a.m. Three days, three animals, and each an excellent example of their particular species. In addition to my trophy accumulation, the meat from each animal was helping to feed the local population. Some went to the safari camp, and some we consumed ourselves, but the remainder provided protein for the local people. Nothing was wasted.

I learned that Etienne's only source of income was from hunters like me and the surplus animals that he culled from the herds. For example, he estimated that he had about 1,500 impala on his concession and if he did not occasionally harvest some of them by means of a cull hunt, he would face a habitat disaster within just three years. By managing the population of the various animals carefully, their health and wellbeing were thus assured.

While it may seem contradictory to many, hunting is, in fact, both species and habitat conservation.

That evening we were invited to participate in something completely unplanned. Etienne wanted to hunt for some predator animals, mainly jackals, but perhaps also a bush pig, hyena, or civet cat. The strategy was to sit in the dark in the open vehicles, play a CD offering the sound of a wounded animal, and shine a red spotlight into the dark and look for the reflection of animal eyes. Back home we'd call this poaching, but here in Africa, on private land, it was predator control.

We didn't see anything other than some hares and several other unknown small animals. However, while driving to and from the spotlighting area we did see numerous impala, duiker, steenbok, and wildebeest. The animals seemed somewhat more at ease under the cover of darkness when they had only predators to contend with and not the other threat of hunters. Conroy had made a point of informing me that while most game animals in North America face minimal danger from predators other than man, in Africa, virtually everything is a walking meal to some other creature. Only through continual vigilance could the inevitable be forestalled.

While I'd gained a bit of confidence in my shooting skills that day by taking the nyala, another event, though lesser in magnitude, was till nagging at me. For the second time since our arrival, Conroy had pointed out to me a common "animal of opportunity" and I'd decided to take advantage of that opportunity. The animals in question were gray duikers, diminutive members of the antelope family. A large gray duiker only weighs about 30 or possibly 35 pounds and sports a set of horns perhaps just four to five inches in length. However, they are a common animal taken by many safari hunters. If I'd been at home, I'd have put them in the same class as gray squirrels.

In both instances, my shots were at considerably less than 100 yards. And both times, my shots never even touched the animals. Not only was I embarrassed at my ineptitude, but it was becoming a bit of a private joke among the people on the truck, including me, that I was not destined to take a gray duiker.

Later reflection offered some solace in that these shots were from the back of the truck and using the side rails as rests and not from my well-practiced stance of taking aim from shooting sticks. Still, I should have made the easy shots. And now, gray duikers were on my self-proclaimed endangered species list.

One animal that was not on my trophy list was giraffe, which we saw several times while driving about on the Spoor Safari concession. They are amazing creatures to see. In one area we saw a small group of them, about five, traveling through a wooded area. The trees were perhaps ten feet tall, just high enough to conceal the bodies of the giraffes so that it appeared as though disembodied necks and heads were gliding above the treetops. Conroy mentioned that once he had a client that wanted and took an 18-foot-tall giraffe and intended to have a full body mount done. I could only imagine the trophy room in that hunter's home.

Other creatures that we often spotted were a bit more terrifying than the giraffes and they nearly ensnared us several times. I'm talking about some rather large and fearsome-looking spiders. As we rode in the back of the truck looking for other animals, we were at exactly the right height to become tangled in spider webs. The spiders would stretch their incredibly strong silk lines from tree to tree during the night and then position themselves in the middle of that web. Conroy and I developed a sort of sign language to indicate to one another when we were approaching one of these traps so we could duck down in time. I don't recall that we were ever captured.

Duikers, zebras, and dancing

The next day Conroy was at our cottage when he spotted some zebras on a hillside facing us. We hustled after them on foot and eventually had them somewhat corralled in a group of trees. As they slowly moved towards an opening, we did the same. The herd stopped while we waited in position for a shot. All the herd had to do was walk about four or five more yards and they'd be in the open. Instead they turned and trotted up the hill, still in the trees, and then out of sight. We hiked back to the cottage and got in the truck to look for more animals.

We resumed the quest for my nemesis, the gray duiker. Conroy quickly spotted one near where we saw the zebras and we headed toward it, this time in the Hilux. As we neared the spot, we dismounted, but the duiker seemed to have vanished. A few minutes later, the tracker, Peter, spotted another one, or perhaps the same one, and we tried to sneak up on it. It took me several tries at looking through my scope before I could make out the duiker's shape. When I finally did, Conroy had me use his shoulder as a gun rest, something I'd never done before.

My third try at a duiker worked. The animal dropped and quickly expired. It was interesting that there were exit wounds on both sides of the duiker. My bullet had struck a small branch in front of the duiker and we believed that the core of the bullet must have separated from the jacket once it entered the duiker's body. Regardless, my duiker jinx was broken.

By now I'd hunted four days and taken four animals, but none of them were of the species that I had listed as desired before the safari began. It wasn't a concern, but I did make a mental note that I was rapidly spending my allotted trophy fee budget on other species. I mentioned this to Conroy and he said that I should not be concerned. If I went over my budget, he would be happy to trust me for the balance until I returned to the United States. As he put it, "I never worry about Americans. They always pay." He said that the same could not be said for some other to-remain-nameless nationalities.

A word about shooting stances might be appropriate here. I've talked about shooting from tripod sticks which is what I had practiced and what is generally seen on television safari hunting shows. I also took some shots from the back of the truck and, as described, once rested the rifle on Conroy's shoulder. Some readers might question the ethics of shooting from the elevated position within the truck. Here's the rationale on that. Whenever possible, we did leave the truck and shoot from ground level off tripod sticks. However, in some circumstances, such as when the game was in chest-high grass or reeds by a river or lake shore, the only ethical shot, short of wading in after the animal and more than likely spooking it, was from an elevated position. In retrospect, I wish I had practiced more of a variety of shooting stances prior to my trip. Experience is always an excellent teacher.

So with my trophy-fee money worries allayed and the duiker brought to the skinning shed, we headed out once more. This was to be my final full day at Spoor Safari and I didn't want to waste a minute of it.

We stopped on several hillsides and spotted impala and hartebeest, but no kudu or zebra which were what we were after. We headed off to a sparsely forested area where we'd seen some small kudu earlier and were just coming up from a wet area when the Hilux abruptly halted. A small herd of zebras were about 150 yards away in a clump of trees. Only one was clearly visible and Conroy said it was a shooter.

Nature has played a cruel trick on zebras by imprinting a perfect aiming point on the animal. Just on and very slightly behind the front shoulder, the zebra's stripes form a perfect triangle. With the animal standing broadside, the top point of the triangle is the spot to hit.

This zebra was slightly quartered towards me so I adjusted my aim to a spot just in front of the triangle point and fired. I heard but did not see the bullet hit. I did see the zebra hunch up so I was pretty certain it was a good hit. Immediately after the shot the animal bounded away in line with one of the trees so I was unable to see if it went down.

We checked the area where the zebra had stood, but found no blood. Then I saw one zebra standing and watching us and then bound away at full speed, obviously unhurt. Had I made another bad shot? Seconds later, self-doubt turned to elation. Peter pointed to a depression in the chest-high grass and there lay my zebra. I'd finally taken one of the animals on my list.

During the trip back to the lodge, Brian mentioned that zebras are the most wounded and non-recovered animal in Africa. Despite their public image of being little more than a cuddly horse in striped pajamas, in reality, zebras are a very tough animal. Unless hit solidly in a vital area, they can and often will run for miles only to die a slow death far away. Also, if the lead stallion of the herd is killed, whichever animal assumes control of the herd will often set about killing any young colts so that only his offspring will go on to populate the herd. The animal I shot was a mare so I was happy that the carnage would be limited to just the animal I had taken.

Before I went to Africa, I talked to my taxidermist who made a suggestion about the zebra, if I took one. Most people just have a flat hide tanned and use it as a throw or as a rug for the floor. The taxidermist suggested that I consider having the zebra mounted in a similar fashion to that of a bearskin rug, that being with the hide lying flat, but the attached head being mounted in a lifelike whole fashion. Ultimately I decided to do this and today am very glad I did so. The mount is quite distinctive and I can use it in any manner I choose…flat on the floor, on the wall, or as a cover over a pool table, which is how mine is currently used.

That last evening at Spoor Safari camp we were the guests of honor at quite the party. The people from the surrounding village all visited after dark and entertained Molly and me with native dances, songs, and music around the campfire. I'm not much of a dancer, but Molly really got into it. I also learned that if you take photos or movies of these events, make sure to include everyone equally. Anyone that is left out will be offended by the omission.

I hunted with Brian for a couple hours the following morning, but did not shoot at anything. In my mind I was replaying the first four days of the safari and all the adventures it had presented. I could only imagine what the next days and destination had in store for me.

Pangola delights

I'm a bit the rustic (said with pride, by the way). Spoor Safari camp was wonderful. Just the right mix of earthiness and contemporary. Had I been on safari without my wife, it was absolutely my kind of environment. In fact, I probably would have gone for more primitive, like a tent camp safari.

Mvubu Lodge at Pangola Game Reserve, our next destination, was over the top in terms of the type of luxury I'm used to. Molly was ecstatic. Imagine a cottage with bamboo walls, a thatched roof, and yet air conditioning for comfort. It had a full bath with shower, electricity, nice furniture and appropriate appliances. Young nyala wandered across the grounds and the steep hillside setting provided a view from the balcony that encompassed a wide swath of the river, including the resident crocodiles. This was truly a "pinch yourself, I'm really here" destination. I like to think that in addition to the rustic, I'm also a renaissance man. I can handle the primitive, but I can also "sacrifice" and adapt quickly to the modern when necessary. It was, and I did.

The reserve encompassed approximately 18,000 acres. The main lodge held a full bar, a restaurant, gift shop, and large reception area. Wi-Fi Internet connection was available and a spa offering massage services was just a short drive down the road. Between our cottage and the lodge was a nicely appointed swimming pool which Molly used several times during our stay. Several hippopotamus skulls were strategically placed along the walkways for atmosphere.

We had arrived at Pangola fairly late in the day, but still had a couple hours of hunting time available and Conroy suggested that we take advantage of it. I didn't need convincing and we were soon ferrying the Hilux across the river. The one courtesy that the Pangola resort asked was to not shoot any animals within sight of the resort itself. Not only was Pangola a safari destination, but also a resort used by wedding parties, vacationers, and other non-hunters. We happily complied and did not shoot at any animals in front of the tourist shutterbugs.

We didn't shoot any animals in the short, first-night excursion, but did see impala, kudu, wart hogs, giraffes, and even a black rhino mother with a calf that bluff-charged the truck. (Note to the reader: Do not openly approach rhinos, especially black rhinos. These are the more aggressive of the two species. Caught in the open, you stand a good chance of becoming rhino toe jam.) Conrad made note of some fairly substantial kudu and impala with hopes to revisit them later in the stay. We dined outdoors on venison (the name given to any wild game meat) while seated around a central fire on a slate-covered patio. Different tables hosted different groups, some hunters, some vacationers. Pangola was setting and delivering on some high expectations.

Just the trip from the Mvubu lodge to our hunting area was an adventure in itself. We drove down a dusty road to the boat landing and then drove the Hilux onto the raft which an attendant used to motor us across the river to the hunting area. The river came complete with fearsome tiger fish as well as the crocodiles. As on the arrival day, we did not harvest any animals on the first full day of hunting at Pangola though we did nearly get a chance at a large kudu.

We saw a herd of about eight or nine elephants that second evening. All were either cows or calves and the cows made it very clear that it was not permitted to approach within a certain distance. Conroy told us that there were not many animals more dangerous than an enraged mother elephant when she thought her calf might be in peril. We took him at his word.

Wildebeest tales and wildebeest tails

The next morning saw us spot-and-stalk hunting once again, but this time on the same side of the river as the lodge. Conroy, Brian, and I were joined by a new tracker named Javulani, whose name I was told translated to "Happy." We came close to kudu and wildebeest, but never got shots.

It was during this morning that I mentioned to Conroy that while I knew it was impossible, I was sure that for the second time since our arrival I was smelling the unmistakable odor of home-fried potatoes even though we were miles from the nearest kitchen. The first time I'd passed it off as just some figment of my imagination and my nose, but here it was a second time.

Conroy, as I should have known by this time, knew immediately what it was. A certain shrub had the nickname of the potato bush. The belief was that the odor had something to do with the times when the plant was switching back and forth in producing oxygen while taking in carbon dioxide. Whatever the cause, the pleasant odor on the morning breeze was a nice reminder of home.

A short time later we approached a saddle area between two ridges and spotted a small herd of about ten blue wildebeest milling around approximately 75 yards away. Conroy said there was a nice bull in the group and I set up on the sticks while he glassed the herd to pick him out for me. Eventually the bull was clear of the cows that had screened it from me and stood quartering towards me facing to the left. I took the shot.

The bull bucked up at the shot so I was sure I'd hit him, but he didn't go down. Instead he ran directly away from us through the tall grass with the rest of the herd. As I thought more about the shot, I began to think that I might have pulled it just a bit to the right to be sure I was shooting clear of the cows. We waited a short time and proceeded to where the animals had stood. We found no blood or other evidence of a hit, though Conroy and I were both certain the bullet connected.

After about 20 minutes, Brian found one small leaf with a speck of blood on it, even smaller in size than a whole drop. Five minutes later we found another blood spot so we had a direction of travel. Every now and then we'd find another drop or two, but no large amount of blood or a pool of it indicating the wildebeest had stopped moving. I was starting to have more serious doubts about my shot. Eventually we found a small splash of blood with some frothiness in it, indicating a lung shot.

We went a bit farther on the trail with Conroy in the lead when he signaled for me to come running with my rifle. He had caught a glimpse of the wildebeest and thought it was down, but it quickly ran off. I managed just a glimpse. The general consensus was that I had probably nicked one lung and that it was best to wait a bit. A hit in one lung would ultimately prove fatal, but the question was would that happen close by in an open area or a long ways off and perhaps in some thick and inaccessible spot?

We waited about an hour and resumed the pursuit. At one point Conroy motioned for me to join him in the lead. I was fully expecting to see the wildebeest, but what he'd seen was what he described as a monster wart hog. When I reached the spot, the wart hog had headed for the thick stuff. I never saw it.

Luckily it seemed the wildebeest was sticking to the dirt road and we could see his tracks and the occasional drop of red. Brian told me the story of one hunter who had shot a large blue wildebeest square in the chest with a .375 magnum. The animal was knocked off his feet, bellowed, got up and ran off never to be seen again. The story did little to boost my spirits. After all, I was using "only" a 7mm magnum.

We reached a point where it was not clear if the wildebeest had stayed on the road or strayed to the side. We spread out to look for tracks or blood. Conroy spotted both in short order and we were on a new path. We marched along in single file, Conroy in the lead, then Javulani followed by Brian and me bringing up the rear. The blood trail was now redder, meaning that it was fresher, and my spirits rose.

Everyone was looking well off to either the sides of the trail or into the distance straight ahead. As we entered a grassy area with protruding black volcanic rocks scattered about, I caught sight of one rock that seemed odd and out of place. The rock grew a set of horns and from that transformed into my wildebeest lying stone dead about 15 feet off the path. We could see by the blood trail that he had been walking along and had become woozy and then staggered to the right and collapsed in a heap.

In all, the wildebeest had covered about a mile and a half from where I'd first shot him. Conroy said he had a great set of horns and weighed about 300 kilos (660 pounds). In addition to the trophy, I was much impressed with the animal's toughness. For me, no other plains animal signified an African safari more than the blue wildebeest and I now had mine to bring home. It was my sixth animal, but only the second on my list. I still wanted an impala, a wart hog, and a kudu.

Brian made a point to tell me that in addition to taking the cape, horns, and some of the back skin, I should also keep the wildebeest's tail and that it was considered the most valuable part of the animal. The tail with its coarse brush of black hair on the tip is what tribal medicine men wave around during their dances and incantations. Thinking back to the last-evening dance at Spoor Safari, I recalled that the medicine man (also the skinner) had such a ceremonial wand as part of his costume. I saved the tail.

African plains game shot placement

I was amazed at the toughness of the plains animals I saw and shot in South Africa. In addition to their heart and lung areas being farther forward than in North American animals, they also have disproportionately larger adrenal glands, no doubt out of evolutionary necessity for self-preservation. Once alarmed or shot, they give themselves a huge dose of adrenalin and this partly accounts for their ability to keep going even after receiving a well-placed fatal shot. In some species, their sheer size and bulk also account for their ability to absorb lead. It's critical, as I too well learned, to hit an animal in a vital area with the first shot.

The rule of thumb for African plains animals is to divide the animal's body into thirds and aim at the top of the bottom third. This establishes the right height for shot placement. Next, establish horizontal placement. If the animal is facing broadside, aim for the front shoulder. If he's quartering towards you, aim just inside the shoulder. For quartering away shots, aim just behind the shoulder. For straight-on shots, shoot just under the jaw.

> Following these bullet placement guidelines, as well as keeping in mind entrance and exit wound trajectories, will help ensure cleanly taking your animals and minimizing lengthy tracking expeditions, or worse, lost animals. In addition, if you are going on your first African safari as I was, be sure to spend a lot of time at the shooting range and shooting from a variety of stances. Then double that amount of practice time.

Into the reeds, ground pepper, and black snow

The next day we headed out for the three animals I still wanted to take: impala, wart hog, and kudu. We saw several of each species, but no shooters. We also saw some white rhinos.

Conroy explained to me that while they often inhabit the same areas, the two species of African rhino do not compete with one another. The white rhino has a squared-off nose and mouth and crops grass very low to the ground. On the other hand, the black rhino has a more pointed and prehensile snout, similar, though much shorter than an elephant's, and uses it to feed on foliage and grasses higher up from the ground.

After a short excursion, Conroy spotted a nice example of a common reed buck along the shore of the river. Another animal of opportunity was presenting itself. The common reed buck is interesting in that while most plains animals have horns that either slope back or point straight up, the reed buck's actually curve forward.

Brian positioned the truck and I took a fairly quick shot at a distance of about 150 yards and made a complete miss. We moved a few feet forward and the buck appeared again. This time I slowed down and fired again. We heard the bullet hit, but saw the animal bound ahead and disappear into some riverside reeds. We waited 15 minutes and then waded through the reeds that were well above our heads.

Javulani spooked a nearby female reed buck and quickly found the wounded male which I dispatched with another shot. Conroy mentioned that the reed buck is one of his favorite species because they tend to be less common and also because of their distinctive horns. Animal number seven taken.

After emerging from the reeds, Conroy asked me if I'd suffered any tick bites. I said that I had a few. He also had some and said that there was a good chance that I might develop tick fever in a couple weeks. The symptoms would be headache for about four days accompanied by nausea. While Molly and I had taken shots for hepatitis and other contagious diseases prior to our departure, as well as medications to prevent malaria, we were unaware of ticks. Brian described tick infestations in Mozambique that sounded quite unpleasant. Imagine animals covered from head to hoof with the blood-sucking beasties!

The ticks we faced in South Africa were a bit less dramatic, though still irritating. Whenever I shot an animal, almost immediately I would see large, blood-engorged ticks dropping off the animal. Perhaps they could sense that the flow of blood had stopped within the creature's body and their free meals were at an end. In any case, these ticks were easy to spot and didn't concern me.

What was a concern were the pepper ticks. Their name was derived from the fact that they were about the size of ground pepper and thus, difficult to see. If your arm looked like it had a coating of dust on it, and the dust moved, it was time to take some preventative action in the form of lotion, which I didn't have, or a shower as soon as convenient. On any future safari, I'll be sure to bring along appropriate treatments as I did come down with tick fever shortly after returning home. Strong antibiotics offered a cure.

While driving and walking along the shore of the river, we noticed quite a number of crocodiles sunning themselves on the shore. One of the trackers relayed a story of a client shooting and wounding a reed buck similar to mine and that the buck decided to swim for it rather than face the next bullet from the hunter. The crocodiles saw to it that nothing was wasted. Apparently the crocs' bodies are attuned to the slightest bit of thrashing in the water and interpret it as a dinner bell.

Later that day I saw what looked like black snow settling out of the air. Conroy and Brian explained that this was from grass and sugar cane fires in neighboring Swaziland. Burning the sugar cane is part of its harvesting process. Also, the scorching of grasslands to stimulate new growth is another common occurrence. While the smoke and flames of these fires were well beyond our sight, the scene of black ashes falling from a clear sunny sky certainly seemed odd.

The most-wanted list dwindles

The next day we went after impala first and other species second. There had been no shortage of impala. We'd seen hundreds, if not thousands, but since nearly every predator apparently loves an impala sandwich or two, they were extremely skittish. Whenever we managed to get near a small herd of them, they'd stand still only for a few seconds and, with all those eyes on the lookout, it only took a twitch of movement to spook them all bounding away.

Conroy and I set off for one group of impala in some moderately thick cover and walked two or three hundred yards in pursuit. There was at least one good ram in the bunch. As was usual, they spotted us and took flight. However, a few individuals stopped behind a small clump of trees to take a second look at us. I'm sure they thought they were concealed safely from our view. In a flash, Conroy had the sticks up and within a couple seconds I had the ram in my crosshairs with a clear lane through the branches.

Sometimes a shot just feels perfect and this was such an example. Everything happened in one smooth motion and at the crack of the shot from the rifle the impala dropped on the spot.

It was a beautiful animal, probably the prettiest and most graceful of all those taken during my safari.

We were well out of sight of the truck and Conroy told me to stay with the impala while he went for the Hilux. I knew we were near where we'd seen the cow and calf elephants earlier and also the rhinos. I asked Conroy about this and he calmly advised me to climb a tree if either species appeared and threatened. I'm sure he got a good chuckle out of this. No tree was taller than about ten feet; easy hunter-plucking distance for an elephant. And as for the rhinos, yes, I could probably have found safety up a tree, but with three-inch thorns protruding from every branch all the way from bottom to top, I'd probably bleed to death before any rhino could reason out what was impaled in the branches above him. Conroy arrived back with the truck in short order and no elephants or rhinos showed up. Animal number eight checked off.

This left only the wart hog and kudu and one day left for the two of them. I was content no matter what happened. As we started out on the final day, we passed through an area that contained an enormous number of animal spines, rib cages, skulls, and other assorted bones. Conroy said it was where the remains of all the harvested animals were placed. They were tossed here once they had been picked clean for their protein by the reserve's butchering staff. The area was affectionately known as the Vulture Restaurant—a very fitting name.

Since wart hogs spend their nights in their underground burrows and wait until the warmth of the day to emerge, we hunted for kudu first. We drove for several hours and eventually stopped for our morning tea and coffee break. We saw more kudu that day than any previous one, but they were all either females or small juvenile males.

We resumed our hunt and about mid-morning came across a grassy slope and spotted a herd of kudu among some trees. They were all females except for one lone bull. Conroy said he was a shooter. I set up the shot quickly on the quartering away animal, aiming just behind the front shoulder.

As I fired I saw the kudu flinch and heard the bullet strike solidly. The bull charged off behind the trees and out of sight. I thought I might have hit just slightly back from my intended spot so we waited about 20 minutes before setting off after him. We didn't see any blood, but did spot the distinct hoof impressions of the smaller females with the bull in pursuit. Five minutes later, Conroy turned to me, smiled, and pointed at my trophy kudu bull lying dead under an acacia tree. It was a very respectable kudu.

The bullet had struck a bit to the rear of where I wanted, but the 7mm did its work and the kudu had only traveled a short distance before dropping. Javulani said something to Conroy in Zulu and I asked what it meant. The translation was that my rifle seemed to pack a pretty good punch. For myself, I knew that the rifle was better than I was, but together we were a respectable team. We loaded the kudu into the back of the Hilux and headed back to the lodge.

We went out one last time that afternoon to see if a wart hog would make the ultimate sacrifice. It was not to be. I had an average animal in my sights and maybe should have taken the shot, but decided to pass. I rationalized that doing so might give me a reason to return someday.

Molly, Conrad, and I, along with one of the lodge's staff members took a boat tour down the river and saw more crocodiles, hippos, and a variety of other wildlife and birds. I even managed to catch a small tiger fish. It was a very relaxing end to the safari portion of the trip.

Molly, Conroy, Brian, and I spent the next several days at the Hluhluwe/iMfolozi National Park. During the drive there we stopped at a taxidermy shop to have the hides, horns, and skulls treated for their eventual trip back to the United States. We saw animals at the park that we might not have otherwise seen. These included cheetah, hyena, and close-up encounters with cape buffalo, otherwise known as dugga boys. I was told that "dugga" means "mud" which is what the older cape buffalo often cover themselves with by rolling in it once they are outcast from the herd. Another nickname for the cape buffalo is Black Death.

They've earned the name through their mean disposition and their habit of turning the tables on hunters after they've been wounded.

We did some souvenir shopping, much to Molly's delight, and spent several hours touring an authentic native village and showering the children, as well as the adults, with pieces of hard candy. On our last evening in South Africa we were treated to a fine dinner in Durban by Conroy, Brian, and Brian's wife, Louise. That night we stayed at a quaint bed and breakfast run by Conroy's mother. In the morning, Conroy took Molly and me to the airport and shepherded us through all the airport formalities. We readied ourselves for the long plane ride home.

My safari clothing seemed to fit a bit better than it had at the start of the trip and I definitely felt considerably less naked than when I first arrived in South Africa.

Looking back at Africa

I spent some time thinking about the trip and evaluating the experience as the safari wound down and after my return to the United States. I've also been asked many questions about the adventure and I'll attempt to answer some of them here.

First, would I go back to Africa again? The answer…how quickly can I get to the plane? Not only would I go again, but I've already made a new list of the animals I'd like to take on a second trip. Since my wife has more of a "been there, done that" attitude about such a repeat trip, I'd opt for a more primitive safari the second time around, perhaps in more remote country and with fewer amenities. I'd still hire Conroy as my P.H. if he was available.

I've also been asked, sometimes rather indelicately, what the safari cost. I prefer not to discuss financial matters outside my immediate family so my answer has typically been as follows. If I hadn't gone on the safari, and figuring in all the costs, including the taxidermy fees, today I could be driving a new full-size pickup truck equipped with all the extras I'd want and it would be fully paid for. While that might sound like a lot, bear in mind that my wife accompanied me on the trip so airfare was doubled and while the safari fees were not doubled, there was an additional daily rate for a non-hunting guest. Also, on any future trip I would likely not add in the four days of sightseeing.

An additional item to factor into the cost is the number and choice of animals. Trophy fees are less expensive for the more common species and increase for those that are more exotic or dangerous. Another aspect to cost is basing it on a per-animal basis. A western U.S. lodge-based deer or elk hunt can reach $10,000 or more for one animal. On my African trip I took nine different animals, so dividing my imaginary new pickup into nine separate pieces would result in a cost of considerably less than $10,000 per segment.

One final aspect of cost is the old axiom, you get what you pay for. Packaged hunts are available for a fixed price that includes several specific animals, depending upon the concession. These trips might be more economical, however there is generally less control over the quality of the trophies taken and the personal attention provided by the P.H. Hunting with two hunters per P.H. versus one-on-one may also lower expenses, but can introduce more complications, such as who takes which animals.

What about disease and inoculations? Depending on what country or countries you include in your safari, you may or may not require immunizations, boosters, or preventative measures. South Africa did not require any such precautions at the time of our visit, but my wife and I opted to be on the safe side and got several different ones. Discuss these with your doctor and do so three to six months in advance of your trip as some immunizations take significant time before they offer protection. Documentation of those immunizations will be required in order to enter certain countries. Any prescription medications carried with you should be in their original vials or packaging.

Even though Molly and I had extensive and very productive discussions with our booking agents, Tim and Valerie Farren of Farren Global Adventures, I strongly recommend talking directly to your P.H. in advance of your trip. Make sure he knows your likes, dislikes, and expectations in advance, as well as similar priorities for others in your party. Talk about your food and drink preferences, health issues such as allergies, accommodations and degree of luxury or lack thereof, and your animal species and trophy expectations. Do you want to only take record-class animals or will good representations of your selected species be acceptable. Let the P.H. know about your level of shooting proficiency and what firearms you will be bringing and whether or not they are appropriate for your desired species. Ask where he will be meeting you. Talk about any side trips you might want to take. Obviously you should discuss anything related to financial matters, including payment of any trophy fees. Bring adequate photography equipment and a journal to write down your observations and thoughts as they happen.

One last note about Conroy and Brian. Not only were they wonderful guides and superb P.H.s, they were also incredibly attentive hosts. Molly has some significant health issues and yet I never felt she was even once at risk. Two specific examples of their attentiveness depict this especially well.

One evening as we sat talking during the sightseeing portion of our trip, Molly mentioned how as a child she enjoyed sitting around a campfire toasting marshmallows. The next evening when Conroy served the grilled chicken he had prepared on the braai, he also brought in several toasted marshmallows for Molly. For me, that was a most memorable demonstration of the level of thoughtfulness we both experienced during our entire stay in South Africa.

The second example demonstrates Conroy's and Brian's unflappable sense of humor and composure. I had warned Conroy and Brian early in the trip that Molly had a tendency to occasionally ask somewhat outrageous personal questions and I'd been waiting all trip for one to come out. One evening towards the end of the trip Molly delivered. As we sat around talking, she suddenly asked of all present, "Where were you when you first had sex?"

I burst out laughing as I'd been waiting for just such a question from her for nearly two weeks, but didn't expect it just then. I don't remember Brian's specific answer, but I do recall that it was quite over the top in terms of one-upping Molly, a game the two of them had engaged in during the entire trip.

Conroy's response, once he also regained his composure, was that he had been a professional hunter for many years and been asked literally thousands of questions over that time, but this was the first time he'd ever been asked that one. I think he may have also mentioned something about the backseat of a car, but I could be mistaken.

When Molly and I first met Conroy and Brian we were strangers to one another. When we parted at the end of the trip, we were good friends who had enjoyed a great experience together. I am exceptionally grateful for that.

Brian Kelly's special amarula dessert recipe

Boil three or four ripe unpeeled bananas for three minutes. Peel them, split them lengthwise, and lay them split side up in a casserole dish.
Pour in approx. ½ cup Cointreau, flavored brandy, or, preferably, amarula liquor.
Top with a layer of coconut-encrusted marshmallows.
Broil just long enough to toast the marshmallows (approx. two minutes).
Serve topped with vanilla ice cream and a dash of cinnamon.

Epilogue

I've hunted and fished nearly all my life. During the last twenty or so years I've come to realize just how passionate I am about these hobbies. That passion is in my blood and helps define who I am today and will be tomorrow. I live somewhat vicariously through television hunting and fishing shows. I have my favorites and am inspired by them. I'm honored and often surprised when friends and former coworkers tell me they live vicariously through my adventures.

I wrote the first of this collection of stories in 2001. It took me six years before I wrote the second. At some point thereafter I realized I'd been collecting similar stories in my head all my life and that I'd better put them on paper before they slipped from my mind forever. I thought the total number might come to about ten. It ended up being double that. Perhaps I had a book in me. It turned out I did. Maybe I'll have a second someday.

I have more hunting and fishing adventures planned. In the immediate future are another New Brunswick spring bear hunt; another September return to the Leaf River in Quebec for caribou; a trip to Lake Oscar north of Montreal for brook trout, walleye, and northern pike; and my annual trip with my sons to Lower Richardson Lake in Maine for landlocked salmon and brook trout. I try to always have one or more future trips on the calendar. Anticipation is at least half the fun and it motivates and inspires me.

I want to continue planning, taking, and documenting these and similar trips for as long as I'm physically able to do so. I can draw a bit of inspiration from my caribou hunting companion on my most recent trip to Leaf River. Ted Tolman was an F105 fighter pilot during the Vietnam War. It was an honor and privilege to hunt with him. Ted was 82 years old at the time of our hunt. He climbed the tundra hillsides and withstood the rain and snow without complaint with people a third his age. His excitement at taking his caribou and in catching several nice salmon was infectious. He had his own stories to tell. And some war stories he literally couldn't talk about.

I was once part of a caribou hunting party that included two 80-plus-year-old brothers. At the end of the day they had to help take one another's boots off, but they each got their caribou. That's another example of how I want to be. Age is just a state of mind. Ted and those two brothers knew that already. I'm realizing it.

If I eventually reach the stage where I can no longer go on these adventures and pass from this world, my children say they have a plan for me. It's called a Viking funeral. My remains are to be placed on my boat. Then the boat is to be lit on fire and set adrift. It's occurred to me that my children might actually be serious about this. If so, is there fishing and hunting in Valhalla? I sure hope so. Be sure to send me off with my fishing tackle and firearms on that boat. I'll be needing them.

About the Author

Peter (Pete) Popieniuck is a retired marketing communications manager who worked in the high-technology industry in his native New England. At an early age, Pete developed a deep affection for hunting, fishing, and other outdoor activities. He continues to enjoy these passions today. He lives in a log home in Lunenburg, Massachusetts, with his wife, Molly.

Appendix

Tips, Tricks, and To-dos

Every hunter and fisherman has his own set of tips, tricks, and to-do items that he or she uses to make their outdoor experience better, safer, more comfortable, or more productive. I have mine too. I'm not talking about common-sense practices like always having a compass with you, spare batteries, a cell phone, a means of starting a fire, toilet paper, or a basic first aid kit. Anyone that ventures into the wilderness or onto its waters should always have these essentials with them, especially if they are hunting or fishing alone. I'm referring to more obscure items or practices that might not normally spring to mind. In no particular order of significance, here are mine. Use them as you will, or not.

Duct tape

No surprise here. Duct tape can be used for thousands of things. Repairing leaky waders, torn duffel bags, backpacks, rain gear, even clothing. The list is endless. The trick is to save the remnants of one or more rolls so you don't have to carry around an entire heavy roll of tape. This is especially appropriate when weight is an issue, such as on a remote fly-in trip.

Put the right lid on it

Nearly everyone wears a baseball-style cap when hunting or fishing. But these are of little use in two particular situations. The first is if you're using a head net to keep bugs off your face. Without a full brim, the net will be close to the skin on your neck, cheeks, and ears and allow mosquitos and other biting insects to make their annoying presence fully and painfully known. The same is true during spring bear hunts. I've learned this lesson, like many I've learned, the hard way.

The second situation when a wide brim comes in handy is during rain or snow storms. Sure, rain gear will help, but pulling a hood over your head also restricts hearing and vision. A hat with a full brim keeps the wetness from running down your neck and still lets you see and hear what's going on around you.

Rod tip tip

During my last caribou hunt, a guy I was with accidently broke the tip of his fishing rod just as we were about to start salmon and trout fishing. Even the guide thought he was in trouble. But I fixed the situation quickly. I carry a rod tip repair kit with me. These can be purchased in most sporting goods stores and consist of an assortment of rod tips and adhesive. Or, you can make up your own kit from pieces of old rods and a tube of super glue. This is another lesson I once learned the hard way. I also include a bottle of clear women's nail polish and dental floss. These items come in handy to repair rod guides and the floss can be used for many other purposes, like maybe to stitch up that incision where you had to remove the fishhook from your partner's forearm. Better him than me.

Grin from ear to ear

How does a dental repair kit come in handy? Have you ever been on a fishing or hunting trip and lost a filling or had a crown come loose? I have. Most drug stores carry a small kit that includes a small vial of dental adhesive and an applicator with which you can temporarily fill a cavity or re-attach a crown. I also stash a few toothpicks in the kit. Few things are more annoying than a chunk of bacon that gets wedged between two molars and refuses to let go at the start of a long day on a deer stand.

The walking dead (battery)

On another recent trip, my partner caught a nice Atlantic salmon and asked me to take a photograph of him and it with his camera. When I tried, the digital camera shut itself off seconds after being turned on. The battery was not a standard size and my partner didn't have a spare. However, we ended up taking several good photos of his salmon. Here's how. Unless the battery is completely and totally dead, remove the battery from the camera or other device, such as a GPS receiver, radio, or cell phone, and hold it in your warm hands for a few minutes. Then re-insert it into the device and power it up. A warmed battery will recover some of its power and enable further use for a limited time. Another way to accomplish this is to keep the battery-powered device as close to your body as possible, such as in an inside pocket. I tell my wife I have a warm heart. Now I can prove it.

Bagging it

Sandwich bags and elastic bands are indispensable in my pack. The sandwich bags, of which I prefer the zip-locked variety, can carry dry socks, loose pieces of anything, my dry wallet and licenses/permits, the earlier mentioned kits, and any of a thousand other items. And the elastic bands come in handy for such things as keeping compressed items compressed (such as a dry pair of gloves or mittens in one of those sandwich bags), holding two- or three-piece fishing rods together prior to use or during transport, wrapping around a spool of fishing line to keep it from unravelling, fastening your tag to the deer or turkey you just bagged, or, like the sandwich bags, for innumerable other uses. A half dozen safety pins also can come in handy.

Old underwear never dies

Specifically, just the elastic waist band can be reincarnated. How could this possibly come in handy? Here's how. I've tried dragging a small, scent-coated cloth behind me when I'm heading to a deer stand to leave a scent trail. Invariably, the cloth gets caught on brambles and branches and becomes a nuisance. Instead, rip the elastic waistband from a pair of your used underwear and wrap it around the toe of your boot and under the instep. Apply whatever attractant scent you prefer to the top or bottom of your boot and onto the band and walk to your stand.

With each step you'll leave that scent along your trail with no extra effort or inconvenience. If I ever market this idea I think I'll call it BVDeer. By the way, your wife will be happy that you're finally getting rid of some of that old ratty underwear from your bureau drawer.

Fool-proof water-proof

Sure, we all water-proof our footwear and wear water-proof, or at least water-repellent, outerwear when the environment requires it. But what about backpacks and hats and other garments? A few days before a trip I liberally spray my pack, wide-brimmed hat, knit or baseball-style caps, and cloth gloves with a retail water-repellent spray and then allow them to completely dry before packing. It makes a very noticeable difference when you get that first downpour on your fishing or hunting adventure.

Treat yourself

I always pack some special snack treats with my other essential gear. If I'm sitting in a tree stand for deer for what might be the entire day, I pack a handful of mini candy bars. Every hour I allow myself one of them. It helps make the time pass and gives me something to look forward to. Some of my favorite snacks back at camp are sardines, smoked oysters, and kippered snack whitefish. A couple cans of these along with two or three plastic forks will not only satisfy your own appetite, but also make you popular with your guide or hunting or fishing buddies. Jerky works well too. Bring a big container of homemade venison or caribou jerky and you'll be a downright hero. I've found a flavor that mixes sweet and hot is best. Be sure to bring those toothpicks.

The tale of the tape

Yes, we all want to make sure that trout or salmon is legal size before stuffing it in the cooler or keeping it for the shore lunch fish fry. But a tape measure also comes in handy to settle bets on the pool for the biggest fish, widest spread of antlers, or, in my case, determining the true length and girth of that huge Atlantic salmon I released so I could have an accurate replica made when I returned home. A small mechanical, or better yet, cloth sewing tape measure weighs little and make these judgments much easier. Hint: don't borrow one from your wife's sewing kit and return it after measuring fish with it. She *will* notice.

Blue ribbon winner

No, not for your prize hog at the county fair. I've been on several caribou hunts where all the antlers from thirty or more hunters are shipped back in one bulky jumble of bones. Sometimes the outfitter has put obvious name tags on the racks and sometimes it's just been small pieces of flagging tape with handwritten names. And whether the names of the owners are obvious or not, it's always a bit frustrating to stand amid a jostling bunch of excited hunters eager to get their hands on their hard-won trophy and be on their way home. I minimize this by having my own distinctly colored ribbons to attach to the antlers in addition to whatever identification the outfitter attaches. A florescent green or blue ribbon stands out quite vividly amid a sea of orange.

Pen to paper

You should keep notes. On my African safari I took over 100 pages of notes in the evenings because I wanted to remember as much of the experience as possible. Photos are essential, but so too is a good journal. Sometimes I make notes on things I wish I'd brought on a trip or things I brought that weren't needed or necessary. I make notes of the names and addresses of other sportsmen I might want to keep in touch with or of the guides. Or maybe I just want to do a crossword puzzle while waiting in an airport for my connecting flight. Perhaps a pencil will help me keep track of how many quarters I'm ahead in the never-ending camp cribbage tournament. And I can't very well fill out that tag for my next world-record species without something to write with.

In touch

Hand-held two-way radios can come in handy, space and weight limits permitting, to keep in contact with hunting partners or guides. On a recent trip, two guides connected via radio and helped each other and their clients fill their caribou tags. Depending on where you are, they can also be useful in emergency situations or to ask for help in dragging that huge 10-pointer out of the woods.

Hot stuff

Staying warm for hours in a ground blind or in an elevated stand in the late fall or winter is often a challenge, even when using all the proper clothing and layering techniques. Body suits are effective, but they can cost $300 and more. A simple and cost-effective alternative is to adapt an old sleeping bag for the purpose. Be sure it is a rectangular shaped bag as opposed to a mummy style so your feet have plenty of room. Cotton outer shell bags are quieter than those of synthetic fabric. And if that outer shell is already in a camo pattern, so much the better. A couple elastic straps sewn into the bag will help keep it from slipping off your shoulders and you can even cut two slots for your arms so you can raise your rifle on that 10-pointer with a minimum of noise and movement without having to unzip the bag. Good thing I have women in my life that know how to sew.

Protecting luxury libations

I don't often drink hard liquor. (Kind of sounds like the start of that Dos Equis beer commercial doesn't it?) However, I do enjoy a couple fingers of scotch, or possibly a tad more, in the evening after a long and taxing day afield. While it might not be as impressive as a glass bottle of Johnny Walker Green Label or those red-wax-sealed bottles of Makers Mark, before I pack for my trip I transfer my beverage of choice into a puncture-resistant plastic bottle. Not only does this prevent the potential double disasters of shattered glass and scotch-scented gear in my duffel bag, but it also helps to deter the curious thievery of those scoundrels, the liquor bottle pirates back at camp.

The cool factor

To give due credit, this one comes from Carroll Ware of Fins and Furs Adventures. He has a super-effective way to keep food cold and even frozen for upwards of a week in a cooler without additional ice or refrigeration. First, if possible, have your largest cooler either pre-cooled or even frozen if you have access to a walk-in cooler or freezer. Next, arrange gallon-size, non-clear milk jugs containing frozen water in the bottom of the cooler as tightly packed as possible. (Prior to freezing, fill the milk jugs about seven-eighths full as water expands as it freezes.) Fill all the gaps between the jugs with ice cubes packed as tightly as possible. Shake the cooler to further compact the cubes and add more as needed. Next, pack your previously frozen foods on top of the ice layer *in reverse order.* In other words, put your last day's food on the bottom and stack upward until you have the first food to be used on the top layer. Fill the remaining space in the cooler with more tightly packed ice cubes. Close the cooler and seal the seams with duct tape. (Coolers with gasketed lids may not need to be taped.) Once you are at your final destination, put a canvas tarp (or wet towel if a tarp is not available) on top of the cooler and soak it twice daily with cool water. Drain melted ice water from the cooler once daily. When removing a day's worth of food from the cooler, do so all at once and re-open the cooler as little as possible. Your frozen foods will stay that way, and, as a bonus, you'll have plenty of ice cubes for after-dinner cocktails. Keep an ice pick or screwdriver handy to help chip through the ice.

Cool Rx and it's free

Don't need to keep a giant 120-quart cooler chilled? Here's a great way to keep small coolers colder longer. When diabetics have their insulin supplies shipped to them via mail or freight carrier, the packages typically contain those frozen gel packs to keep the insulin cool and stable. The frozen gel keeps cool longer than frozen water ice. Simply cut open the gel packs and use a funnel to put the gel into an appropriately sized plastic container. Fill the container about seven-eighths full to allow for expansion. I like to use square containers such as quart or half-gallon milk jugs as they help to optimize space inside the cooler and are significantly more puncture resistant than the original gel pack plastic casings. For safety, I use an indelible marker on the jugs to make sure it's known that the contents is not water ice. Refreeze the containers as often as necessary. Empty square plastic saline solution bottles also make suitable containers. Use two and call me in the morning.

Trash bag bonus

I like to keep at least one full-size trash bag in my pack at all times. It can be used as emergency rain gear, as a cover for non-waterproof items, a temporary container for game animal parts, a ground cloth, or as a container for wet or dirty clothing. It weighs almost nothing. A colored bag, such as the orange ones sold at Halloween, can be used as an emergency signaling device. And of course, a trash bag can be used for trash to keep your campsite litter free.

Doggin' it

There are many ways to teach a bird dog to retrieve and all sorts of devices to aid in this effort. Here's mine and it's nearly free. Save the wings from two or three pheasants that your hunting buddies have shot. If you already have a dog, save the wings from several of your own birds. Put those wings in a freezer bag and store them in your freezer until you're ready to use them. Buy yourself a package of the cheapest paint rollers you can find. Thaw out a couple wings and stuff them inside the rollers. Voila! The rollers smell just like birds. Accompanied by the use of a starter or cap pistol, throw those wing-stuffed rollers as far as you can and send your pup after them and praise the heck out of the dog as he brings them back to you. My bird dog, a wire-haired pointing griffon named Diesel, became a trained retriever in one session. And griffons are not supposed to be retrievers. Please don't tell Diesel.

I brake for…gloves?

Never buy work gloves again. Apparently there is an epidemic in our state of people putting work gloves on top of their automobiles and trucks and then driving around until the gloves fall to the street. I call them road gloves. When I spot a pair—and it must be a pair, no singles—I stop and pick them up. If the gloves are oily or filthy, they get a good washing. They come in handy (pun intended) everywhere. The fact that I do this is embarrassing to my grown children, which is all the more reason to continue doing it.

A stab in the dark

This tip I owe to a native guide on a caribou hunt about ten years ago. He was telling me how he once dropped his sheath knife on the ground while quartering a caribou and never found the knife afterwards even though he knew it had to be right there in the ground litter at his feet. Since that time, he ties a piece of florescent string or flagging tape through the handle of his belt knives. He hasn't lost a knife since. Neither will you.

Cold feet

I used to suffer from painfully cold feet when hunting, especially when sitting for hours on a deer stand. I tried all sorts of remedies and nothing was effective. I even tried battery-heated socks. They worked for a time, but very quickly the batteries ran out of juice. Here's what did work. First, be sure to get a pair of good quality boots. I like the rubber-bottom, leather-upper style boots with removable inner liners. Buy an extra set of liners and swap them out daily to let the accumulated moisture evaporate from the used pair. Then I like to use a light breathable pair of non-cotton socks with a pair of heavier woolen socks over them. Do not lace up the boots too tightly as this will cause restricted blood flow in your feet. Finally, if the temperature is going to be below freezing, I insert a chemical foot or hand warmer between the pairs of socks, either under the arch of my foot or on the inside of my leg near the ankle. Select a chemical warmer that matches its hours of operation to the amount of time you plan to be outside. Do not put the chemical warmers next to your skin. They will burn your skin. I still have the scars. The cost of quality boots and the throw-away chemical warmers is well worth the toasty warm feet you'll have.

Forearmed is forwarmed

While on the subject of keeping warm, here's another tip. One of my favorite TV hunting personalities is Jim Shockey. Have you noticed the arm warmers that he wears in some of his shows during colder weather? They are essentially just sleeves that cover his arms from about the elbow to the wrist. Apparently you can buy these, but you can also easily make your own. Just take a worn out (or new if you're so inclined) pair of woolen socks and cut off the foot portion. The remainder can be used as an arm warmer. If you're like me, your hands get cold easily and this can help control that. You can even cut thumb holes to help keep the warmers from riding up on your arms and a little judicious stitching can help to keep things from unravelling. These damn things do work!

Targeted

This one is pretty simple. Rather than going through the bother of breaking down all those used cardboard boxes prior to putting them out for recycling, save the sides and bottoms as targets for the shooting range. Just use a straight edge and a thick marker and make a horizontal and vertical line on the cardboard and you have a target. Add one-inch gradations if so desired. Sometimes I make the target on the bottom of a still intact box and then put all my range gear in the box to make it simpler to carry to the range. Unless I'm shooting lots of birdshot loads or several boxes of rifle ammo, the box will still be intact when I'm done shooting and capable of holding that gear to bring it all home.

Think small and efficient

Most fly-in adventures, especially the remote trips, have baggage weight limits. There are many ways to cut down on unnecessary poundage. Here are a few. Save the small shampoo, toothpaste, mouthwash, and soap complimentary items from your hotel, motel, and dentist visits. They are ideal for outdoor adventures, but be mindful of scented items. I roll up and store an emergency space blanket inside the cardboard tube that my supply of toilet paper is wrapped around. If you shave, use a disposable razor as they weigh much less than the replaceable blade models. I carry my spare batteries in my pockets while traveling so as not to make my baggage weigh more. If you're slightly over or borderline on weight limits, wear your heavy boots and pack your slippers, sneakers, or camp shoes in your duffel. Likewise, wearing a heavy coat versus packing it can save a couple pounds in baggage weight. The point is to think smart, small, and efficient when packing for your outdoor adventures and you can travel lighter or be able to pack more luxury items than might otherwise be possible.

Getting the boot (off)

Here's one I got from a hunting partner during a remote trip. Removing rubber or other heavy and possibly muddy boots after a long day afield can be difficult, especially as you get older. (Note that I might actually use this tip when I do get older in a decade or three.) A neat way to make this chore much simpler is to make a boot block. Simply take a six-inch wide by 10-inch long pine board and cut a V-shaped notch in one end. The notch should be cut with its point with the grain of the wood, not against it. Next, screw, nail, or glue a one-inch by one-inch strip of wood to the first piece crosswise about an inch below the point of the V. The strip should be the same width as the first piece of wood. You're done. To remove stubborn boots without bending over, just stand on the back of the board with one foot and place the heel of the boot on the other foot in the notch and lift your leg. Reverse the process for the other boot. Dimensions can be adjusted depending on foot and boot size.

Get the lice out

If you bird hunt in New England or elsewhere, you will undoubtedly emerge from the field more than once with both you and your bird dog covered in little D-shaped brown "stickers." These miniature burrs are known as Beggar's Lice. They are actually the seed pods of a legume plant similar to beans and peas. Removing them is generally a difficult process and is accomplished by trying to brush them off, comb them out, or tediously picking them off by hand. Here's a much easier way. Put the affected clothing items in your washing machine *by themselves* (no other clothing in the load). Add detergent and run a complete, full-load wash and rinse cycle. Most of the burrs will soften up and go out with the rinse water. The lint trap in the dryer will catch any remaining burrs. You may have to run one washer load with just water and detergent afterwards to fully clean them out of the machine. Too bad you can't put your bird dog in the washer. Maybe I'll name my next bird dog Maytag. By the way, if your wife objects to you using the washing machine for this purpose, you don't know me. Understood?

Prepack, pack, and postpack

Packing for a remote hunting or fishing trip often involves an overnight hotel stay on the way in and another on the way out when the trip is over. Couple this with packing under the burden of a weight limit for the trip itself and all this packing and repacking can be a royal pain in the butt. Here's how to accomplish the task more easily and never have to dig into your duffel bag or suitcase for the trip itself until you arrive at your lodge or final outfitter destination. First, pack and weigh everything you will need for your expedition itself. This includes all the gear and clothing needed from the time you arrive until you depart. Separately, pack what you need for the two overnight stays. By packing in this manner you never have to dig through your primary luggage until you arrive. Be sure to keep toiletries, passports, tickets, and any other essential paperwork available for easy access. I use a small backpack for these items. It may also be possible, depending upon your destination and any applicable regulations or restrictions, to ship some or all of your trip gear ahead of time via a freight carrier.

Keeping the woodstove hotter longer

Many hunting and fishing camps have wood-burning stoves for heat and those stoves are usually not the expensive, airtight models that can cost a couple thousand dollars. Here are two easy ways to have the stove retain and radiate heat longer, even after the fire has died out. One common way is to keep a pot or metal pail of water on top of the stove. The more, the better. The water retains and gives back the heat to the camp in a slow and controlled manner. You'll also have a ready supply of hot water and keep the humidity level of the air in your camp at a reasonable level. Another, not-so-common way to "store" the heat is to put a layer of red clay bricks on top of the stove. These absorb and radiate the heat back to the room over an even longer time than the water. If space on the stove permits, a combination of the two methods can be used. If your camp has electricity, a small low-speed fan helps circulate the heat and diminish cold spots in the camp.

Button it up

If you're like me, when I'm hiking along on a hunt and have my rifle slung over my shoulder by its sling, the sling keeps sliding off my shoulder and requires constant readjustment to keep it there. Here's an easy solution. Sew a large button, like the kind found on Navy pea coats, securely to the top of the preferred shoulder of your hunting coat (both shoulders if you like). The button will keep the sling and your rifle from slipping off your shoulder and yet make it quickly accessible when that next trophy animal suddenly comes into view.

Free hunting time

Some years ago I read an article in an outdoors magazine about how to add 20 percent more time to a hunting trip for free and it made an impact on me. Most deer hunting trips last a week and typically include five days of hunting. The vast majority of hunters know the value of being in the woods at first and last light and for the following and preceding, respectively, several hours. However, many of these same hunters leave their stands and the woods and go back to their camps or vehicles for lunch. If this takes an hour and a half to two hours during each of five days, then one full day of cumulative hunting time is lost, or at best, not used as effectively as it might be. By packing in a light lunch and hunting through the middle of the day, a hunter not only gains back this "free day" of hunting time, but may also capitalize on midday deer movement caused by other hunters who feel they simply must leave their stands or the forest for their noontime break. The deer don't go back to their camps or vehicles during the middle of the day so why should you?

Clear as glass

Buying optics is always a dilemma. One school of reasoning says to buy the most expensive (highest quality) you can afford. But those top-of-the-line optics can cost an arm, a leg, and a side of beef, possibly leaving you a bit short on funds for your hunting trip. What's the right choice? A case in point might help you decide.

I needed a good pair of binoculars several years ago and stopped at a well-known retail outlet in Maine to make the purchase. I tried a pair of relatively low-end Nikon binoculars ($100) that was the display model and was amazed. The sharpness, clarity, and light-gathering capabilities were incredible. I tried two more-upscale models and found that they lacked the performance of the first selection. After deciding to purchase the lower-priced binoculars, the counter clerk handed me an unopened box. I tried these out and found that they too also performed less effectively than the display model. In the end I purchased the pair that had been on display and am still very happy with them twenty-five years later. The lesson learned is to try out the optics before you make your final selection. I'm convinced that while quality and price generally go hand in hand, sometimes, like any piece of fine machinery, all the parts can fit together perfectly and give superior performance above what the price tag might imply.

A tipping point

If you are extra happy with the performance of your guide, show that in his or her tip. This might sound like common sense, but all too often the gratuity given to the most important person on your hunting or fishing trip relative to its success or failure is just a percentage calculation. The general guideline I follow is ten percent of the cost of the trip (excluding airfare), but that's just my starting point. If I feel the guide really went above and beyond to make my trip memorable, I add in some extra money. Depending on the cost and duration of the trip, this might be an extra $50, $100, $200, or whatever seems appropriate. When compared to the total cost of your entire adventure, the extra amount that you add to the tip is a very small piece of the trip budget, but can win you some lasting gratitude from your guide, especially if you book another trip with him or her in the future. I once had my guide come running out to the float plane just as I was boarding for departure. He was all smiles and gave me an even stronger handshake than he had earlier. I like to believe the extra $100 I added to the wad of bills I'd put in his hand accounted for that. And don't forget to tip the second most important person (or maybe the first, depending on your perspective) on your trip, the cook. Cooks work hard and have good memories too.

Let your guide guide

Speaking of guides, let your guide do his work. I once watched a fellow hunter completely disassemble and reassemble the fire pit prior to the guide preparing a shore lunch for us. The hunter thought he was helping out. To his credit, our guide never said a word. He patiently and silently put the fire pit back the way it was originally so he could properly position and balance his cookware. He'd probably prepared many dozen shore lunches at that same location over the past several years and had everything the way he needed it to be. No matter how much you think you know, your guide almost certainly knows more. He's familiar with the terrain, the species, and the techniques that work. The point is to let your guide do his thing. That's what you're paying him or her for. If you'd like to help, ask first or let your guide know that you're available to help if needed. Not only that, but you can learn a lot by listening and watching how your guide does things. I know I have.

Rope-a-dope

There are probably thousands of uses for that length of rope you carry under the seat of your truck. Here's another. If your 4WD or even 2WD vehicle gets bogged down, say on the backside of a snowed-in hillside dirt road that was bare when you entered the woods earlier that day, you can fashion a set of passable tire chains from that rope. Cut lengths of rope long enough to pass through the wheel slots and around each tire and knot the ends of each length together as tight as possible. The makeshift chains will help you climb back to civilization. Cut away the rope once you're back on a good surface. For some added traction, pile logs, rocks, or your brother into the bed of the pickup. The dead weight will help, but tell your brother he's a critical element in your escape from entrapment. Not that I've ever had to actually use this tip, mind you.

String me along

While on the subject of rope, here's another. I always carry a 15 or 20 foot length of para cord in my pack. The uses are innumerable, but one that might not be so obvious is as a clothesline. On my last caribou hunt, my partner and I got soaked on the first day and our small cabin only had a few hooks where we could hang up our clothes to dry. No problem. I connected all the existing hooks with the para cord and we had a line that was able to hold all our wet clothing near the ceiling where it dried completely overnight.

Fake fly fishing

I admit to not being a purist. That is, one day I will become a fly fisherman, but I'm quite slow in getting there. I was recently on a trip where my two companions were happily trolling sinking fly lines and flies and cleaning up on brook trout while I, with my beginner's equipment and only a floating line, was at a distinct disadvantage. If I had listened to myself and brought my standard trolling rig, I would have been my companions' equal.

My standard trolling rig is a bait casting reel such as an Abu Garcia Ambassadeur 6000 series, loaded with 12- or 14-pound test lead line (or its non-lead equivalent), and tipped with about 20 to 25 yards of 6- or 8-pound test monofilament-type line. (I like the hybrid monofilaments that blend strength and flexibility.) Attach an appropriate fly or streamer pattern and I'm in business. I can easily regulate the depth of the fly by the amount of lead line I let out. Let's see…being a purist or catching fish? You call the shot.

Make a kid happy

Ever fish in one of those outdoor show catch-and-keep pools filled with brook trout? More importantly, have you let your child fish in one? Not an easy task catching one of those trout. But here's a way to make your child feel like a hero. Put a small bit of red fabric, like felt, in your pocket as you prepare to go to the show. Before your child dips his fly into the pool, put a small bit of that fabric onto the hook. Chances are he'll hook a trout. Not that my own Dad ever did such a thing for me. And trust me, that brook trout will still be quite palatable after spending several hours inside a plastic bag and stuffed inside a warm coat pocket before it gets home. Or maybe not. But the smile on your child's face is guaranteed to endure.

Double tag it

A mile and a half into the backwoods, you've just bagged a big 220-pound, 10-point buck. It's the biggest, most impressive deer you've ever shot. You put your tag around its leg and now you're heading back to camp, flagging trees as you go, to get a couple friends to help you drag your trophy back to camp. You return two hours later and another hunter and his companion are standing over your deer, your tag is gone, the new guy's tag has replaced it, and he's telling you to get lost in no uncertain terms. Not wanting to risk a potentially violent confrontation, you and your buddies back off and instead follow them to the check station. At the check station the other guy says he's been with the deer since he shot it so your claim is completely bogus. Fifteen minutes later, you're heading home in your truck with your deer in the back. How?

Before you left the 10-pointer to find your friends, you hid a second tag in an empty soda can and jammed it as high as possible up into the body cavity of the deer. When the warden asked you if you could prove that the deer was yours, you said yes, and to the dismay of the unscrupulous hunter, you reached into the deer and pulled out that soda can and the tag it contained. Issue resolved.

Situations like this are more common than you might think. I've even heard of people that have had deer stolen from backyard trees where they've hung them to age for a few days. A little creativity with the placement of the second tag can help make sure you keep your trophy safe and in your possession.

Nearly free decoys

Here's a great wintertime project. Instead of buying another dozen duck or goose decoys, buy just one. Paint the entire decoy with melted kitchen paraffin and let it cool. Apply generous layers of paper mache to the waxed model and let it dry and harden. Use a sharp knife or razor knife to split the dry and hardened paper mache into vertical left and right halves and separate them from the original model. A small slat of wood, one inside and one outside, is used to provide a more substantial point for anchor hooks. Place a weight in the bottom of one of the separated halves along the centerline for ballast and glue it in place. Use plenty of glue. Glue both halves back together. Self-hardening insulation foam can be put in the halves first if desired. Lightly sand the halves to smooth any undesired ridges. Spray or paint the decoy liberally with several coats of waterproof paint or primer as a base coat. Remember, your goal is to make it waterproof. Then paint details as desired. Install desired fasteners. Seal any final fastener holes. It pretty much goes without saying to use waterproof glue, paint, and sealers, so I won't say it again.

Mixed bag hunting

Be mindful of what seasons are open to you. For example, here in Massachusetts during the first week in November, I go to the sportsmen's club I belong to as well as local wildlife management areas and hunt pheasants. However, a quick check of the rules and regulations shows that I can also hunt roughed grouse (partridge), woodcock, ducks, geese, and turkeys at the same time. Be very afraid, winged critters. Be very afraid.

Deer out on a limb

You're a mile in the woods and have just shot a 200-pound deer. You're alone and no friends are nearby or expected. It's going to be a long and tiresome drag to get that deer back to your truck. Here's how to make it easier. Sure, you could have spent some hard-earned dollars on a store-bought drag with a fancy plastic handle. Or you could do this. Pull up the buck's front legs and tie them tightly behind his neck. Find a two-foot length of a solid dried fallen tree limb and tie one end of a six-foot length of rope around its center. Tie the other end around the buck's horns. Grab one end of the limb in each hand behind your back and walk towards your truck. If the rope is too long, shorten it by just rolling some of the rope onto the limb. The buck's antlers and front legs will be off the ground and unlikely to get tangled in undergrowth, making the drag as easy as possible. This tip also works on does.

Within arm's reach

One of my favorite deer-hunting methods is to sit in a tree stand. Even though I always use a safety strap since I'm prone to take short catnaps, I prefer stands that have a bar across the front. Not only does the bar provide an additional measure of safety, if it's properly used it can offer a means of gear storage. Once I raise my pack from the ground by means of a length of cord, I clip the pack to the bar in front of me with the zipper side facing me. This way I can easily open the pack when needed to get at binoculars, snack foods, extra gloves, or anything else and do so with minimum observable movement. A short length of cord and a carabineer make an excellent pack clip.

Double up

Want to increase your shooting accuracy? Double the distance. Most shooting clubs have a standard 100-yard range and if that's the only distance you shoot, then it's the distance at which you'll be most comfortable and it becomes your de facto standard range. I know that's true for me. The sportsmens club I belong to recently built a 200-yard range and before a caribou hunt I decided to sight in my rifle at 200 yards. It took a bit of getting used to, but paid off big. On the hunt I downed a nice bull caribou in his tracks at about 250 yards with one well-placed shot. Shots at 100 yards now seem like child's play. Two hundred yards is my new 100 yards.

Ticked off

I hate ticks. Not only are the little blood-sucking pests a nuisance, they can also spread dangerous illnesses such as Lyme disease. Before I adopted the following procedure, I'd typically return from a fall bird hunting excursion and find one or more of the little creepy-crawlies behind my ear, on my neck, or in some other, more intimate areas. The common insect repellants helped some, but I don't like their odor or the feeling they leave on my skin. Here's what does work.

Purchase a permethrin-based insect repellent spray and apply it to your outer clothing layer several hours before you wear it. (Always follow the manufacturer's instructions and warnings.) The permethrin lasts through several washings and leaves no odor. Since adopting this method, it's rare that I find a tick on my body or clothing after a hunt. And for your canine hunting companion, make sure to regularly use a good quality preventive such as Advantix or Frontline.

Embrace technology

I'm generally suspect of new technology and gadgets. In my estimation, gizmos such as fancy deer scent dispensers and rattling fish lures are mainly designed to catch more hunters and fishermen than game. However, some items actually do work and are worth checking out and the financial investment. I resisted buying a ThermaCell bug repellant device for several years and eventually relented. Damned if the darn things don't work as advertised. Breathable synthetic underwear actually will keep you warmer in the cold and cooler in the heat. LED lights are far superior to ordinary incandescent lights in terms of bulb longevity and battery life. You get the idea. At least give a try to some of these and other innovations and you might be pleasantly surprised. Heck, I might even try to figure out how to operate one of the two GPS units I own. Just as soon as I understand how to use a couple more features on my smart phone. What's an "app" anyway? A hashtag has something to do with breakfast. Right?

Circle of life

Besides being a disciple of the philosophy "if I kill it, I eat it," I like to find ways to get maximum use from the whole creature. I'm personally not enamored of deer hoof gun racks, table lamps, or candlesticks, but other uses do appeal to me. Nearly every trout or salmon streamer fly I tie has a bit of pheasant feather in it from birds I've shot. I give a friend other pheasant carcasses and he skins them and uses the feathers to make decorative women's earrings and broach pins. In addition to the typical buck tails for fly tying, I've saved caribou tails and pieces of hide and hair from bears for the same purpose. Pieces of antler make great buttons, coat hooks, or tool and knife handles. I've had bear teeth made into pendant necklaces. My teenage granddaughter gave two thumbs up for the one she received. So did my wife. Sections of tanned hide have all sorts of practical and artistic uses. The professional hunter on my African safari suggested that I use the extra hide from my mounts to make a framed patchwork "quilt" from those pieces. Every time I look at it, I'm reminded of the animals and of that adventure. Use your imagination.

Pay it forward

Expose others to the excitement and joy of hunting, fishing, and the outdoors. Not everyone will take you up on it, but some will. My five-year-old granddaughter matter-of-factly says "yes" when I offer to take her bear hunting or pheasant hunting with me. I know she may change her mind when the time comes, but I've planted the seed. I get a thrill when visitors look at my trophy room and ask me questions and imply they might like to go along on a trip with me someday. I encourage this. The only thing better than taking an animal or fish myself is watching one of my children, grandchildren, or the children of a friend do it. As sportsmen, we need the next generation, and the ones after that, to promote these healthy forms of recreation.

Balance

This might be my most important tip. I've been blessed with being able to pursue my passions for hunting, fishing, and the outdoors. But this pursuit would not be possible or at least not possible to the extent I've enjoyed without the support of my wife. Molly is not a hunter or fisherperson, but has consistently encouraged me in my efforts. In return, I've been careful to return the appreciation. For every trip I've gone on, we've also gone on one that is more to her liking. These have included trips to the

Caribbean and Europe as well as visits to several United States vacation spots. I just hope Molly understands the heavy sacrifice I make when I'm sitting on a white sand beach in St. Maarten, sipping rum punch amid a sea of bikinis when I could be resting comfortably in a frozen tree stand all day in late November in the deep woods of northern Maine. I guess we all have our burdens to bare...I mean bear.

Be active

Lastly, join and support at least one pro-hunting, pro-fishing, pro-sporting, or pro-firearms organization. There are dozens of anti-organizations out there and they are well funded, have large followings (albeit uneducated), and equally ignorant celebrity spokespeople. Your support is needed and necessary. Without it, you may find your passion for the outdoors might have no outlet. Be and act responsible. Get involved.